Punk and Disorderly

Punk and Disorderly

Acting Out Gender and Class in First-Wave British Punk

Karen Fournier

BLOOMSBURY ACADEMIC
NEW YORK • LONDON • OXFORD • NEW DELHI • SYDNEY

BLOOMSBURY ACADEMIC
Bloomsbury Publishing Inc, 1359 Broadway, New York, NY 10018, USA
Bloomsbury Publishing Plc, 50 Bedford Square, London, WC1B 3DP, UK
Bloomsbury Publishing Ireland, 29 Earlsfort Terrace, Dublin 2, D02 AY28, Ireland

BLOOMSBURY, BLOOMSBURY ACADEMIC and the Diana logo are
trademarks of Bloomsbury Publishing Plc

First published in the United States of America 2026

Cover design by Louise Dugdale
Cover image: Siouxsie Sioux by Paul Natkin/Getty Images

Library of Congress Cataloging-in-Publication Data
Names: Fournier, Karen author
Title: Punk and disorderly : acting out gender and class in first-wave
British punk / by Karen Fournier.
Description: [1]. | New York : Bloomsbury Academic, 2026. | Includes bibliographical
references and index. | Summary: "This book foregrounds the participation of women
as performers and songwriters in early British punk, despite the fact that the genre has
tended to be more commonly associated with its male musicians. Through a close reading
of punk art, fashion, and music, this book examines how female contributors to the early
British scene responded uniquely to the alienation expressed by their male peers, and
demonstrates how social alienation was inflected both by classism and sexism in the work
of those women who helped to shape the early British scene"– Provided by publisher.
Identifiers: LCCN 2025029021 | ISBN 9798765124710 hardback | ISBN 9798765124758
paperback | ISBN 9798765124734 pdf | ISBN 9798765124727 epub
Subjects: LCSH: Women punk rock musicians–Great Britain | Punk rock music–Great
Britain–History and criticism | Rock music–Great Britain–1971-1980–History and criticism |
Women–Great Britain–Social conditions–20th century |
Punk culture–Great Britain–History–20th century
Classification: LCC ML82 .F68 2026 | DDC 782.42166092/52–dc23/eng/20250812
LC record available at https://lccn.loc.gov/2025029021

ISBN: HB: 979-8-7651-2471-0
         PB: 979-8-7651-2475-8
     ePDF: 979-8-7651-2473-4
   eBook: 979-8-7651-2472-7

Typeset by Integra Software Services Pvt. Ltd.
Printed and bound in the United States of America

For product safety related questions contact productsafety@bloomsbury.com.

To find out more about our authors and books visit www.bloomsbury.com
and sign up for our newsletters.

Contents

Illustrations

Acknowledgements

There are too many people to thank for seeing this book from its genesis in my youthful passion for punk to the final project. First and foremost, I want to dedicate this book to all the amazing female artists who refused to be sidelined by the music industry in the 1970s and who grabbed the spotlight for themselves through their mastery of musical performance, songwriting, visual art, fashion, music journalism and (more recently) life-writing. The women whose work I describe in this book have been my inspiration over the decades since I first heard punk as a teenager in Canada. The music and lyrics created by these artists, their bravery in the face of misogyny (and worse) and the general attitude that they embodied have shaped my perspective as a woman and have given me the strength to face many challenges in my own life.

At the University of Michigan, my mentor Abigail Stewart looms large over this project. She was one of my most ardent supporters during the project's earliest incarnation, when she steered me towards the intersectional approach that figures prominently in this reading of punk. Her groundbreaking work on standpoint epistemology has been transformative in my work. My colleague Patricia Hall, who served as my department chair as I wrote the first version of this book and who has become a close friend, has been another invaluable source of support and encouragement. It has been a joy to share aspects of this work with her in conversations over the years. My friend and former Michigan colleague Andrew Mead (now at Indiana University) has served as a scholarly role model for me because of his broad and genuine curiosity about all aspects of music, including punk. I have relied heavily on his foundational concept of 'kinaesthetic empathy' for the analysis that appears in Chapter 4. Andy is among my most treasured colleagues in the field, and his presence in my life has left an indelible imprint on me, as it has for so many in the field of music theory. None of the transcriptions would have been possible without Stephen Lett's keen ear and computer skills, and I would like to credit him for his work on that aspect of the project. I am also indebted to several colleagues at the School of Music, Theatre and Dance for their support and friendship, notable among whom I include Christi-Anne Castro, Áine Heneghan, Nancy Murphy, Aleksandra Vojcic and Leah Frederick (who left Michigan for greener pastures before I finished this book). My doctoral students remain an inspiration to me, and I would like to thank Cecilia Hiros, Sylvie Tran and Evan Ware for bringing different analytical perspectives into our many conversations. The editorial team at Bloomsbury, and in particular Leah Babb-Rosenfeld, deserve particular credit for seeing the potential in this project and for enabling me to focus exclusively on the British scene when many other editors tried to encourage a comparison with its North American counterpart. Leah knew instinctively that while these two scenes might be called 'punk', they responded to very different historical and cultural pressures, and it would have been a mistake to combine their analysis into a single project. Closer to home, I would like to thank Christian Matijas-Mecca, with whom I share a lifelong interest in punk and whose insights have helped to shape my understanding of certain aspects of the genre. Christian and our furry family (Eliot, Josephine, Cassiel and Isabel) exhibited enormous patience as I disappeared for hours and days into my thoughts as this project unfolded. Additionally, this book would not have been possible without the unwavering support of my parents, Bob and Denyse, and my sister and brother-in-law, Leslie and Rob, all of whom are keenly aware of the many ups-and-downs of writing a passion project and who have stood behind me all the way. Bob and Denyse raised their two daughters to be punk long before we had a term to describe it.

The women described in *Punk and Disorderly* modelled a new brand of female identity premised on self-determination and a refusal to accept the gendered status quo. I dedicate this book to these remarkable women and to every woman who has acted out against the patriarchy in their quest to make things better for the next generation.

Introduction

More than any popular music scene that preceded it in Britain, the punk scene that emerged in the mid-1970s encouraged the participation of women in all aspects of the scene, and women created a rich tapestry of social critique in punk through songwriting, performance, art-making, fashion design, photography, music journalism and, later, historical and autobiographical reflections on punk. Musicians and visual artists in the British scene used punk as a way to 'act out' against the country's political establishment and their social values and mores, which largely reflected the experiences of white, Oxbridge-educated men. Those who helped to create punk and who populated its fandom maintained that the experiences of those in the country's ruling class were diametrically opposed to those of everyday Britons who struggled through a decade of labour disputes, inflation and chronic unemployment. Amply documented from a male perspective, British punk has typically been characterized as a form of resistance to classism and its denial of employment and educational opportunities to working-class male youth.[1] However, a handful of (largely female) scholars have also examined punk from a female perspective. Some of these studies have served to introduce their readers to lesser-known female punks through interviews with those musicians and their fans and through historical accounts of their involvement in the early British scene.[2] Other scholars have examined the societal and institutional forces that conspired to marginalize women once the punk scene was colonized by the male-dominated music industry. These studies note that women were typically denied equal access to the field of cultural production that afforded their male counterparts with more opportunities to record and distribute their music on major record labels. Without the means to extend their reach beyond local or regional audiences and to preserve their music through recording, the contributions of many female punks have been lost and forgotten.[3] In *Punk and Disorderly*, socio-economic class and gender are examined as co-contributors to the oppression experienced by British women in the 1970s and expressed by women in punk. As in many studies of punk, class is defined in this book in terms of the socio-economic conditions experienced by individuals or groups, their place within an existing socio-economic hierarchy and, in the case of some punks, as a romanticized identification with those who are marginalized within this structure. *Punk and Disorderly* argues that punk produced by females in the British scene was often animated by intersecting systems of oppression that were experienced uniquely by the working-class women who populated the scene or with whom women in the scene identified. While the frustration experienced and expressed by male punks was largely rooted in their perception of a lack of political and economic power in Britain's rigid class system, female punks also pushed back against a patriarchy that questioned their claim to any kind of power at all, including the power of self-determination and the right to gender equality. In the 1970s, women were idealized in the media as submissive, passive and subordinate to boyfriends, husbands and other men in positions of power. A woman's success, according to this construct, was inextricably tied to the success of her male partner, and her main tasks were to attract a successful male and to reflect his success through her comportment, appearance and domestic skills. *Punk and Disorderly* argues that female punks in the British scene acted out against these patriarchal depictions of femininity not only because they reflected a particular class perspective that marginalized working-class punks regardless of their gender but also because their narrow and conservative depictions of gender roles were especially infantilizing and harmful towards women.

To examine how women in the British punk scene responded to the double-bind of classism and sexism, *Punk and Disorderly* draws its analytical methodology from third-wave feminist standpoint epistemology, which locates female identity at the confluence of such social matrices as gender, class and race. While this approach might seem surprising, given that punk was roughly contemporaneous with feminism's second wave and often reflects some of the philosophical ideas of that earlier wave, a third-wave approach offers a more nuanced reading of class than most studies of punk provide because it teases out the experiences of class oppression by those who are also oppressed by gender and race. *Punk and Disorderly* therefore defines a new set of analytical parameters for punk by looking back at the scene through the lens of feminism's third wave. This study rests on the premise that class is experienced differently by women than it is by men, and it proves this point by examining the various ways that the gendered experience of class oppression is expressed in a subset of musical and artistic works created by women in the British punk scene.

This book will focus exclusively on the early British punk scene, which is understood as a counterpart to, but as different from, the American scenes with which it is often compared. While punk also took hold in urban centres like New York City, Washington D.C., Akron, Cleveland and Los Angeles in the mid-1970s (and in many other geographical locations besides), none of these scenes grappled with the same class constraints as their counterparts in Britain. Many American punks were born into middle-class suburban families and used punk as a means both to comment on the boredom and predictability of their suburban youth experiences and to resist any expectation that they would aspire to the middle-class suburban lives of their parents. American punks rejected what they perceived as the phony, constructed façade of suburban life that was packaged and sold to American consumers. They believed that media portrayals of suburbia created an image of white, middle-class success that the Nixon and Reagan administrations used as propaganda. By focusing on an idealized suburban lifestyle, they argued, the government promoted a myth of American prosperity that downplayed the fall-out from the war in Vietnam and the harsh realities of the economic recession of the 1970s. To expose the various societal failings that were erased by the suburban myth, punks congregated in decaying and often violent American inner-cities, where they moved in search of a more 'authentic' lifestyle.[4] Bands like the Ramones and the Dictators also appropriated earlier musical genres like surf, garage and bubble-gum pop to recreate the music that was marketed to American suburban teens in the 1960s and to critique a system that socialized teenagers into lives of mindless suburban consumerism. These bands, and others like them, drew a stark opposition between the suburban teen fantasies recounted in their lyrics and the urban decay that surrounded the clubs in which they performed and that was reflected in the seemingly dirty, cast-off clothing that was worn by many of the performers themselves.[5] American punk was a political statement by middle-class youth against the suburban myth and its ideals, while for British punks, the images of suburban comfort and prosperity that circulated through the media merely highlighted the extent to which the United States – and not Britain – appeared to have reaped the rewards of post-war economic growth. As the British working class struggled through the fiscal challenges of the 1970s, images of American prosperity reinforced the stark economic differences that were embedded into the British class system. The distinction between American and British punk is therefore rooted largely in differences in class perspectives between the middle-class ennui felt by American punks and the working-class anger felt by their British counterparts. A thorough study of the intersection of class and gender, like the one offered here in relation to British punk, must make certain choices in its point of departure. By exposing the inherent male-centeredness of British punk's resistance to class oppression, *Punk and Disorderly* proceeds from a British perspective. A study of American punk would necessarily examine its female subjects through a different set of critical lenses and potentially come to different conclusions about the ways in which women were able to contribute to that scene and the forms of protest that they created there.

Additionally, *Punk and Disorderly* focuses on the period from 1977 to 1981, which encompasses Britain's 'punk' and 'post-punk' scenes. In an attempt to untangle the terminology that has been used to describe these two scenes and their musical practices, Mimi Haddon (2020) explains that the term 'post-punk' is a misnomer that has been applied to a genre that actually overlapped with punk beginning in 1977.[6] Haddon notes that the term 'post-punk', while admittedly slippery, can be distinguished musically from punk because it featured 'an emphasis on artiness, eruditeness, or a "new" musical language' that was structured 'outside of punk's most limited musical parameters'.[7] In his foundational study of British post-punk, Simon Reynolds (2005) adds that, early on in the formation of the punk scene,

> the fragile unity that punk had forged between working class kids and arty, middle-class bohemians began to fracture. On the one side were the populist 'real punks' (later to evolve into the Oi! and hardcore movements) who believed that the music needed to stay accessible and unpretentious... the angry voice of the street. On the other side was the vanguard that came to be known as postpunk, who saw [the early days of punk in] 1977 not as a return to raw rock 'n' roll but as the chance to make a break with tradition.[8]

Accordingly, punk (and later Oi! and hardcore) was conceived as a direct and critical response to a particular set of socio-economic circumstances experienced at a specific historical moment. By contrast, post-punk was destined to live beyond the moment of its conception through its experimentation and constant reinvention. Reynolds suggests that, in broad terms, the distinction between these two scenes and musical genres underscores a class tension between those who identified as working-class (and who expressed their class identity through punk) and those who identified with the working-class from their vantage points in the lower- to middle-classes (and who expressed their solidarity with working-class Britons through post-punk).

With the differences between punk and post-punk in mind, it is important to return to the point of punk's overlap with post-punk at the end of the 1970s to explain some of the choices made in this book. I have not limited this study exclusively to bands that appear to exhibit the 'limited musical parameters' described by Haddon as a defining feature of punk, and I have opted, instead, to include more 'experimental' post-punk bands among my case studies. Using the date of each band's formation as a central criterion for my choices, this study includes bands that formed between 1976 and 1979. My rationale for the inclusion of bands that might fall more squarely into Haddon's definition of 'post-punk' is that they formed in the immediate wake of punk, and many cited earlier punk bands as influences on their own music and image. *Punk and Disorderly* therefore explores a selection of female musicians and artists who engage politically through music that aligns with punk *or* post-punk (or that lies in the liminal space between these two genres). Because some of these artists may be unknown to the reader, I will provide a short introduction to each band that can be used as a point of reference for the ensuing chapters. In chronological order of their formation, this study will focus on the following bands:

- **The Adverts** was formed in London in 1976. This band was unique at the time because it featured a female bassist, Gaye Advert (née Gaye Black), who is often credited as Britain's first female punk icon. Over the course of two years, The Adverts released one single, 'One Chord Wonders' (Stiff 1977), and two studio albums, *Crossing the Red Sea with The Adverts* (Bright 1978) and *A Cast of Thousands* (RCA 1979). The band performed for the last time on 27 October 1979 at Slough University and disbanded shortly thereafter. Allegedly disillusioned with the music industry, Gaye has become a visual artist who expresses herself largely through the medium of stained glass.
- **Penetration** was formed in 1976 in County Devon, allegedly after the band's lead singer, Pauline Murray, saw the Sex Pistols in live performance. The band played its first live gig in January 1977 at The Roxy club in London's Covent Garden. Penetration released their first single, 'Don't Dictate' (Virgin 1977), which was followed by the studio albums *Moving Targets* (Virgin 1978) and *Coming Up For Air* (Virgin 1979). After disappointing critical reviews of their second album, the

group disbanded in October 1979 but reformed in 2015 for the release of their third studio album, *Resolution* (Polestar 2015). More recently, Murray published her autobiography, *Life's a Gamble* (Omnibus 2023) and the band continues to tour.

- **X-Ray Spex**, which formed in London in 1976, featured the lead singer Poly Styrene (née Marianne Joan Elliott-Saïd) on vocals and Lora Logic (née Susan Whitby) on saxophone. Other band members included Jak Airport (née Jack Stafford on guitars), Paul Dean (bass) and Paul 'B.P' Hurding (drums). On 2 April 1977, X-Ray Spex recorded a live set at The Roxy club that featured many songs that would later be released commercially on the Virgin label. These included the band's iconic 'Oh Bondage Up Yours!', which was released as the band's first single on 30 September 1977. Logic left the band before their first studio album, *Germ Free Adolescents* (EMI 1978), though she appears on the tracks 'Oh Bondage Up Yours!' and 'I Am a Cliché'. Poly Styrene left the band in 1979 and joined the Hare Krishna movement a year later. In 1995, X-Ray Spex reunited to release their second and final studio album, *Conscious Consumer* (Receiver 1995). Poly Styrene died in 2011. In 2021, her daughter, Celeste Bell, released a film about her mother's life in and after punk entitled *I Am a Cliché*.

- **Siouxsie and the Banshees**, which formed in London in 1976, became one of the most commercially successful and enduring groups from the period. The band was fronted by the iconic punk figure Siouxsie Sioux (née Susan Ballion), who made her first public performance on 20 September 1977 at the 100 Club Punk Festival, where she performed a spontaneous musical rendition of the Lord's Prayer. The band released their first single, 'Hong Kong Garden' (Polydor 1978), followed soon after by their debut studio album *The Scream* (Polydor 1978) and their follow-up album, *Join Hands* (Polydor 1979). In total, the band released eleven studio albums between 1978 and 1995 that explored such genres as punk, post-punk, goth, neo-psychedelia, art rock and alternative rock. Siouxsie continues to maintain an active musical career.

- **Poison Girls** was formed in Brighton in 1976 by the forty-one-year-old guitarist and mother of two Vi Subervsa (née Frances Sokolov). The band was an active participant in Britain's anarchist movement and used their music to advocate for nuclear disarmament, animal rights, environmentalism, anti-fascism and radical feminism. Poison Girls worked closely with the band Crass, with whom they coexisted for a time at an artist commune in Essex known as Dial House and purchased by members of Crass in 1967. Between 1979 and 1985, Poison Girls released four studio albums, beginning with *Hex* (Small Wonder 1979). The group disbanded in 1987 but reunited in 1995 to celebrate Subversa's sixtieth birthday. Subversa died in 2016.

- In its first incarnation, **The Slits** was an all-female quartet that formed in London in October 1976 and originally comprised the fourteen-year-old lead singer Ari Up (née Ariane Forster, vocals), Viv Albertine (guitar, vocals), Tessa Pollitt (bass) and Palmolive (née Paloma Romero, drums). The band supported The Clash during their White Riot tour in March 1977 and recorded sessions with John Peel in 1977 and 1978. By the time the band released their debut album, *Cut* (Island Records 1979), Palmolive had left to join The Raincoats (see below), allegedly over a disagreement about the album's iconic cover. The Slits released their second studio album, *Return of the Giant Slits* (CBS 1981), before breaking up at the beginning of 1982. In 2005, Ari Up and Tessa Pollitt teamed up to release the EP *Revenge of the Killer Slits* (SAF Records 2006) and the band's third studio album, *Trapped Animal* (Sweet Nothings 2009). Ari Up died in Los Angeles in 2010.

- The anarcho-punk band **Crass** formed in London in 1977 as an art collective and punk band. Like Poison Girls, with whom they shared Dial House for a brief period in the late 1970s, Crass embraced anarchism as their political philosophy and expressed their social critique in music, poetry and artwork. The band was formed by the poet and activist Penny Rimbaud (née Jeremy Ratter) and the musician Steve Ignorant (née Steven Williams), who were soon joined by the visual artist Gee Vaucher (née Carole Vaucher). Vaucher provided the artwork for the group, including the iconic cover image for the band's first studio album, *The Feeding of the 5000* (Crass 1978). Crass was highly critical of other punks for 'selling out' in order to secure recording contracts with major labels, and the album quickly established the band as one of the most politically uncompromising punk acts of the period. The band's second studio album, *Stations of the Cross* (Crass 1979), was largely financed by Poison Girls, with whom they performed frequently during this period. The band's third studio album, *Penis Envy* (Crass Records 1980), was the first Crass album to feature the female singers Joy de Vivre (née Joy Haney) and Eve Libertine (née Bronwyn Lloyd Jones) and to engage explicitly with feminist themes. The album sparked a backlash because of its cover image of a blow-up sex doll. In total, Crass released six studio albums before their breakup in 1984. Under the name 'Crass Agenda' (later, 'Last Amendment'), Rimbaud has continued his advocacy work through poetry, music and performance art. A retrospective of Vaucher's creative work was published in 1999, and Vaucher was awarded an honorary doctorate from the University of Essex in 2016.

- **The Raincoats** was an all-female band that was formed in 1977 by Ana da Silva and Gina Birch, who met as students at the Hornsey College of Art in London. The pair were allegedly inspired to form a band after seeing The Slits in live performance, and they appeared as a live act for the first time on 9 November 1977 with Ross Crighton on guitar and Nick Turner on drums. By 1978, the band had coalesced into an all-female line-up with the addition of Vicky Aspinall on violin and Palmolive on drums (having left The Slits over disagreements with the band). Aspinall was classically trained as a violinist at the Royal College of Music and often used the instrument to mimic the sounds of whining and shrieking in the band's music. The all-female line-up made its debut at Acklam Hall in London on 4 January 1979 and released their debut single, 'Fairytale in the Supermarket', three months later (Rough Trade 1979). The band's first studio album, *The Raincoats* (Rough Trade 1979), would be cited by Kurt Cobain as such an important influence on his band, Nirvana, that he wrote the liner notes for its 1993 re-release on CD. By the time the band's second album, *Odyshape* (Rough Trade 1981), was released, Palmolive had left the group, which freed the band to experiment with different drummers and to reconceive the role played by the percussion in their songs. The band subsequently recorded their only live album, *The Kitchen Tapes* (ROIR 1983), and their third and final studio album, *Moving* (Rough Trade 1984), before breaking up as a band. The Raincoats has reformed occasionally for the purposes of special events.

- **Mo-dettes** was an all-female band formed in London 1979 by Kate Korus (guitar), Jane Crockford (bass), Ramona Carlier (vocals) and June Miles-Kingston (drums). Korus started her career as an original member of The Slits, but was replaced by Viv Albertine before that band recorded their first Peel Session in 1977. She had also played briefly with The Raincoats. Mo-dettes released their debut single, 'White Mice/Masochistic Opposite' (Mode 1979), which became an indie hit. Decca Records subsequently signed the band to its subsidiary label, Deram, where they released their only album, *The Story So Far* (Deram 1980), and their final recording, the single 'Tonight/Waltz in Blue Minor' (Deram 1981). After several line-up changes, the band broke up in November 1982.

- **Au Pairs** was a Birmingham-based band that was formed in 1979 by the female musicians Lesley Woods (vocals, guitar) and Jane Munro (bass). Munro claims to have modelled herself on the Talking Heads' bassist, Tina Weymouth. With male colleagues Paul Foad (guitar) and Pete Hammond (drums), the band released their debut album, *Playing with a Different Sex* (Human May 1981), which explores topics like gender and sexual politics, racism and political tensions between Britain and Ireland. The band toured the album in the United States, where they played at Los Angeles' Whiskey A Go-Go club on 30 September 1981 and the Market Street Cinema in San Francisco on 2 October 1981. In mid-1982, the band released its second studio album, *Sense and Sensuality* (Kamera 1982), but broke up during the planning of their third album because Munro opted to leave the band. Woods currently works as a lawyer in London, and Munro works as a therapist in Birmingham.

- In 1979, the band **Delta 5** was formed by a trio of female art students at Leeds University that included Julz Sale (vocals and guitar), Ros Allen (bass) and Bethan Peters (bass). Later additions to the band included Kelvin Knight (drums) and Alan Riggs (guitar). Delta 5 was an important member of the Leeds punk and post-punk scenes along with such (admittedly more familiar) bands as Gang of Four and The Mekons. After releasing their first three singles – 'Mind Your Own Business/Now That You've Gone' (Rough Trade 1979), 'Try/Colour' (Rough Trade 1980) and 'Anticipation/You' (Rough Trade 1981) – the band toured America and signed to Pre, which was a subsidiary of the Charisma label. The band released their only studio album, *See the Whirl* (PRE, 1981), before breaking up in 1982. The band's first single, 'Mind Your Own Business', brought renewed attention to the band after it was used in a 2019 episode of the British comedy series *Sex Education*, a 2020 episode of the BBC series *The A Word*, and a 2021 Apple commercial promoting iPhone privacy. Knight died in 2015, and Sale died in 2021.

While these bands have been chosen for this study because they feature women in prominent roles as performers (and, in many instances, as songwriters), the women who comprise this group represent a diverse set of experiences that are shaped variously at the intersections of gender, class, race and age. This group consists of women who began their careers in punk and others who came to punk through art school. The case studies encompass working-class and middle-class perspectives. The women in this study range in age from fourteen to forty-one, and among a group of women who were largely free from the demands of motherhood, the sample also includes a mother. One member of this case study is biracial, and the impact of racism on her experience of classism and misogyny gave her a unique perspective on exclusion in British society. Given the diversity of the individuals described in this study, *Punk and Disorderly* does not aim to construct a single, totalizing feminist theory of punk, which would miss the point of punk's DIY ethos entirely. Additionally, some of the performers cited here would have resisted any attribution of 'feminism' to their creative motivations and would merely have considered themselves as punks who happen to be women. Instead, this study takes each artist on her own terms as she responded to the social forces that excluded her and as she presented her responses to these exclusions in her work.

Over the course of five chapters, *Punk and Disorderly* explores a subset of British punk that was created and performed by women and that coalesced around the topics of gender, patriarchy, misogyny and gender-based violence. The opening chapter of the book outlines the various historical and social conditions that surrounded punk, with a specific focus on the messages of the second-wave feminist movement that predated punk by roughly a decade and that were reflected in some of the songs and artwork produced by women in the scene. The songs that emerge from women's creative work in the scene express aspirational messages of female empowerment through a network of signifiers encoded in the lyrics of songs produced and performed by the bands cited above, which I describe in Chapter 2. Female empowerment is also reflected in various visual signifiers that are worn by female punk musicians and created by visual artists to represent those musicians and their work, as I argue in Chapter 3. Finally, the music created and performed by women in the British punk scene conveys its rejection of gender norms through its subversion of conventional song forms and instrumentation and its resistance to the suppression of the female voice, which I demonstrate in Chapter 4. What emerges from my study of this important body of punk repertoire and its associated visual artwork is a set of creative strategies used by women in the British scene to expose the particular vulnerabilities of working-class women to abuse and neglect and to critique the social conditions that allowed these experiences to go unchecked. Women in the British scene spoke openly about taboo issues like sexual violence and partner abuse, critiqued the gendering of social spaces that relegated women to subordinate roles as wives and mothers, pushed back against conventional standards of female beauty and femininity, and created parodies of mental illness to debunk the common attribution of 'hysteria' to non-compliant women.

Recently, the punk musicians Viv Albertine and Pauline Murray and the punk style icon Jordan Mooney have revisited their experiences in the British scene through the medium of autobiography, or life writing. Poly Styrene's career in (and after) punk has been reconstructed posthumously by her daughter, Celeste Bell, from her mother's diary entries and from live interviews that she shares in the 2021 documentary *I Am a Cliché*. This film can be added to the existing autobiographies as another form of reflection on the British scene. These memoirs present a unique opportunity to conclude *Punk and Disorderly* with the musings of women who contributed to the British scene. In the final chapter, or epilogue, I will let these groundbreaking women speak for themselves as they reflect upon the scene that they helped to create and as they consider how their contributions to popular music might have opened doors for other women to claim space for themselves in the music industry.

Notes

1   See Romain Garbaye and Gérôme Guibert, eds. *Musical Scenes and Social Class: Debating Punk and Metal* (London: Palgrave Macmillan, 2024); David Simonelli, *Working Class Heroes: Rock Music and British Society in the 1960s and 1970s* (Plymouth: Lexington Books, 2013); David Simonelli, 'Anarchy, Pop and Violence: Punk Rock Subculture and the Rhetoric of Class, 1976–1978', *Contemporary British History* 16/2 (2002), 121–44; Jason Toynbee, 'The Clash, Revolution and Reverse', in *Working for the Clampdown, the Clash, the Dawn of Neoliberalism and the Political Promise of Punk*, ed. Colin Coulter (Manchester, CT: Manchester University Press, 2019), 35–51; and Nathan Wiseman-Trowse, *Performing Class in British Popular Music* (London: Palgrave Macmillan, 2008).

2   See Rebecca Binns, *Gee Vaucher: Beyond Punk, Feminism and the Avant-Garde*. (Manchester: Manchester University Press, 2022); Vivien Goldman, *Revenge of the She-Punks: A Feminist Music History from Poly Styrene to Pussy Riot* (Austin, TX: University of Texas Press, 2019); Maria Raha, *Cinderella's Big Score: Women of the Punk and Indie Underground* (Emeryville, CA: Seal Press, 2005); Helen Reddington, 'Lady Punks in Bands: A Subculturette?' in *The Post-Subcultures Reader*, eds. David Muggleton and Rupert Weinsierl (Oxford: Berg, 2003), 239–51;

and Simon Reynolds and Joy Press, *The Sex Revolts: Gender, Rebellion, and Rock 'n' Roll* (London: Serpent's Tail, 1994).

3   This argument is central to the discussion the erasure of women in punk in Helen Reddington, *The Lost Women of Rock Music: Female Musicians of the Punk Era* (Aldershot: Ashgate, 2007).

4   See John Taylor, '"Society Stinks": Suburban Alienation and Violence in the Early Films of Penelope Spheeris', in *Filmurbia: Screening the Suburbs*, eds. David Forrest, Graeme Harper, and Jonathan Rayner (London: Palgrave Macmillan, 2017), 13–28.

5   This aspect of the Ramones' music is described in Bill Osgerby, '"Chewing Out a Rhythm on My Bubble-Gum": The Teenage Aesthetic and Genealogies of American Punk', in *Punk Rock: So What? The Cultural Legacy of Punk*, ed. Roger Sabin (London: Routledge, 1999), 154–69.

6   Theo Cateforis (2011) argues that punk also splintered into new wave in 1978, a genre that does not concern the current study.

7   Mimi Haddon, *What Is Post-Punk? Genre and Identity in Avant Garde Popular Music 1977–1982* (Ann Arbor, MI: University of Michigan Press, 2020), 54.

8   Simon Reynolds, *Rip It Up and Start Again: Postpunk 1978–1984* (London: Faber and Faber, 2005), 1.

1

'She doesn't have political views': Historical context

The year 1977 represents the moment when British punk rock broke onto (or perhaps into) a popular music scene whose charts had been dominated by what many punks would describe as the vacuous hits of pop and disco and the self-indulgent anthems of progressive rock.[1] The year also marked the Queen's Silver Jubilee, during which Britain was in the throes of nationwide celebrations despite a period of economic stagnation that forced Britons to ration to an extent that recalled the conditions under which they were asked to live during the Second World War. The coexistence of punk and the Jubilee was likely no coincidence. In the view of many punks, one of the problems with mainstream culture, as it was represented by the popular music that it consumed, was that it reinforced societal distinctions between those who were authorized to participate in its construction (as trained musicians, sound engineers, producers and distributors) and those who were relegated to more passive roles (as listeners and consumers). Disco, pop and progressive rock were vilified by British punks not only for their musical content but also because they reflected the tastes and values of the middle-class and ignored the interests of the working-class from which many punks originated or with which they empathized. Citing an emphasis on perfection in musical performance as one strategy used by the music industry to minimize the contributions of the working-class to popular music-making, punk appeared to embrace musical 'imperfection' as a way to encourage the participation of anyone who aspired to perform.[2] Musical mistakes, unpolished musical techniques and seemingly poor recording qualities were championed in punk as strategies designed to invert the power dynamic between those who were authorized to make music and those who were not. While the creation and performance of mainstream popular music seemed to demand a certain degree of musical aptitude, punk merely asked its participants to master three chords, as the British punk fanzine *Sideburns* suggested with its famous quip 'this is a chord, this is another, this is a third; now form a band'. Imperfection, as a reflection of the voice of the 'everyday working-class Briton' (and perhaps even as the musical equivalent of the 'undesirable' working-class accent that rubbed against the grain of the more 'polished' Oxbridge accent), became an oppositional strategy used by punk to critique the middle-class. Having said this, it is important to note that while punk's early claims to musical naïveté are intended to lend a sense of authenticity to a genre that purported to speak for the working-class, these claims often ignore or downplay the raw talent and musicality displayed by many punk musicians early in their careers and perfected as these careers evolved. Nonetheless, one important aspect of the 'three-chord' credo is that it did not discriminate within the punk subculture between those who were allowed to participate in the creation of punk and those who were not.

Given its claims to inclusiveness and its tendency to eschew conformity in favour of individuality, punk resists any singular definition except, perhaps, that it embraced the status of 'other' in relation to mainstream culture and its social conventions. Those who played a part in the creation of punk were encouraged to embrace their 'otherness' as a means to critique mainstream societal norms; however, what it meant to be 'other' was entirely dependent upon the experiences of each individual punk. Because the 'three-chord' credo dispelled any notion of the 'ideal' popular musician, it opened a performance space not only for the 'other' embodied as the working-class male but also for groups that found themselves marginalized for other reasons. In particular, the scene invited the participation of women (and, albeit to a lesser extent, of those who traced their cultural heritage elsewhere), who found themselves unfettered by their status as the gendered or racialized 'other' and free to assume creative roles in the construction of the scene in ways that were prohibited elsewhere. For young women who watched the scene unfold, like this author did in the late-1970s, the liberation of the guitar and the drum-set from its male stronghold, the contributions of female songwriters to the lexicon of the scene and the roles played by female journalists and photographers in chronicling the scene seemed to promise a revolutionary change in the gendering of popular music. Punk allowed its participants to explore how the broader societal matrices of gender, sexuality, class and race intersected in their own lives to create the oppressive conditions under which they lived. Each social critique posed by punk, whether it was expressed in music, lyrics, fashion, artwork, zines or in the on- or off-stage behaviours that added to the scene's notoriety, was created from a unique confluence of these social categories within the life of each individual punk.

Despite the prevailing perception of punk as a resistance to classism, the idea within the scene, then, was not necessarily to mount challenges to conventions from one particular disadvantaged standpoint (say, that of class) but to critique mainstream culture from multiple standpoints as each was reflected in the experiences of those individuals who participated in the scene. What happened for 'othered' punks in the wake of punk will be examined in the concluding chapter, but for now, we should note that the sense of optimism that punk provided for female participants has rarely been reflected in the ways in which we define the term 'punk'. Rather, the category of gender has tended to be overshadowed or eclipsed by the category of class in most discussions of the scene, and it is the purpose of the current study to rectify this skewed impression of punk with a refinement of existing definitions of the term 'punk'.

Defining punk

It is commonly understood that punk rock struck an oppositional stance towards mainstream popular culture, but the diversity and multiplicity of the modes of resistance adopted by punk has frustrated most attempts to define the term. In part, the problem lies in a monolithic understanding of 'class' as a social category populated by people who experienced oppression in the same way. In reality, punk was a heterogeneous subculture whose oppositional stance took many, and often disparate, forms that recognized the varied experiences of those who comprised the working-class or who identified with working-class punks from their position in the middle-class. Punk's heterogeneity has complicated the quest for an over-arching definition of the term because punk acknowledged and embraced 'difference', whereas many definitions of 'punk' look for 'sameness' (i.e. they attempt to explain the genre in terms of characteristics held in common across the various and varied artistic contributions that coalesce around the term 'punk'). The definitions that currently exist, of which some will be described below, help to characterize some examples of punk but fail to capture the qualities of other examples. Perhaps most importantly, the definitions that have emerged in studies of punk have tended to assume an androcentric perception of the genre that ignores the stark differences between male and female punk and, by extension, that envelopes the latter into the former. In what follows, I will examine the gendered perspective that is tacit in many existing definitions of punk and explain how these definitions intersect with certain historical and cultural events that shaped the British landscape in the 1970s (specifically, the economic collapse in Britain following the energy crisis of 1973, the end of Bretton Woods and the strengthening of trade unions). Following this, I will pose a rereading or redefinition of punk that emerges from the consideration of these alongside other historical events (specifically, the rise of second-wave feminism and its various challenges to conventional assumptions about gender and sexuality).

From a purely musical standpoint, the term 'punk' has been used to characterize a repertoire of popular music in which 'the unnecessary complexities of existing music were to be challenged not by a purer, simpler sound but by a frontal assault. The sounds were to be distorted, dirtied and destroyed, so that meanings were mangled'.[3] Those who have focused on the musical aspects of punk as a source of a definition for the term often point to its purported origins in earlier rock 'n' roll, garage or pub rock to emphasize how punk's seeming return to these musical roots allowed its practitioners to imagine a future of music without the technological or performative intricacies that were more characteristic of the genres with which punk coexisted in the late 1970s, like disco and progressive rock. Moreover, the sense that the meaning of punk lies in the 'purity' or 'simplicity' of its 'sound' (assuming that there is a single punk 'sound') is a direct outgrowth of punk's self-constructed mythology, according to which anyone who could master three chords – or, as the Adverts' debut punk single, 'One Chord Wonders' (Stiff 1977), suggests, even just one – could form a band. But any description of punk as a form of musical expression provides only part of the picture, since the term is also used to describe a subculture of 'disenfranchised youths gathering around some shared interests in music and fashion [who hold common] attitudes to society, to "the establishment," and to previous music-oriented subcultures, particularly hippies and progressive rock'.[4] Those who participated in punk's subculture positioned themselves in diametric opposition to mainstream popular culture, whose conventions of beauty, taste and respectability were often the source of parody and ironic reinterpretation by punks. Finally, the term 'punk' is also used to refer to a general sense of antagonism, manifest in some cases as a sort of political proto-ideology expressed by members of the punk subculture towards exclusionary societal structures that defined, and were governed by, hegemonic class (and, to a lesser extent, by gender and racial hegemonies). The privileging of class as a defining feature of punk runs throughout definitions of the genre, as, for example, in Nathan Wiseman-Trowse's interpretation of punk as 'an exploration, sometimes implicit, sometimes explicit, of class relationships. This preoccupation with class, particularly in the (at least supposedly) more socio-realist bands, has lead to the perception that punk is primarily working-class music, an extension of the folk voice'.[5] To complicate matters even further, the term 'punk' is both historically and geographically non-specific, and is applied to music, subcultures and sets of attitudes that have emerged out of locales that are separated in space and time. The broad application of the term to New York punk, which began in 1974 as an expression of suburban boredom and as a critique of the American middle-class, and London punk, which appeared two years later as an expression of working-class anger and disillusionment and which is the focus of the current study, obscures the cultural and historical differences that lie behind each. The focus on class in definitions of these two distinct cultural strands of punk – where the British form is viewed as a form of working-class protest, while the American form is a reaction to the values of the suburban middle-class – further cements 'class' as a defining feature of the genre.

While 'the resistance to classism' is a theme that informs the do-it-yourself punk 'sound', punk's anti-establishment stance and the cultural variants of the genre that emerged on both sides of the Atlantic, the genre's response to various historical events of the 1970s supports the common reading of the genre as a reaction to class oppression. To understand punk, one needs to understand the political and economic climate of the 1970s. At the same time, I will argue that this historical framework provides only part of the picture, and that various social changes that were taking place in the 1970s – specifically those that challenged conventional gender roles – must also be taken into consideration in our redefinition of punk as an expression of the gendering of classism.

Britain's politics of difference: The rationale for 'class' as central to punk

In Great Britain, punk rock emerged as Britons were suffering through one of the worst economic crises to have been experienced in the country since the 1930s, and the economic climate of the mid-1970s has often been cited by observers of the British punk movement, and by punks themselves, as a factor in the music's 'have-not' sensibilities. Many, but not all, punk musicians were raised in lower-middle-class or working-class families, and came of age at a time when jobs were scarce and the future for underprivileged Britons looked bleak. At the same time, disparities in wealth and the rigidity of British class system were accentuated by the 1977 commemoration of the Queen's Silver Jubilee, where elaborate parties were mounted in communities across Britain to celebrate the monarchy despite the financial constraints under which many in these communities were forced to live. The emergence of punk rock in the midst of this contradictory set of historical events is no coincidence, and, at its best, the genre offers an emotionally charged commentary on the social inequalities that denied opportunities to those at the lower end of the class system. To a large extent, punk provided first-person accounts of the impact of the worldwide financial crisis upon those Britons who suffered the most in the mid-1970s, but its focus on working-class unemployment and the lack of 'career opportunities' (in the famous words of The Clash) has tended to shift attention to the plight of working-class *male* youth. Punk's semiotic landscape is littered with references to the emasculation felt by males who were unable to support their families or to dream of a brighter future for their children. (The flipside, of course, was a generation of women who would be required to work in order to help with family finances, although this aspect of the narrative has tended to be ignored in discussions about punk.)

Britain's economic crisis, which set the stage for the class protests mounted by punk, began in October 1973, when the Arab-dominated Organization of Petroleum Exporting Countries (OPEC) responded to foreign intervention in the Yom Kippur War by raising the worldwide price of oil and decreasing exports to those countries, like the United States, who sided with Israel in the conflict. The move caused an immediate fuel crisis in the United States, whose industries relied heavily upon oil imports from the Middle East, and exacerbated an inflationary spiral in that country that had already been set in motion by overspending on the war in Vietnam and by the deregulation of the American dollar in 1971. Britain's refusal to support the American efforts in the Middle East meant that the country was exempt from the embargo, but although their supply of oil was not curtailed, Britons, like everyone else who relied upon OPEC, saw the price of fuel quadruple between the fall of 1973 and the beginning of 1974. The rising cost of fuel had drastic consequences for the British consumer, who was left to contend with rocketing heating bills and the higher prices for food and consumer goods that resulted from an increased cost of transport. Further, worries about the cost of oil in Britain were compounded by a dispute in December 1973, spearheaded by the National Union of Mineworkers (NUM) on behalf of British coalminers who sought an increase in their wages. In response to concerns about waning energy stocks, the British Parliament legislated a variety of austerity measures that cut speed limits on British roadways and that restricted the use of heating and lighting in households and businesses across the country. Although these measures proved to be an enormous inconvenience for most Britons, a more contentious and financially devastating consequence of the fuel shortage was a 'three-day week' order that legislated the reduction of all non-essential services to a Monday-through-Wednesday or Thursday-through-Saturday operating schedule. This legislation was implemented in early 1974, and as factories were forced to downscale production in the face of a shortened work-week, massive lay-offs and long queues for unemployment benefits quickly ensued. With fewer goods to sell to fewer customers with disposable income, many of those who worked in the retail sector soon found themselves unemployed, while those who were lucky enough to retain their jobs in the face of the three-day week were forced to work in unheated and dimly lit offices, stores and factories. By the end of January 1974, almost 1.5 million workers had registered themselves as unemployed as a result of the three-day week legislation. As one economist has noted from his vantage point a decade later, the crisis sent the British economy into a steep economic decline as the purchasing power of the pound fell continuously and precipitously through the mid-1970s and inflation topped out at 24 per cent in 1975.[6] Few employment opportunities existed for British youth who were poised to enter the job-market in the mid-1970s, as many punks would have been, and the sense of hopelessness about the future is a common theme in punk. Interestingly, the punk response to the economic crisis tended to originate in male punk, where songs like Chelsea's 'Right to Work' (Step Forward Records 1977), The Clash's 'Career Opportunities' (*The Clash*, CBS 1977), The Sex Pistols' 'God Save the Queen' (*Never Mind the Bollocks*, Virgin 1977) and The Stranglers' 'Peasant in the Big Shitty' (United Artists 1980) painted a grim picture for young men who sought jobs in a jobless economy. The impact of unemployment on the male ego was satirized in songs like The Strangler's 'Down in the Sewer' (*Rattus Norvegicus*, United Artists 1977) or Alternative TV's 'Love Lies Limp' (Step Forward Records 1977), the latter of which implies that a man who cannot fulfil his role as a breadwinner is unlikely to be able to fulfil his role as a virile sexual partner, either. Although class and gender are often conflated in discussions about punk, themes of class oppression like those in the songs listed here were typical of male punk but were more uncommon in its female counterpart, whose songwriters responded to a set of historical events that were more reflective of their gendered experiences of class.

Redefining punk at the intersection of class and gender

Historically, the term 'punk' has defied any simple explanation, except, perhaps, that it seems inextricably intertwined with class. If we accept that 'punk' is a fluid term, we might argue that it should be understood as a 'scene' that comprises individuals who bring different ideas to bear on the construction of the social critique that constitutes punk for a particular audience at a particular time. The term 'scene', as defined by Sara Cohen (1999), fits the bill for a musical activity, like punk, that is, as she would argue, 'fluid, loose, cosmopolitan, transitory, and geographically dispersed'. Cohen counsels that 'rather than linking scenes with notions of a clearly defined and place-bound community or subculture with a relatively fixed population … scenes are created through heterogenous "coalitions" and "alliances" based on musical preferences, thus linking scene with cultural change and interaction'.[7] What a definition like Cohen's invites us to do is to look more closely at the individuals who populate a subculture (like punk) and who negotiate what the terms of that subculture will be. For a study of female punk, this approach is particularly helpful because it acknowledges 'difference' within the scene and also forces us to examine how 'difference' arises out of the particular experiences of those who comprise the various subsets of punk (based on their gender, their geographical locale, their ethnic backgrounds, their chronological age and so forth) and how 'difference' expresses itself in approaches to punk fashion, song-writing and performance.

Implicit in Cohen's statement is the assumption that scenes or subcultures (like punk) emerge at the intersection of a number of social categories (of which 'class' is only one). The theory of intersectionality to which this approach alludes is a sociological method that traces its origins to feminist theory, where the gendered identity category of 'woman' (and, by implication, its counterpart, 'man') has been critiqued as a superficial and one-dimensional (mis)representation of a subject who comprises more than her gender. As with the category of class, 'gender' is not a monolothic category but must be read through its intersection with class and other social categories, such as race or ethnicity, to name just two. As the term suggests, 'intersectionality' construes the subject as an individual whose identity resides at the confluence of each social field to which that subject can claim membership (of which gender is merely one). The basic aim of the theory is to critique second-wave feminism and to ask whether it is 'possible for us to think of a woman's "womanness" in abstraction from the fact that she is a particular woman, whether she is a middle-class Black woman living in North America in the twentieth century or a poor white woman living in France in the seventeenth century'.[8] (Of course, we can reformulate the question in a third-wave context to ask if it is possible to consider an individual's 'working-classness' apart from that individual's gender, sexuality, race, nationality and historical position.) A question like this, which is central to intersectionality, not only differentiates subjects on the basis of gender but also differentiates the gender categories into which subjects can be placed on the basis of class, ethnicity, and historical context. However, while it may seem obvious that a given subject can describe herself, or be described by others, as an aggregate of identifiers, the binarisms that are implicit in such identity categories as gender, sexuality, class and race imply power differentials that become important ingredients in the analytical process. The point of intersectional theory has been to foreground the experiences of those individuals who might otherwise fade into the background of sociological research by virtue of their association with a particular subordinate social group or set of groups. The intersectional approach has been particularly useful to Black feminist scholars, for example, because it provides a way to highlight forms of oppression that are unique to their experiences but that would otherwise go unnoticed in research that categorizes subjects either by gender or by race, but not by both simultaneously. Intersectional scholars have argued that, in feminist research that describes oppression merely in terms of gender, 'the experience of black women is apparently assumed to be synonymous with black males or white females; and since the experiences of both are equivalent, a discussion of black women in particular is superfluous. It is mistakenly granted that either there is no difference in being black and female to being generically black (i.e., male) or generically female (i.e., white)'.[9] In a sociological approach that fixates exclusively on one or the other identity category, the Black female subject disappears either into the category of race or gender and is thereby given no attention separate from these two generic categories where she is subordinate to the male subject, on the one hand, or the white subject, on the other. Although the study of the Black female experience might appear on its surface to have very little to do with a study of a predominantly white musical genre like punk, the statement can nonetheless be mapped onto the current study with a different set of parameters. In studies of popular music that focus on an abstract notion of 'class' as the prime factor in the creation of punk, the experiences of female working-class participants are often seen as synonymous with, and enveloped within, those of the scene's male working-class participants who, by virtue of securing recording contracts at a greater rate than women, have come to represent the genre for posterity. At the same time, the recent trend towards scholarly studies of women in popular music has tended to assume a non-specific category of 'woman' that equates the experiences of working-class women with those of their middle-class sisters. To paraphrase the given quotation, one mistake to avoid in punk scholarship is to assume that there is no difference in being working-class and female to being generically working-class (i.e. male) or generically female (i.e. middle-class).

The perspective of the oppressed subject is foregrounded in intersectional research because it is believed to present the most honest assessment of the historical and cultural environment that fosters the biases that control her life. Donna Haraway (1991) explains that

> the standpoints of the subjugated are not 'innocent' positions. On the contrary, they are preferred because in principle they are the least likely to allow denial of the critical and interpretive core of all knowledge. They are savvy to modes of denial through repression, forgetting, and disappearing acts – ways of being nowhere while claiming to see comprehensively … 'Subjugated' standpoints are preferred because they seem to promise more adequate, sustained, objective, transforming accounts of the world.[10]

As Haraway suggests, intersectionality provides a conceptual apparatus that allows for critique of societal systems by those whose lives are most affected by decisions and interpersonal dynamics over which they have little control. Despite their lack of power, or perhaps because of it, the oppressed subject must be more attuned to her surroundings than a subject who has more power, and from this canniness, her experiences will capture a more complete picture of what her society is like. To give a familiar example from the intersectional literature, a Black maid who is employed in a white, middle-class home must understand the traditions and mores of a culture and class that is not her own if she hopes to retain her job, whereas the specifics of her life can pass unnoticed by her employers.[11] The oppressed subject is therefore able to see her social surroundings more clearly and comprehensively than those subjects who are not required to consider any standpoints but their own. Intersectional theory argues that the perspective of the oppressed individual provides a better point of departure for an analysis or critique of her social environment than the perspectives of those who hold power within that environment.

Like the Black maid in the middle-class home, many British punk rockers and their fans found themselves marginalized in a society that was controlled and dominated by socio-economic groups that held power over them because of their comparative wealth. Traditionally, the British working-class, from where many (though not all) punks originated, existed to serve the needs and interests of the middle- and upper-classes, who profited from their labour but who were required to pay little or no attention to the values or interests of the class that they exploited. Despite their invisibility, the Black maid or the punk rocker is not required to accept the situation in which she finds herself and, instead, can use the information that she gleans from her standpoint relative to her oppressor to construct a threat to the status quo in which she is imprisoned. Put another way, to propose a viable critique of mainstream culture, punks needed to understand the middle- and upper-classes in order to subvert their values. Punk's claim to musical naïveté is a prime example of a subversive act (and one of many that characterize the genre, as I will demonstrate in the ensuing chapters) because it exposes the conventional notion of musical 'expertise' as prejudiced against those whose economic status presumably prevented, or at least hampered, the development of their musical abilities. Similarly, the visual aspects of punk's subculture deliberately positioned punks against conventional practices in fashion, make-up and hair design, and the myriad punk personae that were conceived within the scene were intended to pose a direct threat to established attitudes about beauty and respectability. The extent to which punk understood the class structure that it sought to critique can be measured by the reactions of those whose values were targeted by punk rock. The Sex Pistols, for example, sparked vitriol when they famously appeared on Bill Grundy's television programme on the evening of 1 December 1976. Their odd appearances, coarse language and seeming intoxication scored a palpable hit against the middle-class viewers of the show who had tuned in just after dinner. Despite Grundy's own inebriation during the interview, the band became the target of verbal attacks in the press, where they were depicted as a threat to Britain's culture and way of life.[12] The reaction, which initially misrepresented Grundy as the victim of punk aggression rather than the dismissive provocateur who goaded the Pistols during the show, demonstrates the limited perspective that Grundy and his supporters in the press brought to bear on their interactions with the band. The Pistols, on the other hand, were successful in their quest to challenge the societal status quo because they understood how to offend their adversary and, in the end, to expose his bias.

Though the identity category of class is an obvious starting point for any discussion of punk, particularly since it is a recurring theme throughout the scene, I have argued that this category can, and should, be nuanced. What I propose here is a redefinition of punk in which 'class' provides only one piece of the puzzle. The reason for this is that the punk landscape was populated by those who performed class in decidedly different ways, each of which was meant to reflect a particular perspective on an identity category that was shaped by factors beyond class. Given the emphasis upon individuality in the construction of punk, it makes sense that 'class' should be construed as one of many identity categories, each of which intersect in different ways within the lives of those who participated in the scene. Although this study purports to focus on the contributions made by female punk musicians to a scene where they were embraced as active participants to a degree that was unparalleled in mainstream popular culture, gender, like class, will be used merely to narrow the scope of identity categories in the study. Like the intersectional scholars in feminist scholarship from whom I derive the conceptual framework for this examination of punk, the subjects to whom I will turn my critical eye will be those who represent an oppressed 'other.' As members of a scene that was already 'othered' in relation to mainstream popular culture, female punks potentially inhabit what Haraway describes as a 'preferred standpoint' in their roles as 'others' within a group that is already subordinated. Haraway would argue that their double subjugation by class and by gender allows female punks to 'see (more) comprehensively' than their male peers as they construct challenges to a mainstream culture in which they have been made invisible. While the male punk perspective could focus on class as the most notable source of societal oppression, the preferred standpoint of the female punk revealed how oppression on the basis of class was experienced differently, and perhaps more acutely, by women.

The modes of resistance adopted by female participants in the punk scene can be understood as a response to the social changes that took place in Britain in the 1970s, in part as a result of second-wave feminism and the advancements in reproductive technology that allowed women to map out biological destinies that differed from those of their mothers. Although I have no solid evidence that female punks, many of whom were teenagers at the time that they joined the scene, had read any feminist literature or joined the ranks of the feminist organizers in the mid-1970s, the themes explored in many female punk songs suggest that this subset of punk responded, at the very least, to ideas that were 'in the air' at the time. Where male punk tended to ruminate on the impact of class inequality on the ability of men to fulfil their traditional role as the breadwinner, female punk railed against gender inequality in such songs as Au Pairs 'Diet' (*Playing with a Different Sex*, Human Records 1981), Siouxsie and the Banshees' 'Suburban Relapse' (*The Scream*, Polydor 1978) or The Slits' 'Typical Girls' (*Cut*, Island Records 1979). The idea in songs like these, and the many others within punk that protest the subjugation and objectification of women, was to voice the unspoken plight of working-class female youth who found few role models in mainstream culture. Further, these songs (and the appearances and behaviours of those who performed them) also sought to invite the gaze, while at the same time objecting to the idealization of women that was the product of the gaze. To understand this strategy, which emerged in female punk from the confluence of gender and class in the experiences of those who produced the songs listed above, the observer must understand the social conditions under which this subset of punk originated and to which it responded. While working-class British women lived through the same economic crises as their male partners in the 1970s, they also witnessed the rise of second-wave feminism as a political movement designed to protest gender inequalities in the private space of the home and in the public space of workplace, where women found themselves in increasing numbers as the decade unfolded.

British second-wave feminism: The rationale for the 'gendering' of punk

While the economic climate in Britain helped to underscore the financial disparities in British society, it also forced an examination of stereotypical gender roles, spurred on in part by the economic circumstances faced by working-class women who were often required to seek work outside of the home in order to contribute to the family finances. Paradoxically, the post-war British family tended to be defined through the 1970s in traditional terms by those in positions of power who had inscribed a gendered division of labour into various post-war reconstruction policies aimed at revitalizing Britain in the 1940s and 1950s. For example, policies like William Beveridge's *Social Insurance and Allied Services* Report (1942) framed gender stereotypes that continued to resonate through the 1970s, whereby the British family was idealized as a partnership between a working husband and a dependent stay-at-home spouse whose proper role in the reconstruction effort would be to 'ensure the continuation of the British race' through childbirth and the unpaid domestic labour associated with child-rearing.[13] To assist families in this task, the Beveridge Report took such proactive steps as the establishment of a family allowance to offset the cost of raising children, the creation of the National Health Service to provide free health care and the commitment to full employment in the wake of the war for its male citizens (a guarantee that admittedly vanished in the economy of the 1970s). As medical breakthroughs and changing attitudes towards female reproductive rights began to present choices to women who would otherwise have been destined to roles as housewives and mothers, a workplace that was marked as male seemed increasingly outdated and impractical, particularly as the economic crises of the 1970s began, quite literally, to hit home. As early as December 1961, the roles prescribed for women in the Beveridge Report were challenged when Enoch Powell, in his role as Minister of Health in Harold Macmillan's Conservative government, announced that married British women would be given access to birth control pills under the National Health Service. Women would now be allowed to decide when, or even if, they would become mothers, and could opt for different kinds of lives than those led by their mothers and grandmothers. This legislation was followed in 1967 by the Abortion Act, which made it possible for women to receive a legal abortion if a physician determined that a continued pregnancy would threaten their physical or mental health. This new reproductive freedom may account, at least in part, for the increase in female participation in the British workforce through the 1970s: as the feminist movement was gaining steam in 1971, women comprised roughly 38 per cent of the British workforce, a number that climbed to 43 per cent by the end of the decade.[14] What the figures fail to reveal, however, is that despite their increased participation in the job market, women tended to find themselves in gendered employment where they performed jobs that were viewed as traditionally 'female' (such as sewing, light manufacturing, typing or domestic service) and that were paid less than jobs that were viewed as traditionally 'male' (such as heavy industrial work, transportation and office management). Disparities in pay between male and female workers became a topic of heated contention by the late 1960s, and the extent to which women's work was undervalued in the workplace was corroborated in a 1969 pamphlet entitled *Women's Liberation and the New Politics*. Its author, the British feminist Sheila Rowbotham, proposed that the conventional image of the housewife led directly to discrimination in the workplace, where she suggested that jobs performed by women merely replicated the kinds of tasks that they performed at home.[15]

Although access to birth control facilitated the pursuit of employment by all women, working-class females, in particular, joined the workforce in growing numbers through the 1970s because of the economy and to offset financial losses incurred by husbands who were un- or underemployed or who found themselves on the picket-lines as the economic crisis deepened. Although the ideal of the at-home wife and mother was touted by the British government, it was rarely a feasible option for families at the bottom of the economic ladder, where women were often forced to perform what has been described as a 'double-shift' or 'double-day' of labour as housewives within the home and as secondary breadwinners in jobs outside of the home.[16] While this was especially true for working-class women of the 1970s, the British feminist Hannah Gavron revealed that the trend traced back several decades in her study of female employment in Britain, *The Captive Wife* (1966). Gavron reveals that exhaustion and frustration were common complaints among working-class women who tended to be consigned to unskilled or semi-skilled jobs in the manufacturing sector and who faced few opportunities for advancement and lower wages than their male counterparts.[17]

Despite their hardships, working-class women were central to the fight for equality in the workplace, and their plight was a key issue in the establishment of female trade unions in the late 1960s. Disparities in pay and employment mobility fuelled a growing militancy among working-class women that culminated in a landmark strike for equal pay in 1968, during which female sewing machinists at the Ford plant in Dagenham demanded both a raise in pay and a change in the classification of their jobs to bring them on a par with similar jobs performed by men. The strike, which began on 7 June and lasted for three weeks, eventually yielded a pay increase that brought the female machinists to within 8 per cent of what their male counterparts earned, but without a reclassification of their jobs. (Surprisingly, this last demand would not yield a positive result until 1984.) The Dagenham strike served as a template for ensuing demands for equality in pay that resulted in the February 1970 walkout of female clothing workers at forty-five factories in Leeds, the May 1976 shutdown at the Trico-Folberth windscreen wipers factory in Middlesex and the two-year strike by Asian women at the Grunwick Film Processing plan in North London from August 1976 through July 1978. Although, or perhaps because, the issue of reclassification remained unresolved after the Dagenham strike, female workers decided to form a trade union that would represent their interests. The National Joint Action Campaign for Women's Equal Rights (NJACWER) focused initially on the issues of parity in pay and access to employment and held demonstrations in London that prompted Barbara Castle, then the Secretary of State for Employment and Productivity in Harold Wilson's Labour government, to push for the Equal

Pay Act of 1970 in the wake of the Dagenham walk-out. When the Equal Pay legislation was implemented in 1970, women earned only 64 per cent of what men earned for full-time work, and although this differential shrunk by 10 per cent by the middle of the decade, when the Equal Pay legislation came into full effect, equal pay for work of equal value remained illusory because jobs held by women continued to be classified at lower ranks than similar jobs held by men.[18]

The formation of the NJACWER represented the first organized effort for women's liberation in Britain, and the group met annually through the 1970s to establish a series of demands for legislative reform aimed initially at addressing the issue of job reclassification, among other things. At its 1971 meeting, the group demands included equal pay for equal work, equal access to employment and education, abortion on demand and twenty-four-hour day-care to facilitate female participation in the workforce. These demands were publicized on 6 March 1971, when the group held its first International Women's Day march in London, and became a theme in the British feminist magazine *Spare Rib*, which launched its first issue in 1972 with a mandate to explore alternatives to the traditional female roles of housewife and mother. In 1974, the NJACWER added two more demands to the original four at its annual meeting when its membership agreed to campaign for legislation that would ensure financial and legal independence for all women and that would end workplace discrimination on the basis of sexual orientation. While the original demands focused upon women's rights in the workplace, these later demands sought to challenge existing societal structures by establishing a legal foundation for single women and gay couples. The debates that took place at the 1974 meeting encouraged activism among gay feminists in the group, some of whom subsequently organized the first National Conference of Gay Women later that same year. In 1977, the NJACWER was dominated by discussions about rape, violence against women, classism and child custody, in the wake of the Yorkshire Ripper murders that were occurring in and around Leeds and that would eventually leave thirteen women dead before Peter Sutcliffe was identified and convicted in 1981. The attacks prompted feminists to organize the first 'Reclaim the Night' march in Leeds on 12 November 1977, which was replicated in dozens of British communities and held annually thereafter. At the 1978 meeting of NJACWER, members agreed upon a demand for stiffer penalties for domestic violence and sexual coercion, but the discussions that preceded the demand were particularly divisive and ultimately led to a split between radical feminists who believed that female liberation could only be attained by a wholesale rejection of patriarchal social structures and socialist feminists who argued that men could play an important role in enacting social change. Despite their differences, both strands of the British feminist movement worked together to identify key issues that would coalesce into a feminist mandate. By the end of the 1970s, British feminists had identified financial equality and independence, reproductive rights, sexuality and male violence against women as key elements of women's liberation.

Female punks were surely aware of feminist activism in the 1970s, and although we have little evidence that any female punks took part in the kinds of activities described above, the themes explored in their music reveal a keen awareness of the 'women's issues' that lay at the heart of the feminist movement, as Chapter 2 will reveal. We can assume that female punk's interest in such topics as the captivity of the housewife, the difficulties of the 'double-day' work schedule faced by working women and the constant demands placed upon women to prioritize the quest for 'beauty' (in spite of everything else that they were expected to do) emerged out of personal experiences of class and gender oppression in the lives of those who created punk from a female perspective. These were topics that female punks sought to expose in their music as a means to critique what has already been described as conventional assumptions about 'womanness' both as they reflect a hegemonic (middle-) class perspective and as they reinforce a subordinate (female) gender perspective.

While economic and social history informs our understanding of punk and helps to tease out the differences between the gendered subsets of the scene as we work towards a more nuanced definition of the term, one further aspect of punk needs to be examined. As I have said in my opening remarks, one of punk's most famous quips was its invitation to punk wannabes to learn three chords and form a band. Tacit in this credo is the suggestion that punk was meant to be an 'outsider' genre in a popular music environment that privileged musical aptitude and thereby limited participation to those who, perhaps by virtue of training or, at the very least, access to well-crafted instruments, could meet the standard set by the music industry. British punk was as much a response to its historical and cultural circumstances as it was to the constraints placed by the music industry upon participation in the construction of popular culture. In what follows, I will frame the intersectional argument once again – this time discussing the relationship between class (coded first as male) and the music industry (also coded as male), and reconsidering the relationship of class-and-gender (now coded as female) to the music industry (again coded as male). I will foreground the difficulties faced by women who sought to break barriers within the music industry in the 1970s both to highlight how extraordinary many of punk's female artists were and to demonstrate biases within the industry that ultimately privileged male punks (despite their association with a subordinate class) with recording contracts in larger numbers than their female counterparts (because these women were 'acting out' of their subordinate gender). It is important to note that the privileging of male participants in the scene likely explains why issues surrounding class oppression have often taken precedence over issues of gender in punk scholarship.

Historical constraints on women in the music industry

Recent studies of the popular music industry have demonstrated that female participation in the construction of popular culture has been inhibited and restricted by an institutional framework that is dominated by males. Institutional barriers to women in the popular music industry have been relatively easy to discern by scholars because they are so overt and can be measured statistically from comparisons of the ratio of males to females in such settings as record companies and studios, radio stations or in music journalism. However, while institutional bias in popular culture might be obvious, some of its effects are less easy to detect and therefore prove to be more difficult to combat. Specifically, male authority over the production and distribution of popular music has had a significant impact on the ways in which this music conveys its meanings to the consumers for whom it is intended and, perhaps more important, on the ways in which those consumers come to perceive themselves both relative to each other and to the musicians whose recordings they share. Consumer identity is linked to the semiotics of popular culture, which is coded strongly as male and which skews its signifiers in such a way as to trivialize or to exclude the female perspective on that culture. The same is true of performer identity, which embraces the male musician as 'normative' and which dismisses the female as 'aberrant'. Institutional power and symbolic power are thus intertwined, with the former reinforced by the latter and the latter produced by the former. My concern, for the moment, is not to explain how females who aspire to careers in popular music might break this cycle of power or, failing that, how they might clear a space for their contributions to popular music in a male-dominated environment. This will occupy the next section of this chapter. To set the stage for that discussion, we need to examine how the female 'other' is constructed in popular culture by pointing out the institutional and symbolic barriers faced by women in popular music. Admittedly, much of the research done in this area has focused upon the last forty years and has tended to make only passing reference to the 1970s, when punk rock made its debut (and also saw its demise) in Britain. Despite this shortcoming in existing research, a picture of the constraints placed upon women in the production of 1970s popular culture emerges from a study of record charts and music magazines of the time, both of which reinforce observations of female 'otherness' in more recent forms of popular music-making.

In her study of British 'indie' music in the 1980s and 1990s, Mavis Bayton (1998) has argued that participation in the institutions within which popular culture is constructed has historically reflected and reinforced a traditional gendered division of labour in which females typically find themselves in subservient roles to their male counterparts. Her study reveals that while men employed in the music industry will scout for new musical talent, assume key managerial positions in recording companies, make production decisions in the engineering booth, oversee the packaging, marketing and distribution of recordings, select songs for radio playlists and report upon musical trends as journalists, women have largely been excluded from these key decision-making roles. By contrast, she demonstrates, women have often found themselves in supporting roles within the industry, 'contributing' to the creation of popular culture from such faceless and powerless positions as secretary, receptionist, personal assistant or factory worker. One early study of female representation in the music industry shows that in the mid-1970s, or the period immediately preceding punk, only 7 per cent of jobs in the industry were held by women, and of those, 10 per cent were classified as secretarial positions, with the remainder of women employed in the areas of publicity and art direction.[19] Not surprisingly, because the history of the popular music industry has tended to chronicle the contributions made by those in (male dominated) managerial positions, females in the industry have been largely written out of its history, and this has proven to be as true for the 1970s as it is for the period studied by Bayton. In the ensuing discussion, I will examine the various ways in which women have been excluded from the popular music industry, with special focus on Britain.

During the heyday of British punk, the British music industry was dominated by four major recording labels that produced the bulk of the 'hit' popular music recordings of the period: these labels included Decca, EMI, Polygram and WEA (Warner-Elektra-Atlantic).[20] Despite the prominence of these labels in the UK market, smaller labels existed in Britain alongside the so-called 'big four', noteworthy among which were Island Records, Virgin, RSO, Rough Trade, Chiswick and Stiff, with the last three of these notable as the labels that signed and recorded many punk artists at the beginning of the punk movement. Without exception, each of these labels, both big and small, was founded and directed by a man, and in the 1970s, men continued to monopolize key managerial roles within each of these companies. Although a comprehensive list of British record executives in the 1970s would be too sizeable to include here, a few notable examples of male executives who were directly associated with British punk include Bob Mercer (the managing director of EMI who signed, and then dropped, the Sex Pistols in 1976), Richard Branson (who founded Virgin Records in 1972 and signed the Sex Pistols in 1977), Geoff Travis (who founded Rough Trade in 1978), Roger Armstrong and Ted Carroll (who co-founded Chiswick in 1975), and Dave Robinson and Jake Riviera (who co-founded Stiff in 1976). Beyond these directorship positions, other important roles within the recording industry have also been dominated by males.

Some of the most influential middle-management positions in the recording industry are to be found in the 'artist and repertoire' (A&R) area, where musical trends are monitored and influenced by personnel who seek to discover and secure a contract with the 'next big star'. The commercial success (or failure) of a recording company depends largely upon the abilities of its A&R personnel to predict or respond to trends in popular music and to identify artists who will reflect those trends. Any misstep on the part of an A&R representative either to identify a potentially lucrative artist or to convince a recording company to secure that artist with a contract can be costly. (Perhaps the most famous example of this kind of blunder occurred when the Decca label ignored the advice of its A&R representative, Hugh Mendl, and opted against a contract with The Beatles.) For a variety of practical reasons, women were historically shut out of the A&R area and have therefore had little input on decisions about the music that will enter the marketplace. The task of securing new talent is a job that requires long hours, many of which are spent in bars, pubs and nightclubs. Obligations to family and children often limited the extent to which women were available at night, but perhaps an even bigger obstacle to potential female talent scouts (and an obstacle that was also faced by aspiring female musicians) was the safety of the venues in which new musical acts were often found. In her study of the Liverpool scene of the 1990s, Sara Cohen describes a situation that is neither unique to that city nor to that time-period when she observes that 'many of its venues … are situated in narrow back streets around and behind the main city centre thoroughfares. These are areas that many, particularly women, might feel uncomfortable venturing into at night'.[21] Despite this observation, the potential for sexual attack is something that male A&R representatives have to consider less than their female counterparts as they perform their jobs, and in this way, male talent scouts were less hampered by the conditions under which they had to work. Without sizeable representation at the level of the talent scout, then, it is hardly surprising that women have only rarely ascended through the ranks to A&R directorships, where recording contracts are negotiated and signed and where decisions are made about the musical directions that a company will take.

Production and sound engineering has been another area that has been the near-exclusive purview of men, not because of any latent physical dangers in the working environment of the recording studio but, instead, because the studio has traditionally been viewed as a male domain. Much of this has to do with the gendering of education, from where those who inhabit the recording studio have come to perceive 'a culturally understood "fit" between masculinity and the "mastery" of "complex" technologies (i.e., those that are not concerned with domestic work)'.[22] This observation is supported by Lucy Green (1997), whose research on gender differences in music education has shown that young girls were often discouraged by their teachers from studies in science and technology and were therefore largely ill-equipped, and therefore reticent, to pursue careers in sound engineering. The comparative lack of females in the studio has had a significant impact on female participation in the construction of recorded artefacts, because, as one observer has noted, 'the ideology of rock, and therefore its meaning, revolves around sound. Recording technology, as the means by which sound is manipulated and reproduced, is the site of musical and political power in popular music'.[23] The process of recording produces a musical document that is often more widely accessible than a live performance and that therefore becomes the sole point of reference to the majority of listeners who may have no access to live versions of a given song or set of songs. In the recording studio, artistic and technical decisions made by record producers can alter a song considerably and thereby can contribute new meanings to the 'live' performance upon which the recording is based. However, since 'historically few women have been producers in the traditional sense', the female voice has been largely silenced in the process of constructing any new meanings that might come to be inscribed onto the musical object during the process of its recording, editing, mixing and mastering.[24]

Once an artist has been signed to a contract and their music has been captured and processed in the studio, the industry must find strategies to market that artist to an audience of consumers. Writing at the time of punk, Chapple and Garofalo (1977) demonstrated that this was one of the few areas within the recording industry where women have found ways to participate in meaningful ways, although in lesser numbers than men. Women in marketing positions have tended to be called upon for their perceived expertise in areas like wardrobe and hairstyles or for their opinions about staging for photographs, and have therefore played a central role in the construction of the public image that will be used to 'sell' an artist (and, by extension, his or her music) to the consumer. This is a significant contribution because, without a convincing or compelling image that captures and retains the interest of an audience, an artist might be hampered in his or her quest for success in the marketplace. However, while women may have assumed advisory roles in the areas of marketing and packaging, they rarely produced or edited the images that were released into the marketplace and therefore had little power over how the meanings associated with those images were contextualized in the promotional materials in which they appear. Often, these meanings have tended to reflect the well-worn narrative of 'sex and drugs and rock 'n' roll', which has been invoked repeatedly in the popular music press to depict the kind of lifestyle that musicians are assumed to enjoy and which pushes women to the periphery of popular culture as mere purveyors of 'sex' for male musicians (and for their male fans). Since 'media messages can act as teachers of values, ideologies, beliefs and … can provide images for interpreting the world whether or not the designers are conscious of this intent', the ways in which images of popular musicians are deployed have tended to cancel out the contributions made by women to the construction of those images.[25]

Before the advent of music videos in the early 1980s, 'media messages' were conveyed largely through images that appeared as album-cover artwork or in photographic records that were published by the popular music press. In both of these promotional arenas, depictions of females belie any participation of women whatsoever in the construction of popular music iconography and serve, instead, to reinforce gender stereotypes and to draw a stark contrast between the roles of men and women in the campaign to sell popular music. Perhaps the most obvious examples of differences in gender portrayals lie in the visual depiction of females in album cover artwork, whose history is replete with examples of graphic sexual imagery that diminishes and belittles women and that portrays them as mere playthings that exist solely for the gratification of the male artists upon whose album covers they appear. Female models have been used variously on album covers in nude still photographs, either alone or with other female nudes, or engaged in staged sexual acts with men, other women, animals or objects, while in more 'benign' examples of album-cover art, women are portrayed as scantily clad or in bikinis, sometimes wet and often oiled. While instances of female nudity are so numerous that they have become almost prosaic and unremarkable – except in cases where the brutality or tastelessness of an image is particularly strong, as in a case like the Dwarves' 1990 gruesome album cover for *Blood Guts & Pussy* (Sub Pop 1990) – the few instances of male nudity on album covers stand out as unusual and noteworthy – as, for example, in the case of Prince's nude cover for *Lovesexy* (Paisley Park 1988), which caused an uproar at the time despite featuring the artist in the kind of modest pose denied to many female models on other album covers. The hyper-sexualization of women on the album covers of male musicians also extends to depictions of female artists themselves as they are portrayed on their own album covers. Rarely are female musicians represented by degrading images of men, and instead women often represent themselves as objects whose sexuality is highlighted for the purpose of increasing sales.

In their portrayals in popular music tabloids, women fare only slightly better, although the ways in which female musicians are objectified and sexualized by marketers nonetheless have a discernible impact on the ways that they are regarded and discussed in the press. In large part, the female personae that are constructed by the industry are given their meanings by the press, which has traditionally been dominated by male critics, photographers and editors whose gender biases reinforce the stereotypes that they inherit from marketing executives. Like many other areas in the production of popular music, journalism has been a difficult career for women, in part because of the rampant sexism in the field. In reflections upon her career, one former female journalist has noted that 'several women [in the popular music press] use the "locker room" analogy to describe the fraternity of rock critics as well as the atmosphere surrounding rock stars – particularly the backstage area, where, if you're a woman, it's assumed that you're a groupie'.[26] Statistically speaking, male predominance in rock journalism has been demonstrated by Kembrew McLeod (2002), whose study of the field reveals that, by the late 1990s, women comprised about a third of the journalists at *Melody Maker* – figures that are corroborated by a headcount of females in

Rolling Stone and *Spin* during the same period, where women held less than 20 per cent of the editorships or journalist positions.[27] Male control over popular music journalism has meant that decisions about which artists and bands merit attention and about how these musicians will be portrayed in popular music tabloids have reflected a decidedly male perspective. Bayton's (1998) work has shown that the press has focused upon male musicians more often than their female counterparts, chronicling their 'lives' (or, at least, the lives constructed for public view by marketing executives in the recording industry) in photographs and interviews more often than those of female musicians by a ratio of 9:1.

Like the history of the popular music industry, where female contributions to the construction of popular culture remain largely unrecognized by those who have documented the music industry, the various histories of rock that are represented in music tabloids have frequently overlooked the contributions made by female musicians. The careers of male artists have been carefully documented in the press, and their music can therefore be more easily contextualized within a broader history of (male) popular music, but the same kind of continuity has not been offered to female musicians by the few journalists who opt to discuss their music. Instead, women have been presented in the press as novelties, with each new female artist or band heralded by rock journalists as something new, unexpected, and without a prior history. These kinds of descriptions of female musicians are common in popular music journalism, where the 'otherness' of women has spawned various 'special issues' devoted to women in music over the years. Some of these include 'Cute, Cute, Cutsy Goodbye' (*NME*, March 1980), 'Riot Grrrl! The New Girl Revolution' (*Melody Maker*, October 1992), 'The Women's Movement' (*Rolling Stone*, September 1989), 'Women of Rock' (*Rolling Stone*, November 1997), 'Women in Rock: 50 Essential Albums' (*Rolling Stone* 2002), and 'The Girl Issue' (*Spin*, November 1997). Such descriptions of women have also seeped into the mainstream press, where opinions about the behaviours of female musicians are aired in such headings as 'The Girls – Letting Go' (*Newsweek*, July 1969), 'Chick Singers Need Not Apply' (*Time*, January 1980), and 'These Big Girls Don't Cry' (*Time*, March 1985). As Marion Leonard has noted, 'the very phrase "women in rock" is itself problematic. Rather than simply pointing to the activity of female musicians within a particular music genre, the phrase usually works to peculiarise the presence of women rock performers.'[28] It is noteworthy that an issue that would focus on 'men in rock' would seem to be too self-evident to the (male) readerships of these, and any number of other, rock tabloids to warrant the kind of attention that the topic of 'women in rock' has received in the popular press, which suggests that while male participants in the construction of popular music culture are viewed as normative, women are anomalous and therefore merit a different kind of attention and description.

The disproportionate focus of journalistic writing on male popular music is also reflected in the many photographs that fill the pages of music tabloids. Bayton (1998) has shown that men, as the subjects of more journalistic essays than their female peers, are also photographed more often than women. Further, in many visual depictions of male performers, and in particular in shots that capture live performances, tabloids have manufactured the idea of the 'woman as wallpaper', where female fans and groupies, seen dancing, screaming and fainting at popular music concerts by male musicians, provide a backdrop to the actions of men. When they *are* photographed in the press, female musicians are objectified and more highly sexualized than their male counterparts, according to Bayton, and are often captured on film without their instruments in tow and more frequently depicted in 'still' portraiture than in 'live' performance. Similar to the way that female models are objectified on album-cover art, in the popular music press, 'the emphasis in photos of women musicians is on their bodies. … Women are often photographed from below, with the camera looking up their skirts'.[29] The message that these photos convey to the reader of popular music tabloids is that a female musician in the popular realm is valued less for her songwriting abilities or her musical skills than for her appearance and, in that sense, that she is meant to be seen but not heard. Helen Davies (2001) argues that 'the constant stress on women's attractiveness and sexuality is easy to identify and criticise [but] a more subtle form of sexism operates around issues of credibility. In the eyes of the serious music world, credibility is the most important factor in determining the value of a performer of a piece of music'.[30] She suggests that in popular music, credibility is awarded by the press (and, as a result, by consumers of popular music) to those who are perceived by their listeners as both serious and intelligent. She argues that in its focus on the physical aspects of female performers (particularly their weight, their clothing and the size of their breasts), the press downplays or ignores the cerebral aspects of their music and therefore denies legitimacy to females as popular musicians. By contrast, the comparative lack of interest in the physiques of male performers (who can presumably weigh what they want and dress as they may within the limits prescribed by the executives who package their public image for the marketplace) has allowed the press, and by extension its readership, to focus instead on the music that they produce and perform and therefore to authorize male artists as more credible purveyors of popular culture than their female counterparts. Descriptions of musicians in the popular press therefore convey the message that while males contribute musical artefacts to popular culture, females who aspire to performance careers in popular music must also be prepared to contribute hyper-sexualized images of themselves in order to be as marketable as their male peers.

While the foregoing has chronicled a history of female exclusion behind the scenes of popular music-making, consumers may remain largely unaware of the legion of (male) executives, producers, engineers and marketers who lie behind the musical products that they purchase. However, while they might be oblivious to, or choose to ignore, the gender imbalance in the music industry, consumers cannot fail to notice the obvious inequities on the performance stage, where male musicians historically held more prominence as the subjects of media and fan attention and adulation and were therefore the most visible locus of power in a communicative act that the performer appears to initiate and control (albeit, in the case of the recorded artefact, with the input of the producer and marketer). In an industry that promotes male musicians more than their female counterparts, women find many barriers to their full participation in the construction of popular culture, many of which trace their origins to the comparative lack of support and mentorship given to aspiring female musicians within an industry that has few women in key managerial positions. Since male executives dictate the terms by which popular music will present itself, it is hardly surprising that topics and themes that are explored most often in popular music will be coded as male. As Mary Ann Clawson (1999a) explains, 'sexist lyrics and aggressive, misogynistic performance styles comprise a "rock 'n' roll discourse" which … makes it difficult for women and girls to envisage themselves as rock musicians, to imagine themselves on stage, and thus to begin learning the skills that might take them there'.[31] Among the UK chart-toppers in the 1970s, bands like Slade and T-Rex charted with songs that were explicit in their chauvinism, with lyrics that were clearly designed to debase women and to underscore their roles as fans, groupies and sexual playthings. In other hit songs from the decade, particularly from artists like Barry White and Leo Sayers, females are not debased but were portrayed as objects for worship. Other songs, like chart-toppers by Gary Glitter or Queen, ignored women altogether and, instead, focused upon the (male) singer's life and experiences. As long as female fans had few role models to follow, and as long as they were debased, objectified or ignored in the lyrics of the songs that they heard, it would seem that the performance of popular music would continue to be dominated by men. And Bayton suggests that this cycle is unlikely to end, given that popular culture is a training ground where 'young women and men learn how to be feminine, masculine, and heterosexual through listening to rock music, and observing the clothes, bodily gestures, and general preference of rock musicians as they simultaneously perform gender, sexuality, and music'.[32] Female participants in popular culture become entrapped within the gender roles that are prescribed by male popular-music idols and that are described in the songs that they perform, which has meant that it has been easier for a would-be male performer to embrace the role of the 'rock musician' than it has been for a female aspirant in an industry that perceives her as 'other'.

When women *do* contribute their voices as musicians to the creation of popular culture, the stage presents other kinds of barriers to their full and equal participation in popular music-making. Philip Auslander (2004), for example, points out that 'although there were many women in rock by the late 1960s, most performed only as singers, a traditionally feminine position'.[33] Moreover, both he and Nicola Dibben (1999) assert that women have tended to perform songs whose lyrics were often written by men and thereby to inherit a mode of performing gender from a perspective that is not their own.[34] This is certainly true of the 1970s, where female performers tended to find themselves consigned to such 'pop' genres as disco and R&B, fronting for a male band and performing songs that were written by male songwriters. On the British Market Research Bureau (BMRB) charts from that decade, performers like Tina Charles, Kiki Dee, Freda Payne, Diana Ross and Deniece Williams are notable examples of 'successful' female participants in popular culture, although their contributions were restricted to the 'traditional feminine position' of the singer and none participated in the process of songwriting. Only two of the female artists at the top of the charts, Minnie Ripperton and Tammy Wynette, wrote the songs that they performed, although in each case, the work was co-authored with a male songwriter.

Although female singers and singer-songwriters are vastly outnumbered by their male counterparts, female instrumentalists find themselves even further marginalized in the performance of popular music. Philip Auslander's study of one of the first women to make her career as bass guitarist, Suzi Quatro, contends that the instruments common to guitar-based popular music (the electric guitar, electric bass and drums) have become so encoded as 'male' that they continue to seem anathema to conventional constructions of 'femininity'. Auslander remarks that much of the gendering of the guitar lies in its phallic associations, and he argues that the stance used by male guitarists during performance (who tend to hold the guitar with its neck facing forward and who prop it low on the hip) reinforces that imagery. However, this fails to explain Quatro's success on the bass, which yielded two hits on the BMRB charts in the 1970s with 'Can the Can' (RAK Records 1973) and 'Devil Gate Drive' (RAK Records 1974) (both songs were written by male songwriters Nicky Chinn and Mike Chapman). Mary Ann Clawson (1999b) accounts for her success by observing that the instruments to which women have been permitted access in popular music-making are those that are less appealing to men. She asserts that male performers continue to hold the monopoly on the electric guitar, which they find to be more interesting and challenging to play, and have loosened their grip on the bass because they perceive its function as supportive to the more dominant guitar. What this has meant is that 'the star status of the guitar is conflated with its gendered character. If the rock band is, as a unit, a masculinizing institution, then its most visible and flamboyant instrument, the electric guitar, is understood as the masculine instrument par excellence, while the bass is the instrument men are least motivated to monopolize for themselves'.[35] Further, she notes, the bass is seen by musicians as the easier of the two to master and therefore somehow more accessible to female performers. In a series of interviews with amateur popular musicians in the Boston area in the 1990s, she discovered that 'everyone who discussed it agreed not only that the bass is perceived as the rock instrument that can be learned most quickly but assumed that ease of learning would be important for women … [because] women commonly begin playing rock instruments and join bands at considerably later age than do men'. Gender bias in the performance of the guitar therefore rests on a theory of competency, where males are viewed as more adept on their instruments than females, and therefore more appropriately featured as the leading instrumentalist. In the 1970s, however, Quatro was viewed as an anomaly for her instrumental choice, and despite her commercial success as a bassist, she only reached the top of the charts for three weeks in the seven years that preceded punk. So while male guitarists might have dominated the popular music market at that time, men ceded very little control over the bass guitar as well.

Interestingly, while studies of female guitarists have begun to surface in popular music scholarship, there has been comparatively little scholarly attention directed towards female drummers. Clawson's data, albeit drawn from a very small sample and within a very specific geographical location, nonetheless shows that women have made fewer gains in securing access to the drum-set than they have with the bass. She speculates that, unlike the bass, the drums continue to be the near-exclusive purview of males because they 'express the loudness and power that is central to rock music and to an occupation of sonic space that is coded masculine'.[36] What she suggests is that it continues to be more acceptable for a man to be 'loud' than it is for a woman. Moreover, the instrument has been associated with a set of performance practices that are overtly aggressive and that thereby reinforce the masculine coding of the instrument. In the 1970s, female drummers were exceedingly rare, perhaps with the notable exceptions of Maureen ('Mo') Tucker (The Velvet Underground), Denise Dufort (Girlschool) and Karen Carpenter (The Carpenters). Not surprisingly, no female drummer is represented among the female artists who appear in the 1970s BMRB charts, while on the *New Music Express* (*NME*) charts, The Carpenters cover of 'Please Mr. Postman' (A&M 1974) reached the top of the charts in 1975, but with Alvin Stoller credited as the drummer on that track.

From executive positions within the industry to creative positions in the recording booth or on the stage, in both its visual and its aural signifiers, in print and in performance, popular music has been a domain that has been controlled largely by men and that has reflected a conservative perspective on the gendering of labour that curiously contradicts the outwardly liberal façade of popular culture. On occasion, women have made headway in their quest to secure meaningful roles to play in the construction of popular culture; however, this has required them to come to terms with societal expectations of what it means to be 'female'. Put more plainly, it has forced female participants in the music industry to position themselves as 'other' against more typical constructs of the female. At the same time, the 'otherness' of the female participant is highlighted against the male, who is characterized as normative by those who work in the music industry and who therefore comes to be viewed as normative by those who engage with the industry as consumers. In her concluding remarks, Bayton argues that:

> since becoming a musician requires seeing yourself as a bit unusual – an 'artist', a bohemian, a rebel against nine-to-five workaday normality – I would argue that, regardless of whatever else the rebellion is against, for women it is all that it is for men, plus an extra dimension – resistance to gender norms. If male rock musicians are rebellious, then women are doubly rebellious so that any factor which acts to nourish and sustain the revolt against hegemonic femininity will enhance the likelihood of women becoming rock musicians.[37]

Parameters for the study

Because I focus on female punk, my study proceeds from the category of gender to construct an explanation of gender through its relationship to class and other social categories. I argue that females experience class, and class oppression, in different ways than their male counterparts, particularly as the classism that they experience intersects with sexism. We can expect female punk to be different from its male counterpart as a response to these two forms of oppression, of which one is uniquely felt by women. However, class and gender are not the only social categories from which we can posit 'otherness' in female punk. The categories of culture, race and age, all of which are operative in the sample that comprises this study of female punk, bring different perspectives to bear on what it means to be oppressed as a working-class woman. In the chapters that follow, a redefinition of 'punk' will emerge from a careful study of the differences between male and female punk as expressions of resistance. Taking the female standpoint as its point of departure, the study argues that meaning in punk is dynamic, relational and arises from the interplay of signifiers that contributed to punk's social critique from the different perspectives of each participant in the scene.

As I described in the introduction, the group of women that I have chosen for this study of punk is diverse in terms of race, ethnicity, age, educational background, marital status and even socio-economic class. This group ranges in age from fourteen to forty. Some of its members joined punk from an art-school environment, while others started their adult lives in factory jobs. The sample comprises women who were born in England, Spain and Germany. One of the artists identifies as biracial. Most of these women were young and unmarried at the time that they participated in the scene, but a divorced mother of two also claims membership in this group. Finally, some of these women opted to form bands that excluded men, while others embraced men as members of their bands. As the epilogue will also show, the life trajectories of these women were also decidedly different, as some abandoned music to start families, while others pursued careers outside of music (curiously, however, each of these women returned to punk later in life). Despite these differences, the musicians chosen for this study hold in common their gender and an empathy for the working-class, whether or not they claimed membership in it. In the chapters that follow, a clear picture of what it meant to be female and punk in the late 1970s and early 1980s will emerge from an intertexual reading of the texts, images, music and life narratives that were created by a body of pioneering British musicians who changed the parameters for women in music and whose creative work has left an enormous impact on popular culture.

Notes

1   In many accounts, the first wave of British punk actually began on 22 October 1976, when The Damned released the first punk single, 'New Rose', on the independent label, Stiff. The year 1977 represents the year in which the Sex Pistols' various publicity antics brought the genre into view for those consumers of mainstream popular music.

2   This point is central to Mimi Haddon, 'Not Playing Properly: Amateurism as Generic Choice in Three Postpunk Case Studies', *Women and Music: A Journal of Gender and Culture* 23 (2019), 159–83.

3   Dave Laing, *One Chord Wonders: Power and Meaning in Punk Rock* (Milton Keynes: Open University Press, 1985), 26.

4   Christopher Partridge, *Dub in Babylon: Understanding the Evolution and Significance of Dub Reggae in Jamaica and Britain from King Tubby to Post-Punk* (London: Equinox, 2010), 176.

5   Nathan Wiseman-Trowse, *Performing Class in British Popular Music* (London: Palgrave Macmillan, 2008), 127.

6   Noble, Trevor, 'Inflation and Earnings Relativities in Britain after 1970', *British Journal of Sociology* 36/2 (June 1985), 239.

7   Sara Cohen, 'Scenes', in *Key Terms in Popular Music and Culture*, eds. Bruce Horner and Thomas Swiss (Oxford: Blackwell, 1999), 239–45.

8   Elizabeth V. Spelman, *The Inessential Woman* (Boston, MA: Beacon Press, 1988), 13.

9   Deborah K. King, 'Multiple Jeopardy, Multiple Consciousness: The Context of a Black Feminist Ideology', *Signs: Journal of Women in Culture and Society* 14 (1988), 45.

10 Donna J. Haraway, *Simians, Cyborgs, and Women: The Reinvention of Nature* (New York: Routledge, 1991), 191.

11 The maid-as-outsider is a topic explored, for example, in works like Mary Romero, *Maid in the U.S.A* (New York: Routledge, 1994) or Mahnaz Kousha, *Neither Separate nor Equal: Women, Race, and Class in the South* (Philadelphia, PA: Temple University Press, 1999).

12 For a complete transcript of the two-minute exchange between the Pistols and Grundy, I direct the reader to George Gimarc, *Punk Diary: The Ultimate Trainspotter's Guide to Underground Rock 1970–1982* (New York: Hal Leonard, 2005), 49.

13   As quoted in Jane Lewis, *Women in Britain since 1945: Women, Family, Work and the State in the Post-War Years* (Oxford: Blackwell, 1992), 21.

14   Linda McDowell, 'Life without Father and Ford: The New Gender Order of Post-Fordism', *Transactions of the Institute of British Geographers* 16/4 (1991), 409.

15   Sheila Rowbotham, *Women's Liberation and the New Politics* (Nottingham: Bertrand Russell Peace Foundation, 1969).

16   This is a point made in relation to maids by Mary Romero (Romero, 18*ff*), but is just as applicable to working-class women who performed what Rowbotham describes as 'traditional' female roles in the workplace, and then replicated many of these tasks in the evening hours as they performed their 'traditional' roles within the home.

17   Hannah Gavron, *The Captive Wife: Conflicts of Housebound Mothers* (London: Routledge and Kegan Paul, 1966).

18   Linda McDowell, 'Father and Ford Revisited: Gender, Class and Employment Change in the New Millennium', *Transactions of the Institute of British Geographers* 26/4 (2001), 450.

19   Steve Chapple and Reebee Garofalo, *Rock and Roll Is Here to Pay: The History and Politics of the Music Industry* (Chicago, IL: Nelson-Hall, 1977), 290.

20   For a more detailed description of each record label, see Desmond Hesmondhalgh, 'Post-Punk's Attempts to Democratize the Music Industry: The Success and Failure of Rough Trade', *Popular Music* 16/3 (1997), 258*ff*.

21   Sara Cohen, 'Men Making a Scene: Rock Music and the Production of Gender', in *Sexing the Groove: Popular Music and Gender*, ed. Sheila Whitely (London: Routledge, 1997), 29.

22   Marion Leonard, *Gender in the Music Industry: Rock, Discourse, and Girl Power* (Aldershot: Ashgate, 2007), 51.

23   Steve Jones, *Rock Formation: Music, Technology, and Mass Communication* (Newbury Park, CA: Sage, 1992), 2.

24   Albin Zak, *The Poetics of Rock: Cutting Tracks, Making Records* (Berkeley, CA: University of California Press, 2001), 173.

25   William A. Gamson, David Croteau, William Hoyes, and Theodore Sasson, 'Media Images and the Social Construction of Reality', *Annual Review of Sociology* 18 (1992), 374.

26   Evelyn McDonnell and Ann Powers, *Rock She Wrote: Women Write about Rock, Pop, and Rap* (New York: Cooper Square Press, 1995), 18.

27   Kembrew McLeod, 'Between a Rock and a Hard Place: Gender and Rock Criticism', in *Pop Music and the Press*, ed. Steve Jones (Philadelphia, PA: Temple University Press, 2002), 94.

28   Leonard, 32.

29 Mavis Bayton, *Frock Rock: Women Performing Popular Music* (Oxford: Oxford University Press, 1998), 171.

30 Helen Davies, 'All Rock and Roll Is Homosocial: The Representations of Women in the British Rock Music Press', *Popular Music* 20/3 (2001), 304.

31 Mary Ann Clawson, 'Masculinity and Skill Acquisition in the Adolescent Rock Band', *Popular Music* 18/1 (1999a), 102.

32 Bayton, 1.

33 Philip Auslander, 'I Wanna Be Your Man: Suzi Quatro's Musical Androgyny', *Popular Music* 21/1 (2004), 2.

34 Nicola Dibben, 'Representations of Femininity in Popular Music', *Popular Music* 18/3 (1999), 331–5.

35 Mary Ann Clawson, 'When Women Play the Bass: Instrument Specialization and Gender Interpretation in Alterative Rock Music', *Gender and Society* 13/2 (1999b), 199.

36 Clawson, 201.

37 Bayton, 194.

2

'Fairytales in the supermarket': Texts

The categories that we use to define ourselves and to sort out the roles that we will play relative to others in our social environments arise from a set of master narratives through which we view and interpret the world. These master narratives seem real to us because they are rooted in the stories that we tell ourselves about how the world works, even though they are premised upon idealizations of particular role models or ways of behaving in our society that may be difficult, or impossible, to replicate in our own lives. Nonetheless, we embrace and attempt to imitate these exemplars, sometimes actively and sometimes subconsciously, because they reflect what we perceive to be our social reality as it manifests in the roles and behaviours described in the stories that comprise our culture. As the British philosopher Mary Midgley (2003) notes, master narratives 'are not detached stories. They are imaginative patterns, networks of powerful symbols that reflect our surroundings and that are perpetuated in our learned behaviours'.[1] Master narratives therefore serve as repositories of the cultural signifiers that represent our surroundings and that differentiate groups of individuals who are separated in place and time and who coalesce into differing categories based on socio-economic class, gender, ethnicity, race and so on. The feminist theorists Mary Romero and Abigail Stewart (1999) argue that master narratives reflect the perspectives of hegemonic social groups and should be understood to represent not only the ways in which we organize our view of the world but also the structures of power that control our behaviours and that dictate how *not* to be, how *not* to act and how *not* to interpret the world. They argue that master narratives are guilty of 'erasing plot elements that don't fit', thereby marginalizing or erasing those who fail to imitate the exemplars that are centred in a given society's story.[2]

As a strategy used by hegemonic groups to silence and control individuals who reside outside the norms established by those groups, the master narrative is an ideal point of departure for a study of punk since it provides context for the counternarratives devised by punk. Commonly understood as a genre that originated from the standpoint of those who felt oppressed because of class or who identified with those who faced classism, British punk is often perceived as an angry commentary on a society that wrote the unemployed or the working poor out of a master narrative that focused upon, and often idealized, the lives enjoyed by members of the middle- and upper-classes. Punks challenged what they perceived to be a cultural landscape that excluded signifiers of the working-class and responded to this exclusion with counternarratives that were meant to question, and even threaten, the cultural hegemony of the dominant classes. The various stories recounted in the lyrics of punk songs and the themes to which stage names and titles allude combine to form a narrative of resistance to class oppression or, at the very least, a narrative that conveys working-class disillusionment and frustration with a society that stripped the underclass of any power or control over their lives. However, despite its ubiquity in descriptions of the genre, class is not the only social category operative in punk but, rather, represents only one facet of punk's resistance to the master narratives from which the working-class was excluded. Women were notable participants in the punk scene, and their sizeable contributions to punk brought the category of gender into dialogue with class in punk's social critique. As individuals who were oppressed by the economic and cultural hegemony of the middle- and upper-classes *and* by dominant expectations about femininity and domesticity that were imposed by those hegemonic classes, the working-class women who populated the punk subculture and whose experiences were chronicled and fictionalized in punk songs experienced class differently than their male counterparts. These women found themselves erased from view because they were unable or unwilling to participate fully and uncritically in a cultural narrative that expected them to forfeit paid work for domesticity and motherhood, to fixate on their home as the most important marker of their success and to devote their spare time to the pursuit of feminine beauty. The idea in female punk was that if the lives of working-class women were meant to be lived in silence (i.e. ignored or dismissed by the media), punk would command attention by engaging unapologetically in offensive acts and behaviours or by embracing impolite or explicit topics and language that were typically off-limits to women.

A close reading of punk texts as they manifest in names, song titles and song lyrics demonstrates a gendering of perspective relative to class. Where male punks constructed counternarratives that resisted classism through expressions of anger, disillusionment and frustration with a system that offered few employment opportunities and little hope for the future, female punks expressed resistance to the repressive gender norms and expectations that were imposed upon women by the media and circulated through marketing. For women in the punk scene, idealized images of domesticity, like those referenced in The Raincoats' debut single 'Fairytale in the Supermarket' (Rough Trade 1979) and paraphrased in the title of this chapter, were both illusory and unappealing. As this chapter will demonstrate, female punks confronted master narratives by appropriating and subverting the meanings of signifiers drawn from the experiences of middle-class women (like the supermarket) and by imposing new meanings on them. Through the process of turning class signifiers against the hegemonic classes (or *détournement*), plot elements that were conventionally peripheral to, or erased from, dominant master narratives became highlighted in descriptions of the experiences of those who would otherwise have remained invisible because of their class, gender or both.[3] At the same time, plot elements that were traditionally foregrounded in dominant master narratives were parodied or dismissed by punks.

Countering master narratives

Simon Frith (1978) has argued that a community of listeners will coalesce around what he describes as a set of 'lyrical floaters', or themes, ideas and images that recur within a musical repertoire and that refer to familiar social structures or routines. In British punk, these floaters typically originate in narratives about class and reference unemployment and the frustration and despair that ensue.[4] However, songs about the menial labour performed by the working-class, or about the lack of such jobs for youth who are skilled to do little else, tend to assume a male subject. The anger expressed in British punk about the lack of opportunities for working-class youth who sought jobs in the depressed economy of 1970s Britain is predominantly *male* anger. By contrast, many female participants in the British punk scene offered critiques of gender norms that required their female subjects to cede power and control to husbands and boyfriends and to accept roles prescribed for them and reinforced in media depictions of femininity and domesticity. As tokens that challenge gender and class, lyrical floaters in female punk tended to engage with themes of domesticity, romantic love, feminine beauty and consumerism, each of which was subjected to intense scrutiny and challenged by the counternarratives constructed by female punks.

The largest proportion of lyrical floaters in the songs examined for this study originates in the myth of the traditional family, which is critiqued in punk both for the middle-class perspective that it represents and for the restrictive gender roles that it portrays and reinforces. In its characterization by Betty Friedan (1964), the idealized family depicted in the media comprises 'the suburban housewife with an up-and-coming husband and a station wagon full of children' who coexist in a home that is purchased and financially sustained by a male breadwinner and tended by a nurturing wife and mother.[5] While Friedan's statement predates punk by a decade and describes a typically American conception of the family, British families in the 1970s were also held to this standard as it was promoted in women's magazines, among other places.[6] In popular British journals like *Jackie* or the weekly *Women's Own* and *Women's Weekly*, articles devoted to such topics as dating and marriage, cooking and home décor reinforced the traditional belief that a woman's place is in the home. In this scenario, the 'home' is a space designated exclusively for members of the same family, where children are provided a safe and happy environment in which to grow and develop into adults who will replicate the myth of the family in their own lives. Male success in the traditional family is therefore measured in terms of a salary and the ability to secure a space within which his family can be housed and raised, while female success is entirely dependent upon the kind of male partner that a woman can attract and on her ability to keep him entrapped in marriage by surrounding him with tokens of his virility (children) and the material tokens of his success (stylish furnishings, a modern kitchen and a beautiful wife). Where money defines power for men in the traditional family, fertility and domesticity provide vicarious access to power for women who attach themselves to successful husbands and providers in the master narrative of the family.

Because of its perpetuation in 'women's magazines, by advertisements, television, movies, novels, columns and books by experts on marriage and the family, child psychology, sexual adjustment and by the popularizers of sociology and psychoanalysis', the master narrative of the family, and the gender roles that it reinforced, was a source of intense critique in second-wave feminist literature and, later, in British punk.[7] Feminists argued that the family demanded enormous concessions from housewives, who surrendered financial power, and hence decision-making, to their earning spouses. Once marriage and children had taken control of their lives, bored and frustrated wives and mothers were left to wonder if domestic ennui was unique to them, since it was never discussed openly in public. Unacknowledged unhappiness and dissatisfaction with lives devoted to housework and child rearing prompted Friedan to describe the ennui as 'the problem that has no name'. Like their second-wave feminist contemporaries, women in the British punk scene asserted that the nameless problem would only be solved when women were freed from the domestic confines of the home and the nurturing duties associated with their children. In many songs, punk depicted the home and the family as sites of female oppression, where housewives were held captive to the whims of their husbands and often subjected to emotional and physical abuse from which they could never escape. However, unlike their feminist counterparts, for whom gender was the prime source of female oppression, female punks also suggested that the discursive construct of the traditional family represented a middle-class ideal that ignored the working-class realities felt by many British women and their families. In songs that focused upon portrayals of working-class families, female punks argued that media idealizations of the family came to bear an increasingly distant resemblance to the everyday experience of family life in Britain in the 1970s, even though evidence of the power and ongoing pervasiveness of the master narrative of the family in British society was evident not only in the media, but also in various political directives. The Beveridge Report, cited in the previous chapter of this book, continued to encourage British women to contribute to post-war reconstruction efforts through the 1970s by having children and raising them within the nuclear family. Further, the urgency for British nationals to bear children increased in some political circles as the immigrant population began to swell through the decade and to allegedly threaten the primacy of British-born whites in a nation that was becoming increasingly multi-cultural and, in response, xenophobic. More insidiously, social strategies like the Beveridge Report also implied that a woman who sought employment outside of the home jeopardized the stability of the family that she was supposed to nurture from within the home. Social ills like divorce and juvenile delinquency were attributed to female non-participation in the mythic traditional family, and working mothers were therefore vilified as the source of these ills. Further, as I demonstrated in the history surrounding punk, the job market itself reinforced traditional gender roles within the family with rampant disparities in pay and job classifications that buttressed the prevailing view that women made more valuable contributions to British society within the home than in the workplace. Lower salaries for work performed by females ensured their ongoing dependence upon male breadwinners who would continue to be viewed as the main source of income for the family and to whose principal salary women would presumably add their smaller wages. Reinforced by government policies and reiterated in the media, the master narrative of the nuclear family erased working women from its plot by denying their existence or by minimizing the contributions of their labours to the workplace and the importance of their earnings to the family. Working-class women whose financial circumstances required them to seek paid employment outside the home were therefore caught between a dominant master narrative that erased them from view and a reality that demanded them to work outside the home.

As a trap that enticed women into futile lives of domestic servitude within the family, the myth of the fairytale romance was another source of lyrical floaters in female punk. This myth, which was marketed to women in magazines and romance novels, is premised on an idealized male paramour whose interests lie less in his own sexual gratification than in the proper treatment of the woman he adores. In this fictional account of romance, Germaine Greer (1971) argues that the male hero 'knows how to treat women, … nothing hasty, physical, [but rather he engages her in] mystery, magic, champagne, ceremony'.[8] The promises of a 'happily-ever-after' life that ensue from this narrative and that are endlessly reiterated in the lyrics of mainstream popular music were answered by 'happily-never-after' punk narratives in which women found themselves neglected, betrayed or battered by partners who were supposed to worship them but who resented and spurned them instead. Where single females are the object of male adoration in the fairytale romance, they are portrayed in punk as individuals who are trapped by societal expectations that they must 'settle down' with a 'suitable' male partner while they are still young enough to be sexually alluring and to produce offspring. When an appropriate suitor fails to present himself, as it does for many of the female subjects described in punk, women simply make do with any partner who is available, many of whom prove quickly to be indifferent or hostile towards them. Like punk songs about the family, these 'anti-courtship' songs originate from a particular class perspective and suggest that male anger and the spousal abuse that it engenders has its roots in the emasculation felt by working-class men who were unable to find jobs. As the targets of the emotional or physical abuse meted out by their disillusioned partners, the female subjects of punk songs experience depression, paranoia and fear in their romantic relationships. In the end, female punk songs that engage in an anti-courtship narrative conclude that men are shiftless, untrustworthy and prone to violent outbursts that they direct towards their female partners. Out of this stark punk counternarrative, an inversion of gender roles is presented in some punk songs, where female subjects seize control over their relationships by adopting the attitudes and conduct of their male oppressors. The liberated women who are described in this handful of songs tend to be emotionally detached from their partners, self-absorbed and dictate the terms of their relationships to men who are held captive to their emotional whims.

Other lyrical floaters originate in the beauty myth, which held women to an unattainable physical ideal constructed by the fashion and cosmetics industries and perpetuated in the media. Closely aligned with the myths of domestic bliss and fairytale romance, the beauty myth suggests that in order to attract and retain a male breadwinner, a woman needs to aspire to an ideal female type that is, most often, characterized by such attributes as a slim physique, a flawless complexion, a perfect hairstyle and a keen sense of fashion. Thus conceived, a woman is objectified as another token of her male partner's material success: her appearance entices him into marriage and she subsequently coexists with other decorative objects in the 'perfect' home that she creates and maintains for him. Despite its strong associations with the traditional housewife, the beauty myth endured for women who opted out of the domestic narrative and who joined the labour force. Naomi Wolf (1991) has argued that as household technology began to release women from many time-intensive domestic duties, and thereby enabled women to juggle the demands of the home with the demands of paid employment outside of the home, 'the beauty myth took over [domesticity's] lost ground, expanding as [domesticity] waned to carry on its work of social control'.[9] She argues that a woman who works outside of the home is more visible than her domestic counterpart and her appearance is therefore subject to greater evaluation and regulation by those who will determine her success in the employment market. But the problem that women face, according to Wolf, is that they are constantly thwarted in their attempts to respond to a myth that posits a category that is neither natural nor universal but that is, rather, a moving target whose standards change over time and rarely reflect the distinctive physical characteristics of the 'average' woman. Beauty is a form of cultural currency that imposes standardized and unattainable ideals of physical perfection upon women by male institutions that seek to limit and control their access to power. Women who aspire to success in this symbolic economy cannot afford to dismiss beauty as trivial, but must embrace its ideals as a 'legitimate and necessary qualification for a woman's rise in power'.[10] Further, Wolf suggests that the female face and body are sites of symbolic representation upon which a woman displays the degree to which she is prepared to cooperate in the reproduction of societal values. Women who develop and display an ideal body type or who work to rid their faces of the signs of ageing, for example, signal their participation in a culturally meaningful system of values that has been imposed upon them. Conversely, women who embrace, or strive to construct, an appearance that is in opposition to the prescribed female ideal can be said to engage in a form of symbolic resistance to the beauty myth.

Female punks argued that the system of values that determined and reinforced feminine beauty in the 1970s represented the heteronormative, white, middle-class patriarchy. By resisting conventional categories of beauty as antithetical to the experiences of the working-class and non-white populations, female punk not only opposed the chauvinist gender norms that measured female success in terms of beauty, but also challenged class and racial prejudice. Women who expressed themselves through punk suggested that standards of female beauty impose a singular identity upon women and thereby devalue or erase those whose identities conflict with the established female norm. In the 1970s, for example, supermodels like Cheryl Tiegs, Farrah Fawcett and Bo Derek served as templates for those who aspired to conventional female beauty, and the extent of their influence on women can be seen in the adoption of their signature hairstyles, among other things, by scores of women at the time. However, these female exemplars also illustrate the degree to which working-class and non-white women, and white women whose physical and facial features fell short of the desired ideal, were excluded from the narrative of feminine beauty. For example, while Derek's beaded hairstyle appropriated from Black culture, neither she nor the media that promoted her 'look' drew connections to that source for those who imitated her. For others, the designer clothing modelled by these exemplars was out of financial reach and created for a narrow range of unnaturally thin body types. As a counternarrative to the beauty myth, female punk songs parodied the supposed female obsession with cosmetics and vilified fad diets as a potential source of illness. In a reversal of the beauty myth, punk celebrated the 'ordinary' female, and in some cases, touted 'ugliness' as an ideal to which women should aspire.[11]

The myths of the nuclear family, romance and female beauty were reinforced by a myth that suggested that consumers could opt into any and all of these mythic states if they were willing to purchase their material trappings. Writing a decade before punk, the British economist Ralph Glasser (1967) argued that the false promise of happiness through consumption arose as a post-war response to the financial and material constraints forced upon Britons during the war. He suggested that advertisements served as a form of re-education through which post-war spending was presented as a panacea for the stress and unhappiness experienced by many during the war. Post-war consumers were told to believe that money could buy happiness in a process that Glasser describes as 'Aducation'.[12] By the 1970s, advertisements showed family members how they were supposed to look, live and interact with one another within the home, and these representations of British society also idealized aspects of life outside the home in work, love and romance. When working adults were portrayed in the media, they tended to be professional males who held white-collar jobs in stylish offices that were tended by attractive female, yet-to-be-married secretaries (whose roles in the workplace merely replicated the nurturing roles that they would later adopt as wives and mothers). Depictions of the home, by contrast, focused on the stay-at-home housewife who was aided in her domestic tasks by technological innovations and an ever-changing spectrum of cleaning products. Media depictions of the 'perfect home' and the 'ideal housewife', in particular, proliferated in women's magazines and in television and film representations of family life. According to one observer, women were targeted in particular by advertising executives because they acted 'as the guardians of home and family leisure [and were thereby] charged with choosing and purchasing for the house'.[13] Consumers came to think of the home as a site where modern appliances stood as tokens of material success. Access to appliances also helped to drive the beauty myth in consumer culture, since housewives who were relieved of the hard manual work of tending to the house presumably became free to focus almost exclusively on their physical appearances. Since appliances now did all the work, at least according to advertisements, women had no excuse not to look their best. Although it can be argued that the families, romances and individuals depicted in the media rarely reflect the experiences of most 'ordinary' people, that is precisely the point of advertising: exemplars are constructed to convince consumers to purchase products that promise to bring their lives closer in alignment with a given ideal. However, these exemplars also underscore class difference. While many middle-class British consumers could participate somewhat freely in the new consumer culture that emerged in the wake of the war and that was in full swing by the 1970s, most found themselves trapped in an endless quest to keep abreast of an ever-changing landscape of fashion trends, cosmetics, household furnishings and appliances, and other products. By contrast, working-class consumers found that their participation in the consumer myth was financially constrained and, because they were less likely to be consumers, they became comparatively invisible to advertising executives. Moreover, working-class families, homes and workplaces could not be romanticized or idealized to the same extent as their middle-class counterparts, and therefore presented fewer opportunities to those who sought to display and sell the latest consumer goods.

Angela McRobbie (1991) argues that the myths of courtship, marriage, domesticity and beauty that are marketed to female consumers have no parallel in the social spheres that are coded as male. Her study of magazines, in particular, demonstrates that while women's journals fixate on these themes, 'male magazines tend to be based on particular leisure products or hobbies, motorcycling, fishing, cars or even pornography'.[14] Accordingly, songs written by female punks often distinguish themselves from their male counterparts by commenting on, and lampooning, gender stereotypes encoded in certain myths and reinforced in the media. However, the resistance to gender norms by women in the punk scene is also directed towards middle-class values that are represented in social myths about women's lives. Depictions of romance, the family and feminine beauty are heavily coded as middle-class, and thereby marginalize working-class females and the punk artists who sought to represent this class perspective, both by gender *and* by class. In this chapter, I will examine how women resisted sexism and classism in lyrical floaters like stage names, song and album titles, and song lyrics, each of which contributes to the web of meanings that comprises women's contributions to punk.

Names

In popular culture, the names or titles that are attached to musical genres, bands, artists, fans, albums, songs, recording labels and fanzines contribute meanings to musical objects that help to situate them within a particular field of cultural production. Naming in popular music is a representational act in which monikers are chosen to evoke connections between artists or bands and such things as everyday objects, historical or cultural events, emotional states or existing songs and their artists. In choosing a name for themselves or for their band, musicians enter into a dialogue with the world of objects that they share with their listeners, and their choices will convey certain meanings to those listeners. A name like 'The Beatles', for example, connotes both rhythmic energy (expressed as the 'beat') and an intellectual affiliation with post-war, countercultural 'beat' poetry. Alternatively, it might also be understood as a clever pun, reflecting the sense of humour for which the band became known in interviews and lyrics.[15] Similarly, 'The Rolling Stones' might be understood as a play on words in which 'roll', as a component of 'rock 'n' roll', places the band within a particular musical genre, and 'stone' as a synonym for 'rock' reinforces the band's association with that genre. Further, the use of the term 'stone' also connotes a lifestyle of excess enjoyed by its members, whose legendary use (and abuse) of drugs and alcohol meant that they were often stoned as they were 'rocking and rolling'. In interviews, the band also suggests a third meaning for their name when they claim to have derived it from the title of a song recorded by Muddy Waters in 1950. This reading of the name also acknowledges the impact of American blues on the band. Finally, according to the proverb with which the name can be associated, a 'rolling stone' can also imply movement, a lack of rootedness or an ongoing quest for fresh ideas and creativity.

Like their mainstream predecessors, punk musicians sought to harness the semiotic potential of naming, although they tended to construct names from signifiers that challenged existing taboos in popular culture and that tested the limits of social acceptability. As Dave Laing (1985) notes in his foundational study of punk, the name assigned to the genre provides a starting point for the oppositional tone taken by punk musicians and fans towards mainstream culture. In its modern usage, the term 'punk' has come to denote a disaffected young man, typically from working-class origins, who often found himself in trouble with the law. In popular culture, for example, the term tends to characterize the kind of male delinquency depicted in such iconic movies as *The Wild One* (1953) and *Rebel without a Cause* (1955) and has been applied to the characters portrayed in these films by Marlon Brando and James Dean, respectively. Laing suggests that the 'connection between those figures and rock 'n' roll, in the person of Elvis Presley, opened the way for "punk" eventually to become part of popular music stylistics' and, we might add, its lexicon.[16] Those who aspire to 'punk' can presumably find examples in the behaviours of such prototypes as Brando, Dean or Elvis Presley (although Laing fails to demonstrate how, or whether, punks mimicked these popular icons). Matthew Worley (2024) adds that, from a musical perspective, the term 'punk' 'flickered in and out of rock's lexicon as the 1960s turned into the 1970s, gradually transforming from adjective to noun as it connected to recognizable attitudes and styles'.[17] He notes that the term has come to be applied (often retroactively) to such American bands and artists as the Fugs, the Stooges, MC5 and Lou Reed and to various American garage bands. The definitions offered by Laing and Worley reveal the coding of 'punk' as male through its associations with such male outsiders as juvenile delinquents and male artists who resisted the artistic confines of commercialized popular music. Despite this strong association between punk and masculinity, scholars like McRobbie (1991), Reynolds and Press (1994), Raha (2005), Reddington (2007), Goldman (2019) and others argue that the coding of 'punk' as male did not preclude female participation in the subculture. Instead, punk's openness to difference presented possibilities for women in the scene to position themselves as different to their male counterparts in the punk subculture and to create new ways of expressing femininity.

Typically, punk bands and individuals adopted names, and thereby created identities, from 'qualities, objects and activities that established media discourse … could be relied on to find despicable or disgusting'.[18] However, as punk naming illustrates, the ways in which 'disgust' was aroused in the mainstream observer of punks was contingent, in large part, upon gender. For male participants in the punk scene, 'disgusting' punk names often served to challenge and criticize the class bias that seemed to be built into British society whereas, for female punks, these names were often chosen to highlight how classism and sexism worked together to marginalize the country's working-class women. It is important to note the disparity in the reception of 'disgusting' names in punk and the fact that women who created names from taboo terms faced greater backlash (and misunderstanding) than their male counterparts.

For example, we can look to the ways in which male punks sometimes confronted the marginalization of working-class men with names that appropriated symbols of the masculine power to which they were allegedly denied. Names like Buzzcocks, Cock Sparrer, Discharge or Sex Pistols pointed directly and unapologetically at their phallic sources and invoked terms that had rarely been used openly in popular discourse. The stereotype of male aggression was another source of naming in male punk in such names as The Clash, The Stranglers, Killing Joke or Stiff Little Fingers. The threats purportedly posed by male punks to the stability of British society were implied in band names that referenced illness, like Discharge or The Plague, or in names that recalled outside threats to the British Empire posed by the rise of fascism in Europe in the 1930s, like Joy Division or London SS. The tendency towards violence and aggression in male punk naming also extended to independent punk record labels, whose male founders created brand names 'that were meant to assault, shock, and subvert – Rough Trade, a pseudonym for indelicate gay sex; Stiff, for what one wanted a record not to do (sell)' and, of course, the latter can also be understood as a reference either to male sexual arousal or to a corpse.[19] Challenges to middle-class conceptions of popular culture were also posed by individual male punks, a handful of whom opted to adopt stage names that would add a certain quality to their onstage identities. The artist 'Billy Idol', who began his career as a member of the band Generation X, selected a name that can be understood both as a parody of teen adoration for male pop stars and as a reference to laziness and uselessness through its homophone, 'idle'. Names like 'Laurie Driver' and 'Howard Pickup', both of whom were members of the band The Adverts, point to jobs that were typically associated with working-class males. And signifiers of illness like 'Rotten' (of the Sex Pistols), 'Scabies' (The Damned) or 'Lance d'Boyle' (Poison Girls) added to the threats allegedly posed by punk to polite British society.

In contrast to their male counterparts, female punk names were often designed to challenge conventions of femininity that were embodied in the female ideals portrayed in mainstream advertising, created by male advertising executives and marketed to middle-class women. This approach to naming was particularly scornful of media depictions of youth and beauty and echoed a common feminist sentiment that 'glossy advertisements did nothing but convince readers of their own inadequacies while drawing them into consumer culture on the promise that they could buy their way out of bodily dissatisfaction and low self-esteem'.[20] As Angela McRobbie's 1999 study of popular women's magazines from the 1970s explains, 'there is a long history of using "female beauty" to sell products to women … and, rightly or wrongly – mass media consistently reinforce assumed linkages between women's appearance and their feelings of self-worth'.[21] McRobbie's study reveals that these magazines typically 'promoted romance as the means by which women should interpret and practice their sexuality. Inevitably this required submissive and compliant behaviour in relation to men'.[22] Female punk names often parodied gender stereotypes that arose within, and that were repeated across, the media, and although these stereotypes are multifaceted, female punks frequently chose names that focused on media depictions of female place or space, physical or emotional weakness, and female sexuality. In terms of female place, McRobbie argues that the media has instructed 'girls [to] negotiate a different leisure space and different personal spaces than those inhabited by boys. These in turn offer them different possibilities for "resistance".[23] The gendering of physical space reflects an imbalance of power between men, who hold the authority to make decisions that will have broad economic, political or cultural consequences, and women, whose decisions tend to affect only members of her family or those within her immediate social circle. In punk, female naming often pointed directly at spaces that are coded as female (the kitchen, the suburban home, the supermarket) in order to challenge both this power differential and the invisibility imposed upon women by the comparative lack of interest in the positions that they hold within society. Names that were chosen by male punks to highlight occupations associated with working-class men (e.g. Laurie Driver) therefore find their parallels in female stage or band names that referred to domestic servitude, shopping or to everyday objects that were found in the leisure or personal spaces typically occupied by women. In cases where stereotypes of physical or emotional weakness serve as the source of female naming in punk, names that connote male power through references to physical aggression or violence find their counterparts in names that parody female stereotypes of frailty, weakness, and physical or mental illness. In these cases, female subservience is expressed variously in diminutive names that use such suffixes as '-ette' or '-ie' (e.g. Mo-dettes or Siouxsie), or in names that reference ailments, like 'hysteria', that are related to women. Finally, another tactic used by female punks was to pose a direct challenge to the invisibility of women with specific and unapologetic references to aspects of female biology or sexuality in terms that were forbidden at the time (and that continue to be viewed as off-limits). Although this tactic has its parallel in male punk naming, the use of sexually charged names in female punk was even more shocking and potentially threatening to male hegemony because it represented the empowerment of women to reference their own bodies explicitly (and in some cases, clinically) in a culture where those bodies were more typically used in the service of men. Sexual names in female punk were therefore intended to confront taboos that had kept, and that continue to keep, female sexuality unspoken and hidden from view. In the ensuing discussion, a few examples will illustrate the process of naming in female punk.

The marketplace, as a social space in which gender roles are constructed by, and reflected in, the production and packaging of consumer goods, is perhaps the lynchpin that draws together the differing approaches to female punk naming. In some cases, marketing and advertising are referenced directly in the names adopted by female punks in a practice that has no corollary in male punk naming. Two bands that constructed names in this way include

'The Adverts', a band which featured Gaye Advert (born Gaye Black) as its lone female member and bass guitarist, and 'X-Ray Spex', the name of whose lead singer, Poly Styrene (born Marianne Joan Elliott-Said) contributes further meanings to the name of her band. The names chosen in each case connote consumerism, commercialism and mass marketing and are ironic in the context of punk, since advertising tends to assume a buyer whose income will allow them to engage in the purchase of goods. By contrast, The Adverts and X-Ray Spex speak for, and represent, a population that could rarely aspire to the kind of lives depicted or promised in advertising (and who didn't want to, anyway). Instead, by adopting names that reference consumerism, both bands aimed to comment upon the notion of truth-in-advertising and upon their perception of the predatory and exclusionary practices of mass marketing. Clad in leather and sporting thick black eyeliner that emphasizes her otherwise pale complexion, Gaye Advert appears as the model of 'otherness' in relation to the female ideals that were advertised in the mid-1970s and personified by such contemporary icons as Tiegs, Fawcett or Derek. Ironically, Advert is the kind of female who would be unlikely to appear in a glossy magazine advertisement, and her stage name perhaps serves to draw her closer to her female listeners, many of whom would likewise find few role models in the mainstream media. Taking a different approach to their critique of consumerism, the name 'X-Ray Spex' exposes the phoniness of advertising with its reference to a cheap, novelty item that was patented in 1909 as 'X-Ray Specs' and that guaranteed that its user would 'see through fingers – through skin – see yolk of egg – see lead in pencil!' Like the promises of the anti-ageing creams or fad diets whose descriptions fill the pages of women's magazines, those of X-Ray Specs are both implausible and illusory, and the success of the product therefore depends upon the gullibility of the consumer in the face of advertising. It could also be that the promises offered by the product signify the ability to 'see through' or to be wise to the deceptions of marketing. Further, the name suggests voyeurism, particularly in a respelling that substitutes 'Spex' (with its intimation of 'sex') for 'Specs'. The letter 'x', which appears twice in the band's reformulation of the original name, also draws a parallel between the name of the band and the name of its lead singer. The spelling of 'Spex' that is used by the band evokes such synthetic products as Perspex (known in America as Plexiglass) or Lurex, the artificiality of which is also represented in the stage name adopted by the band's lead singer, Poly Styrene. As man-made products, each of these connotes artificiality and signifies an environment that can be scientifically controlled and manipulated in a way that parallels the media construction of individual identity. On the one hand, the name X-Ray Spex exposes the fakery of advertising, while on the other hand (and consistent with the themes explored in many of their songs), it serves as a comment upon the artificiality of the life marketed to the consumer.

References to domestic spaces inhabited by women, and to the objects and activities associated with those spaces, were sometimes used to generate names for individual female punk musicians and for all-female or mixed-gender punk bands. A wonderful example is the name Helen McCookerybook, which is the stage name for the punk scholar Dr Helen Reddington, who was a co-founder of the 1970s punk band, The Chefs.[24] Other examples include the stage name 'Palmolive', adopted by the London-based punk drummer Paloma Romero, who performed with The Raincoats and The Slits, and the name adopted by the Birmingham band 'Au Pairs'. At the time of its use in punk, 'Palmolive' was known commonly as a type of dishwashing detergent whose advertisements promised the 1970s female consumer that the product would 'soften hands while you do the dishes'. The name therefore signifies the kitchen, although it is also rife with broader connotations of domesticity, female servitude and the pursuit of feminine beauty (through soft skin). The irony of its adoption as a name by a female punk drummer is clear, since the aims of a product that touts itself as an aid to a chore performed in a particular female realm contrasts sharply with the performance aesthetic of an instrument that typically symbolizes male strength and aggression. Domestic space is similarly referenced by the name adopted by the Au Pairs, whose music was notable for its explorations of gender roles and relationships. As a term that refers to a job traditionally held by young women, the name appears to point squarely at the two female members of the band, Lesley Woods (vocals and guitar) and Jane Munro (bass guitar). However, the implications of the name go deeper than these surface associations. An *au pair* is typically a foreign woman who lives with her host family and who exchanges her domestic service for a cultural education. As an outsider who lives within, and adapts to, a culture that is not her own, the *au pair* signifies 'the other' in a way that might parallel the 'otherness' of female musicians either within the punk patriarchy or within the broader popular culture whose style is determined primarily by men. However, a more sinister reading of the name emerges when we consider that the *au pair* is also a captive domestic whose complete dependence on her host family makes her both invisible to the outside world and vulnerable to potential abuse by the head of the household.[25] The name underscores a power disparity between males and females that is inscribed into the relationship between the patriarch, on the one hand, and the servant, on the other.

Stereotypes of female illness were another source of naming in female punk, perhaps the most interesting example of which invokes the term 'banshee' to refer to the London punk band that was fronted by the singer Siouxsie Sioux (Susan Ballion). Known as a portent of death in Celtic mythology, the banshee is distinguished by her shrieking or wailing hysteria – a defining characteristic of the banshee that is also reflected in the title of the band's first album, *The Scream* (Polydor 1978), and enacted in its ethereal, untexted opening track, 'Pure'. (I will discuss this song in greater detail in Chapter 4.) Siouxsie's vocals align closely with the voice of the banshee, particularly in this wordless opening track. Tracks without song lyrics are a rarity in early punk, whose meanings tend to be conveyed through the content of their texts. The absence of words makes 'Pure' particularly notable as a punk song that communicates its meanings through parameters other than words. This wordless performance conveys emotions like hysteria, confusion, angst and sometimes anger without recourse to a text. At the same time, the stage name 'Siouxsie', a play on the more conventional name 'Susie', has been interpreted by Dave Laing as a parody of 'an object of male desire in so many songs (e.g. the Everly Brother's 1957 hit "Wake Up Little Susie" on RCA Victor or Bobby Vee and the Shadows' debut single "Suzie Baby," which was released in 1959 on Liberty Records.)'.[26] Following the stereotype of female frailty, the name 'Susie', as the diminutive of the singer's actual name, evokes youth and innocence, both characteristics of which contrast with the dark and brooding image projected by a singer who would later become an icon in the goth scene. Charles Mueller (2017) has noted that 'although Ballion's stage persona and mannerisms may have been aggressive and confrontational during the band's early career, for most of the 1980s she appeared melancholy, misanthropic and introspective during performances, with minimal body movement and a searching gaze that never made eye contact with the audience or any member of the group'.[27] I would argue that the melancholic and introspective qualities that Mueller attributes to her later goth persona trace their origins to 'Pure'.

Like such male counterparts as the Sex Pistols or the Buzzcocks, some female punk names allude to sexuality through signifiers of the female experience of the sexual act or of female anatomy. Band names like Penetration, Nipple Erectors or The Slits are examples of direct engagement with female sexuality in punk naming, none of which requires much interpretation. The name Penetration, for example, originates in the title of song by the

American proto-punk band The Stooges and was used by the Durham punk band fronted by the singer Pauline Murray. The Stooges song 'Penetration' (*Raw Power*, Columbia 1973) takes the perspective of a male heroin addict and draws a parallel between sexual penetration and the insertion of a needle into the arm of a junkie, both of which are described in the song as engendering a similar kind of high. In the hands of a female artist like Murray, by contrast, 'penetration' describes the perspective of the female subject in a sexual act. Alternatively, the word might also signify the incursion of female performers into a territory that is populated and controlled largely by men. In this reversal of its meaning, the word 'penetration' serves as a figurative 'screw you!' to the existing power structure within which women have found themselves subordinated. More blatant, and perhaps more shocking because they have no parallels in mainstream popular discourse, are the names adopted by female punks from direct and uncensored references to the female body. Perhaps the most confrontational depiction of female sexuality in punk naming was provided by The Slits, whose band name serves as the graphic female counterpart to male band names like Buzzcocks and Sex Pistols. A benign interpretation of 'slit' points to the cut that extends upwards from the hem of a skirt and that facilitates walking. This interpretation exists alongside the unmistakable phallic implication of the word, and this reading gains traction when we consider the band's most famous visual image: the bare-breasted photograph of three band members, Ari Up, Viv Albertine and Tessa Pollitt, wearing nothing but mud and loincloths, that appears on the cover of their first album, which is provocatively entitled *Cut*. While these two interpretations point to the female body, the term 'slit' (and for that matter, 'cut') also connotes physical violence and suggests the kind of injury that might be produced by a knife (as, perhaps, in the self-mutilation practices of troubled teens or in executions that involve a slash to the throat). Taken in combination with the title of the album and the album-cover imagery, the name of the band might have been chosen because of the potential threat that it poses to male hegemony by female empowerment: interpreted this way, words like 'slit' and 'cut' might also refer to castration.

Given their origins in female stereotypes and their critiques of media portrayals of women, female punk names differ significantly from their male punk counterparts, which tended to focus on class oppression, violence, aggression and hypersexuality as sources for their inspiration. Female names highlight gender disparities with their references to female space, parodies of physical or emotional weakness, and rejoinders to sexual passivity. The result was a set of names that were unique to the scene and that contrasted not only with male punk naming, but also with mainstream female naming in popular music. Music charts from the 1970s demonstrate a decided lack of oppositional naming among female artists, who either used their given names, hid behind infantilizing stage names or found themselves subsumed within family names like The Carpenters or band names like ABBA or Lady Marmalade. Names like 'Banshee', 'Slits', 'Nips' and 'Penetration' seemed designed to attract attention for those who would otherwise have remained invisible in a cultural narrative that had no roles for them to play.

Titles

Dave Laing's foundational study of British punk explains the genre through a study of a handful of punk albums that were released and gained prominence in Britain in 1977. His study builds its discussion around the first five punk albums: *Damned, Damned, Damned* (The Damned, Stiff Records 1977), *The Clash* (The Clash, CBS 1977), *Rattus Norvegicus* (The Stranglers, United Artists 1977), *Never Mind the Bollocks: Here's the Sex Pistols* (Sex Pistols, Virgin 1977) and the *Pure Mania* (Vibrators, Epic Records 1977).[28] Using these albums as a representative sample, we can see that, in the case of male punk bands, album titles were often chosen to signify misfortune, violence, thievery, male sexuality, agitation, indifference and profanity. In the case of *Never Mind the Bollocks*, the Sex Pistols cued their indifference to society with a phrase used commonly as an instruction to ignore unimportant or trivial details. The title also reinforces the phallic innuendo of the band's name and stands alongside such other signifiers of male sexuality as the vibrator, which represents a male phallus that is eternally erect. These signifiers of male sexuality coexist with themes of violence (*The Clash*) and despair (*Damned, Damned, Damned*), which reflect the sense of hopelessness felt by young men who were marginalized because of class and the violent backlash that might ensue from this marginalization. The ways that society looks upon members of the underclass is cued by the album title *Rattus Norvegicus*, which translates roughly as 'wharf rat' and refers to species of brown rat that is commonly used in laboratory experiments or kept as domesticated pets. Anthropomorphically, the 'rat' signifies a human parasite, a rogue or a good-for-nothing male who lives off the spoils of thievery and petty crime. For punks, the image of the rat echoes the ways in which working-class males are sometimes characterized and caricatured as thieving and dirty.[29]

Following Laing's early study, we might similarly point to a group of albums by female punk artists whose titles can be used to reveal how they challenged mainstream gender norms. Given the lapse between the appearance of many female performers on the punk scene and the release of their first albums, we have to reframe the time period from which our representative titles derive. Unlike like their male counterparts, the earliest female punk albums were released in 1978, almost a year after the purported heyday of the punk scene and the release of many of albums cited by Laing: these include *The Scream* (Siouxsie and the Banshees, Polydor 1978), *Moving Targets* (Penetration, Virgin 1978) and *Germ Free Adolescents* (X-Ray Spex, EMI 1978). The release of *Cut* (The Slits, Island 1979) and *Hex* (Poison Girls, Small Wonder 1979) in 1979 place these albums at the boundary between punk and post-punk, a category that is often used to describe such albums as The Raincoats' eponymous debut in 1979 (*The Raincoats*, Rough Trade 1979), and such later albums as *Playing with a Different Sex* (Au Pairs, Human 1981) and *Penis Envy* (Crass, Crass Records 1981), both of which were released in 1981. Irrespective of the designation of these albums as punk or post-punk, their titles reveal how women in the punk scene mobilized signifiers of gender and sexism for their capacity to shock and to critique mainstream gender norms. Broad categories of critique among this selection of album titles include references to female sex organs and procreation, parodies of hysteria, gender signifiers and more general references to the tenets of second-wave feminism.

Album titles that reference the male phallus (like *Never Mind the Bollocks*) find their female equivalents in titles like *Cut* and *Penis Envy*, both of which construe female sexual anatomy in terms of what it lacks in relation to its male counterpart. *Cut*, for example, suggests a gash or a slit that bleeds and thereby references not only the vagina, but also menstruation, childbirth and as Viv Albertine's life narrative would later reveal, gynaecological cancers for which bleeding is a symptom. The term 'cut' can also suggest the artificial creation of female sex organs through the amputation of the penis, which is also suggested in the title of Crass' album, *Penis Envy*. With its Freudian reference, *Penis Envy* and the cover artwork on which the title is emblazoned challenge the idea of the penis as a symbol of such enviable characteristics of strength and dominance, both of which are conferred upon the man simply by virtue of gender. The album cover features the face of a blow-up doll peering out of a woman's womb through a cutaway heart. With its exaggerated eyelashes and lipstick, the doll presents as an adolescent girl who is made up to look like an adult woman. She is surrounded by amniotic fluid and the body of the mother who carries her is blurred in the background of the image. The doll stares blankly at the viewer with its mouth open, readied to receive the male. Since the image relegates the pregnant mother to the background and reduces the adolescent figure within her womb to the status of a sex toy, it is evocative of paedophilia and incestuous sexual abuse. Alongside the cover artwork, the album title debunks the mystique of the enviable penis and exposes it as an unwanted and violent invader into a woman's life. Less graphically, the title of X-Ray Spex's *Germ Free Adolescents* can also be understood to represent the female sex organ, or its forced absence from view in society. The title points to society's inclination to sanitize the body and, in the case of women, to rid the body of any signs of menstruation and other bodily functions in order to render it inoffensive to the everyday viewer. This reading is consistent with the album cover artwork of *Adolescents* (discussed in greater detail in Chapter 3), which appropriates its imagery from then-recent scientific interventions into the process of conception by placing the members of the band into individual test tubes. The effect of the cover image is to erase the alleged 'messiness' of the female body by replacing conception and reproduction with their clinical representations.

In other cases, the album titles cited above feed on societal fears about female sexual liberation through parodies of hysteria and critiques of social sanctions against female sexual desire. The most obvious example within the sample is the album entitled *The Scream*, which alludes both to an alleged symptom of hysteria and to the expression of sexual release when the hysterical patient is brought to the desired goal of orgasm by her (male) doctor. Given the band's name, the hysteric becomes identified with the frightening, otherworldly and uncontrollable figure of the banshee, who is synonymous with the sexual woman whose urges need to be contained. The banshee's screams foreshadow death, or the sexual release of 'la petite mort'. As a figure of the frightening and uncontrollable woman, the banshee finds her sister in the witch, who is referenced in the album title *Hex*. The title, and the witch that it implies, hints at the underworld through its signifier of black magic, Satanic worship and the paranormal. *Hex* therefore describes the fearsome power attributed to a historic group of women who were persecuted, ostracized and executed both because of a widely held fear of unchecked female power and because these women refused to conform to societal norms.

In titles of many punk albums and in many female punk names, the ubiquity of the letter 'X' is difficult to ignore (particularly when one considers that it also serves as the name of the formative Los Angeles punk band 'X', and forms the basis of the name of the band's female vocalist and guitarist Exene Cervenka). Multiple representations of 'X' in British punk include such female names as X-Ray Spex and Siouxsie Sioux and such album titles as *Hex* and *Playing with a Different Sex*. Phonologically, the letter produces a voiceless, percussive sound that resembles a hiss or the sound of a cymbal. Taken as a statement by a particular demographic, X refers to the post-war 'baby boom' generation into which many punks were born (the phrase 'Generation X' was adopted as the name of the British punk band that was fronted by Billy Idol). The letter also signifies access to education, and thereby class, because X is a signature commonly used by one who is illiterate and who therefore signs her name to documents that she is unable to read. The use of the letter in punk suggests that if education is power, then the uneducated members of the working-class are powerless in the face of those who control their lives in a literate world. Further, the signifier also connotes gender, since 'X' is the sex chromosome associated with the female. Finally, 'X' can also be understood as a display of erasure through which something that is unwelcome or unpleasant is literally crossed out. This reading can be coupled with any of the preceding readings to suggest that the symbol 'X' can be used to erase individuals from view on the basis of age (Generation X), class (the signature X) and gender (the X chromosome).

Finally, some album titles make direct reference to second-wave feminism and its demands for equality for women. A parallel can be drawn between *Playing with a Different Sex* and Simone de Beauvoir's *The Second Sex*, whose author demonstrates, and pushes back against, the historical conception of the female sex as secondary, or 'other', to the presumptive dominant male sex. In the Au Pairs' utopian view, as in de Beauvoir, the gender hierarchy is erased as men and women play together. In this conception, women are seen as 'equal but different', to quote from the title of one of the songs on the album. However, the notion of 'play' also implies that sexuality is a game whose rules we inherit from those who surround and socialize us. The album title might also be interpreted as a call to arms for women who willingly, or unknowingly, accept the rules of a game designed to subordinate them, and this reading of the title is supported by the militaristic female images on the cover of the album. With different rules, the title implies that those who engage in the construction of gender might conceive their roles differently. Gender might therefore be the kind of *Moving Target* to which the album title of Penetration's 1978 debut album might refer.

Lyrics

Writing only six years before the heyday of British punk, Germaine Greer (1971) argued that

> the supreme irony must be when the bored housewife whiles away her duller tasks, half-consciously intoning the otherwise very forgettable words of some pulp lovesong. How many of them stop to assess the real consequences of the fact that 'all who love are blind' or just how much they have to blame that 'something here inside' for? What songs do you sing, one wonders, when your heart is no longer on fire and smoke no longer mercifully blinds you to the banal realities of your situation? (But of course there are no songs for that).[30]

The lyrics composed by female punk songwriters respond to Greer's questions with various narratives designed to challenge the social myths that kept women confined in the service of their families, financially and emotionally dependent upon their male partners and spouses, and controlled by societal expectations about feminine beauty. While stage names and titles often signified punk resistance to the gender stereotypes that are implicit in these myths, song lyrics allowed for a broader critique of traditional gender norms. One caveat in any analysis that focuses upon the content of musical lyrics is that meaning is conveyed not only in the lyrics of a given song but also in the tone of their delivery, their relationships to music, in styles of performance and so on. With that in mind, the content analysis that I provide in this chapter is meant to set the stage for a deeper discussion of the relationship between the text and the music that will occupy Chapter 4.

Resistance to gender norms was not unique to female punk, and is also implicit in its male counterpart. As Dave Laing has noted, using The Clash as his example, 'topics and targets of [male punk] included the royalty, the USA, dead-end jobs, the police, watching television, record companies, ... sexual hypocrisy, war, anarchy, and riots'.[31] Matthew Worley (2017) adds that male punks also positioned their work as an alternative form of media and criticized the press 'as a mouthpiece for nested interests and a means of shaping public opinion on behalf of government, commerce or elites'.[32] Worley and Laing suggest that the anger and outrage that is typical of male punk lyrics arises largely out of a sense of emasculation felt by working-class males who were unable to fulfil the roles prescribed for them in media depictions of the traditional family. Young males who entered the British job market for the first time in the 1970s were often stymied in their attempts to find jobs as the recession deepened, while strikes and the growing gap between wages and the cost of living made it increasingly difficult for those who held jobs to support their families without the help of a working spouse. Working-class men who managed to secure employment during the decade often held a tenuous grasp on jobs that could disappear at any moment, and any possibility of a better life was hindered by their inability to afford an education that might lead to more secure employment. Further, given their financial limitations, working-class fathers held little hope that they would be able to help their offspring escape the confines imposed upon them by class. Sons seemed destined to replicate the lives of their fathers and thereby faced the same kinds of frustrations in their attempts to live up to the roles imposed upon them by the traditional model of the family. Male punk anthems like 'Right to Work' (Chelsea, Step-Forward Records 1977), 'Career Opportunities' (The Clash, CBS 1977) or 'God Save the Queen' (Sex Pistols, Virgin 1977) were designed both as vehicles for social commentary and as outlets for the frustration felt by unemployed working-class male youth who found themselves unrepresented in stereotypical depictions of the family. By contrast, female punk songs rarely addressed the issue of unemployment, which did not carry the same social stigma for women as it did for men. Instead, the purpose of female punk was to critique the assumption that every woman should, or could, aspire to the role of the conventional at-home housewife who entices a suitable husband, bears his children and devotes her life to domestic labour within her home. Dismissed in this scenario as non-participants in the symbolic economy of the traditional family, working-class women often faced financial realities that prohibited their participation in the myth of the traditional family. But unlike their male counterparts, their frustrations lay not in their inability to fulfil their domestic roles but, rather, in the negative response to, or dismissal of, their contributions outside of the home. The female subjects who populate punk songs written by women tend to chafe against the confines of their domestic lives and to demand recognition as equal participants in the labour market. At the same time, they argue that female captivity within the home does not represent an ideal for women but, instead, exposes them to potential abuse at the hands of male partners and spouses upon whom they are financially dependent. The home is not a safe haven in punk songs, but is a space where women are hidden away from view, and where their invisibility makes them prime targets for domestic violence. However, unlike Greer, who tracks a steady decline from the 'fire and smoke' of courtship to the 'banal realities' of married life, female punks proposed that spousal abuse actually germinates in the 'romantic' relationships from which marriages are born. For female punk, the myth of romantic love, in which caring and affectionate partnerships lead effortlessly to a happily-ever-after life, obscures the realities of many romantic relationships, which are often characterized in punk as coercive liaisons in which women are mistreated, beaten, betrayed or ignored by male partners who perceive them as little more than sex objects. Women are counselled in punk songs to seize control over their personal lives by adopting behaviours that are stereotypically coded as 'male' (and this advice likely emerges out of a working-class female reality that required women to 'behave' like men by embracing the breadwinner role when their husbands were out of work). A small proportion of punk songs therefore describe relationships in which female subjects are aloof, non-committal and emotionally abusive towards male partners who suffer in silence but who accept the terms dictated by their female partners. Although fictional, the inversion of gender roles represented in these songs points to changes in interpersonal dynamics within the working-class family, where unemployed or underemployed males were forced to cede status to working females who contributed their wages to the household finances.

A large proportion of the songs examined for this study address the issue of gender roles through critiques of the myths of romantic love and domestic bliss. The lyrics of these songs chronicle a variety of relationships that range from courtships to full-fledged marriages and that examine the personal concessions required of female subjects who aspire to the domestic roles idealized in the media. Some songs focus on the plight of the house-bound wife and mother, who is characterized as a prisoner within her home and whose alienation from the rest of the world tends to present as emotional distress or hysteria. Siouxsie Sioux, for example, portrays the home as a place of drudgery and monotony for an emotionally distraught housewife whose life is described in the lyrics of 'Suburban Relapse' (*The Scream*). Threatening, among other things, to 'throw things at the neighbours' and to 'expose [herself] to strangers', this housewife is placed within a suburban setting, but in a pointed *détournement* of that setting, her home is described as a fraught place where seemingly benign kitchen tools become dangerous projectiles and female sexuality is taken out of the bedroom and unleashed by a paranoid housewife against neighbours that she believes are spying on her life as it unfolds through the windows of her suburban home. The housewife described by Au Pairs in the lyrics of 'Diet' is similarly distraught. On the surface, this woman appears to find satisfaction in her housework and children, and the opening of the song describes a subject who seems content to 'dance with Mr. Sheen' and to 'see the sideboard, sparkling clean'. She accepts that, while her husband 'sits with the [news]papers', her role is not to 'have political views'. However, like Siouxsie's housewife, this character ultimately fails to convince herself to accept the futility and tediousness of her role within the home. Participation in the ongoing charade of her life gives her headache towards the end of the song, and she ultimately turns to medication so that she can surrender to another day of drudgery in the kitchen. The emotional distress experienced by these subjects is depicted more graphically in Siouxsie Sioux's surrealist song, 'Carcass', which depicts a subservient housewife who has reduced her identity to that of the meat that she feeds to her family. With its gruesome references to a dismembered body that is locked away in a freezer, the song describes a female subject who is cut off, or isolated, from society and hidden from view in an appliance that is typically found in the kitchen – a space that is conventionally coded as female. The song depersonalizes its female subject, folding her identity into the meals that she prepares for her family and suggesting that she exists merely to be consumed by those she nurtures. It is only a small stretch from 'Carcass' to imagine a marriage whose female subject is held captive to her husband's frustrations and subjected to emotional and physical abuse, like the relationship described in Au Pairs' cover of David Bowie's 'Repetition' (*Lodger*, RCA 1979). This song narrates a scene of abuse in which a working-class man blames society for his lack of success and directs his anger towards his wife, who he describes as a liability. He imagines that, if he had had access to a better education, he 'could have had a Cadillac' and 'could have married Anne in the blue silk blouse', but instead he is saddled with a wife who is unable to cook and who therefore fails as much as he does to live up to her societal role.

Like the bruises on the arms of the housewife in 'Repetition', themes of emotional distress and spousal abuse that tend to be ignored in popular characterizations of the traditional family are brought to the fore in female punk. They are also embedded in punk's critique of the myth of romantic love, which describes situations in which fictional female subjects who should be feeling elated and infatuated in the early stages of romance instead face loneliness, fear and paranoia in loveless relationships with uncaring and cruel men. While the topic of unrequited love is certainly not unique to female punk, or to punk in general, punk's accounts of female victimization in premarital relationships are perhaps more vivid than those found in many other musical genres. Descriptions of sour love affairs range in intensity from 'No Looking'

(The Raincoats), in which a woman is ignored by a husband who drinks his coffee, smokes a cigarette, gets into his overcoat and leaves the house without acknowledging her presence, to 'I Can't Do Anything' (X-Ray Spex), whose helpless female protagonist attempts to defend herself against a boyfriend who tries to strangle her with her 'plastic popper beads'. Given the neglect and abuse that seems typical in these fictionalized relationships, the irony inherent in 'Love und Romance' (The Slits) would be unlikely to be lost on the female punk listener. Full of girlish giggles ('hee, hee, hee!'), phrases that derive from 1950s rock and roll ('see ya later alligator!') and references to middle-class domesticity ('we can … have a house in the country'), the lyrics are constructed in such a way as to highlight the absurdity and artificiality of mainstream depictions of love and romance. Indeed, the foreignness of the fairytale to the experiences of the fictional women who populate punk songs is underscored by the mock-German title of this song. While we all know what 'Love und Romance' means, the use of the German translation distances the phrase from our everyday experience.

In contrast to these tales of neglect and abuse, a small selection of punk songs describes relationships that are dominated by a new breed of female subjects who dictate their terms to subservient male partners. These songs describe situations in which women take control in the bedroom or look to extra-marital affairs to address any sexual dissatisfaction that they might feel towards their male partners. In songs like 'Triangle' (Delta 5, *See the Whirl*, PRE 1981) and 'We're So Cool' (Au Pairs, *Playing with a Different Sex*, Human 1981), for example, female adultery is presented as the ultimate cure to sexual boredom or frustration and perhaps even as the panacea for an ailing or broken relationship. Both songs focus on a male subject who is unable to gratify a female partner who therefore seeks sexual pleasure from another man. Unapologetic, the female subjects in both songs give their partners the option to accept the betrayal or leave, and in both cases, the male subject convinces himself that the affair was an aberration in a relationship that he perceives to be stable and solid. The Au Pair's subject, for example, tells himself that, despite the betrayal, 'I know that I'm the main man in your life'. However, infidelity is not the only tool used by females to exert control in the relationships described in this group of songs. In some songs, a female narrator demands satisfaction from within her relationship and expresses contempt for a male partner who is either too willing (and therefore viewed as weak or wimpy) or unable to meet their sexual demands. One example is 'Come Again' (Au Pairs), whose female protagonist finds herself unable to climax with a sensitive, obedient male partner who tries too hard to please.

When she finally reaches orgasm at the end of the song, she rolls over and goes to sleep in a move that is often attributed to men in heterosexual relationships. A song like 'Come Again' makes an important feminist statement because, as Luce Irigaray (1985) suggests, 'feminine pleasure has to remain inarticulate in language … if it is not to threaten the underpinnings of logical operations. And so what is most strictly forbidden to women today is that they should attempt to express their own pleasure'.[33] This explanation of the enforcement of female silence about sexual desire and satisfaction is central to an androcentric conception of sex, where 'to deny women native erotic desires was to safeguard man's sexual adequacy. However he performed, it would be good enough. She would not – would she? – ask for more'.[34] In 'Come Again', female sexual pleasure is placed at the centre of a narrative that objectifies its male subject and portrays him merely as a set of fingers that 'ache' and 'hesitate' as they seek to elicit a climax from his partner. Male performance in this song is critiqued and deemed inadequate by a female subject who has to coach her partner through the sexual act. At the end of the encounter, and in a move that reinforces the control exerted by the female subject over the act described in the song, the male, still unfulfilled, is summarily dismissed as having barely fulfilled his job.

Another source of critique in punk is the beauty myth, which is discussed and challenged explicitly in other songs authored by female punks. Challenges to the beauty myth are posed by many female punk bands, but X-Ray Spex led the charge with songs that describe the internal conflict experienced by women who are forced by societal pressures to conceal their true identities behind a mask of cosmetics. In songs like 'I Am A Poseur', 'Identity' and 'Art-I-Ficial', the band argues that women have passively accepted their lot ('that's the way a girl should be in a consumer society') and have tended to blame themselves for their physical shortcomings ('when you see yourself does it make you scream?'). The songs are filled with the anguish and anger felt by women who are told that they are not naturally beautiful, but must construct identities that mirror the physical features of a feminine ideal that has been created by the media. The beauty myth is also addressed by Delta 5, whose song 'Make-up' asserts that although advertising 'will give endless promises', these promises have 'nothing to do with results'. With lyrics that seem to parody advertising slogans, the song asserts that women are told to rely on cosmetics to compensate for their inevitable shortcomings, because they '[make] your face feel important'. However, the conclusion of the song captures the vicious circle in which women find themselves when it asks the inevitable question about cosmetics: 'Do you wear it, does it wear you?'

Those who opt to participate in the symbolic economy of feminine beauty render themselves invisible behind their cosmetic masks, while those who opt out of the economy are erased from view as non-participants in the pursuit of feminine beauty. Performing resistance to the beauty myth through the cultivation of 'ugliness' is a broader theme in female punk that transcends commentary about the cosmetics industry and that extends into the realm of daily behaviours. As one way to challenge the beauty myth, female punk lyrics are sometimes littered with profanities that are shocking and uncommon as female expressions. (These utterances add a shock value to the punk imagery that will be discussed in Chapter 3. For now, suffice to say that profanities merely highlight the bondage attire or the seeming jumble-shop, laissez-faire attitude to fashion adopted by female punks.) More interesting, however, punk songs also describe behaviours that are atypical for women and that clash with the idealized image of the silent, demure and subservient feminine beauty. Punk females get drunk after being dumped by their boyfriends (e.g. 'Now That You've Gone' by Delta 5), suffer from addictions ('Nicotine Stain' by Siouxsie and the Banshees), engage in illegal activities and 'piss their pants' when nearly caught ('Shoplifting' by The Slits) and embrace the kinds of liberated sexual practices described above.

Finally, female punk also helped to dispel some of the myths about masculinity that were propagated in teen magazines. As the supposed objects of female desire, conventional male teen idols were held up to scrutiny in female punk. The Slits, for example, suggested in the song 'Typical Girls' that 'the typical girl gets the typical boy', which implied the need for a new kind of idol for the atypical girls who populated female punk songs. As alternatives to such 1970s teen idols as David Cassidy and Bobby Sherman, punk proposed that atypical girls find their male counterparts in the anaemic heroin addict described in songs like 'Instant Hit' (The Slits) and represented by such personae as the American punk idol Richard Hell or his British counterpart, Sid Vicious. As a punk idol, Hell, himself, is referenced by name in X-Ray Spex's 'Let's Submerge' as an inspirational figure around whom female punks, described in the song as 'Hades ladies', coalesce. Punk females suggested that one way to resist the strictures of the symbolic economy of beauty was to change the object of pursuit, with the assumption that an atypical female may not attract a conventional teen idol but will likely find a partnership with an atypical male. As David Ensminger (2011) noted in his study of punk iconography, 'punk rock … made famous a gaggle of boys so unsuitable for teen pin-ups that they revolutionized the fantasy lives of a generation of girls'.[35]

Closing thoughts on 'talking back' in female punk

X-Ray Spex's lead singer, Poly Styrene, perhaps put it best at the beginning of her anti-consumerist, feminist rant, 'Oh Bondage Up Yours!' when she described the situation for 'little girls' who were told that they were meant to be 'seen and not heard'. The childish naïveté with which this opening lyric was delivered, and its stark contrast to the remainder of the song, underscores the media's objectification of women as ornamental, intellectually inferior and entirely dependent on those who are authorized to speak (namely, men). By contrast, female punks present themselves as unfettered by these social constraints, and free to speak about anything they choose – from critiques of the beauty myth and the fairytale of domestic bliss to blatant references to female sexuality and the effects of domestic abuse. The 'polite' culture of middle-class femininity left open a space for the 'impolite' discussions in which female punks engaged and, in using certain words as their stage names, in their song titles and in their lyrics, female punks not only resisted the gender norms that are parodied by Poly Styrene, but also drew attention to the working-class lives whose details were otherwise hidden away from view. The overarching theme in the words that comprise punk is the refusal to be silenced. In male punk, this refusal translates into a militant cry for employment and for a 'future' in which working-class male youth will be able to support their families. We have seen that the relationship of financial independence and male virility serves as the basis for names, titles and lyrics in male punk, and we have also seen that the attendant impotence felt by those who were unable to act as 'proper' men becomes a recurring thread in these names, titles and lyrics. For women, the refusal to be silenced takes on a different set of meanings that arise both from their economic standpoint relative to their middle-class female counterparts and their gendered standpoint relative to their working-class male counterparts. In the chapters that follow, I will examine how female punk's resistance through naming, titles and lyrics is reflected in its use of images and in the way that its songs are constructed and performed.

Notes

1   Mary Midgley, *The Myths We Live By* (London: Routledge, 2003), 1.

2   Mary Romero and Abigail Stewart, eds. *Women's Untold Stories: Breaking Silence, Talking Back, Voicing Complexity* (New York: Routledge, 1999), xiv.

3   For further reading about *détournement*, I direct the reader to Guy Debord and Gil Wolman, 'Mode d'emploi du détournement', *Les Lèvres Nues* 8 (May 1956), 2–9. See also Chapter 8 of Guy Debord, *Society of the Spectacle* (Paris: Buchet-Chastel, 1967), 204–7.

4   Early examples include Stuart Hall and Tony Jefferson, eds. *Resistance through Rituals: Youth Subcultures in Post-War Britain* (London: Hutchinson, 1975), Dick Hebdige, *Subculture: The Meaning of Style* (London: Routledge, 1979), and Dave Laing, *One Chord Wonders: Power and Meaning in Punk Rock* (Milton Keynes: Open University Press, 1985).

5   Betty Friedan, *The Feminine Mystique* (New York: Dell, 1964), 80.

6   For an excellent content analysis of British women's magazines, see Anna Gough-Yates, *Understanding Women's Magazines: Publishing, Markets, Readerships* (London: Routledge, 2003).

7   Friedan, 80.

8   Germaine Greer, *The Female Eunuch* (New York: Paladin, 1971), 173.

9   Naomi Wolf, *The Beauty Myth: How Images of Beauty Are Used against Women* (New York: Morrow, 1991), 10.

10   Wolf, 28.

11   For more on this strategy, see Karina Eileraas, 'Witches, Bitches & Fluids: Girl Bands Performing Ugliness as Resistance', *The Drama Review* 41/3 (1997), 122–39.

12   Ralph Glasser, *The New High Priesthood: Social, Ethical, and Politic Implications of a Marketing-Oriented Society* (London: Macmillan, 1967), 113.

13   Claire Langhamer, 'The Meanings of Home in Post-War Britain', *Journal of Contemporary History* 40 (2005): 356.

14   Angela McRobbie, *Feminism and Youth Culture* (London: Routledge, 1991), 69.

15   It is interesting to note that 'The Beetles' was also the name of a fictional motor-cycle gang in the 1953 film, *The Wild One*, although no connection has been proven between the two uses of the name.

16   Laing, 42.

17   Matthew Worley, *Zerox Machine: Punk, Post-Punk and Fanzines in Britain, 1976–88* (Chicago, IL: University of Chicago Press, 2024), 27.

18   Laing, 48.

19   Wendy Fonarow, *Empire of Dirt: The Aesthetics and Rituals of British Indie Music* (Middletown, CT: Wesleyan Press, 2006), 74.

20   Angela McRobbie, *In the Culture Society: Art, Fashion and Popular Music* (Oxford: Routledge, 1999), 46.

21   McRobbie, 46.

22   McRobbie, 46.

23   McRobbie, 24.

24 Reddington's book, *The Lost Women of Rock Music: Female Musicians of the Punk Era* (Aldershot: Ashgate, 2007), has been an enormous inspiration for the current project.

25 The *au pair* is also a maid, which draws an interesting connection between punk naming and Mary Romero's discussion of the all-seeing Black maid in her work on intersectionality. I would direct the reader to the first chapter of the current study, where this has been discussed in detail.

26 Laing, 47.

27 Charles Mueller, 'Seduction and Subversion: The Feminist Strategies of Siouxsie and the Banshees', *College Music Symposium* 57 (2017), online.

28 Laing, 27.

29 To my mind, the 'rat' that is reference in title of this album finds it opposite in the title of the Mo-Dette's most famous single, 'White Mice', which describes a gorgeous blue-eyed boy who is the focus of a woman's attention and who is the antithesis of a wharf rat.

30 Greer, 164.

31 Laing, 28.

32 Matthew Worley, *No Future: Punk, Politics and British Youth Culture, 1976–1984* (Cambridge: Cambridge University Press, 2017), 77.

33 Luce Irigaray, *The Sex Which Is Not One*, trans. Catherine Porter and Caroline Burke. (Ithaca, NY: Cornell University Press, 1985), 156–7.

34 Peter Gay, *The Education of the Senses (Volume 1) The Bourgeois Experience: Victoria to Freud* (New York: Oxford University Press, 1984), 264.

35 David A. Ensminger, *Visual Vitriol: The Street Art and Subcultures of the Punk and Hardcore Generations* (Jackson, MS: University of Mississippi Press, 2011), 190.

3

'Seen and not heard': Art and fashion

Although punk rock admittedly represented a particular musical experience for its listening audience, the impact of punk reached far beyond its live and recorded performances largely because of its visual landscape. Punk was notorious for its ability to shock and offend its viewers, and its album cover artwork and fashion statements, in particular, helped to contribute a sense of spectacle, or what Bakhtin (1984) describes as 'carnival', to the punk scene.[1] The carnival of punk was experienced far beyond the confines of the subculture and was on display for mainstream viewers in newspaper articles whose photographs of unruly punk musicians and fans fuelled allegations of the threat posed by punk to 'civilized' British society. Additionally, some mainstream viewers encountered punk's visual landscape first-hand when they witnessed displays of 'outrageous' fashion choices assembled by punks and worn on city streets like London's King's Road. One of the defining hallmarks of the punk 'look' in art and fashion was the use of what Karina Eileraas (1997) has described as 'the performance of ugliness' as a strategy to challenge conventional tastes.[2] Punk visual artists created ugliness through a 'cut-and-paste' technique that defiled familiar images (like the British flag) or that juxtaposed unrelated signifiers (notoriously, the Queen and the swastika) in an attempt to subvert their original meanings and to create new meanings from their forced coexistence. Punk fashion designers similarly aimed to resist conventions about beauty by promoting such 'ugly' physical adornments as facial (and later body) piercings, exaggerated make-up and hairstyles that were chopped, shaved or sculpted into Mohawks and bleached white or dyed in black or various neon colours. The political messages conveyed through punk art were also reflected in certain fashion choices, where chains, pad-locks and bondage wear, or torn and mismatched clothing, were used to create visual statements about class oppression and to challenge dominant norms about style and taste. For a small cadre of early punks, these challenges also involved prominent, problematic and ill-conceived displays of Nazi symbols like the swastika and the lightning-rod icon of the *Waffen*-SS.[3] Considered as parts of punk's visual language, signifiers of ugliness and oppression contributed, on the one hand, to a sense of victimization in punk that was heightened by the predominance of black in punk's colour palette and by the frequent use of red as a contrast to black and perhaps, as a token of blood. On the other hand, punk's 'look' was also threatening to the oppressive hegemonic groups whose values punk sought to critique. Rips and tears in punk clothing can be viewed both as symbolic challenges to the existing social fabric of British society and also as an embodied, or kinaesthetic, response to the confines of the existing social order. The colour black, which was pervasive in the scene, also cued darkness or death to those who viewed the iconography of the punk subculture from the outside.

Punk's visual landscape cut across gender lines and the signifiers used by punk to challenge class oppression were equally prominent in the visual artwork produced by males and females or used to promote all-male, mixed-gender or all-female bands. Similarly, the day-glo Mohawks, fetish wear, safety-pins and torn clothing that were typical of punk attire were not gender-specific, but were freely adopted by all punks in the construction of their individual subcultural identities. Despite the apparent gender equality in the adoption of signifiers within punk's visual field, resistance through 'the performance of ugliness' is inextricably tied to gender because of the different social constraints and expectations conventionally placed upon each gender. For male punks, 'ugliness' was used to challenge the conventional measure of male success through virility, business acumen and career accomplishment. The muscular physique and the business suit that were tokens of success in mainstream male culture were anathema to male punk, where leather-clad performers like Sid Vicious or anaemic Dracula-like characters like Dave Vanian resisted the middle-class narrative of the male breadwinner. Further, male sexuality was deemphasized in depictions of male punks (despite the blatant phallic references of many punk names described in the previous chapter), particularly in comparison with its performance in mainstream popular culture. A famous album cover like the one designed by Andy Warhol for the Rolling Stones' 1971 *Sticky Fingers* (Polydor Records), which displays the crotch of a well-endowed male in tight jeans complete with a functional zipper that entices the viewer to 'take a peek' inside the jeans, has no parallel in punk. Instead, male punk was more likely to express ambivalence towards the pursuit of sex, as illustrated in such songs as Alternative TV's 1977 debut single 'Love Lies Limp' (SG Records) and in the comparative lack of visual allusions to male sexual potency in punk artwork.[4]

Because of the commodification of female beauty through the 1970s through such figures as Farrah Fawcett, Cheryl Tiegs or Bo Derek, female punks had a different relationship with 'beauty' and its corollary, 'ugliness', than their male counterparts. Given their subservience to male breadwinners in the narrative of the traditional family, women conventionally exerted power through their appearance and their ability to attract a prosperous mate. Female 'ugliness', and the assumption that it would lead to the solitude and social invisibility of spinsterhood, was therefore perceived as a failure on the part of women. For female punks, the intentional 'performance of ugliness' became a strategy both to resist conventional gender norms and to critique dire descriptions of female singledom and its underlying threat of female independence. Conventional markers of female beauty, like youth, a trim figure, a perfect (white) complexion or a demure comportment, were dismissed by punks as undesirable female traits. Instead, women in punk sought to redefine a new set of parameters for femininity that were often in opposition to those that defined conventional beauty. In doing so, female punks distinguished themselves both as different from the norm and, perhaps more significantly, as more noticeable in a sea of wannabe Farrah, Cheryl and Bo look-alikes. Uniqueness was prized over conformity to a beauty standard that was prescribed from elsewhere. And conspicuousness became integral to female embodiments of punk as a strategy used to expose and shine the spotlight on working-class women whose inferior social position rendered them invisible to mainstream society. With shocking images that feature women wearing markers of abuse (like chains, razor blades and bondage-wear) and in which their faces are sometimes blank and expressionless, punk imagery forced its viewer to confront the victimization faced by women. In other images, resistance to this victimization was expressed by female subjects who mimic the aggressive and defiant poses of their male oppressors.

Most punk musicians were keenly aware of the impact of visual imagery on the perception and interpretation of punk since many had formal training in the visual arts prior to their participation in the construction of the punk scene. Some women in the punk scene devised their own promotional artwork and created their own punk identities using a do-it-yourself approach to fashion, while other punks relied on established or up-and-coming visual artists and fashion designers to create the imagery that came to identify them within the punk scene. Given the artistic backgrounds of many punk musicians, it is not hard to imagine that even in cases where bands relied upon other artists to construct their punk 'image' for promotional purposes, many punk musicians offered input into any decisions about how they would be represented in staged photographs and in other punk artwork. In the case of female punks, we can assume that themes of victimization and defiance were conscious artistic choices, particularly since these themes are also reflected in stage naming, album titles, song lyrics and certain performance strategies.

To facilitate a discussion of punk artwork, a brief discussion of its major participants will help to initiate the reader. Consistent with punk's ethos of inclusion, which allowed anyone to contribute to the scene in any way they deemed fit, punk's visual-art landscape included contributions from artists of both genders. Notable among female artists in the scene were the photographer Pennie Smith, the collage artists Linder Sterling (Linda Mulvey) and Gee Vaucher (Carole Vaucher), and the fashion designers Vivienne Westwood (alongside her partner, Malcolm McLaren) and Zandra Rhodes. Perhaps best known for the image that she contributed to the cover of The Clash's *London Calling* (CBS 1979) album, Smith served as a staff photographer for *New Musical Express* (*NME*), for whom she captured concert stills of such formative British punk bands as The Clash, Siouxsie and the Banshees, and The Slits. The realism of Smith's photographs provides a visual counterpoint to the cut-and-paste artwork produced by Sterling and Vaucher, who constructed surrealist images and landscapes from photo-collage that were often featured on punk album covers. Based in Manchester and closely aligned with Howard Devoto and Morrissey, Sterling is perhaps most famous for the collaged nude that she contributed to the Buzzcock's 1977 single 'Orgasm Addict' (discussed below).[5] Vaucher's artwork is featured on the covers of albums by such bands as Crass and Poison Girls and used collage to produce post-apocalyptic and surrealist visual landscapes. Emerging from an artistic commune based at Dial House in Epping, Vaucher's artwork became synonymous with the anarcho-punk movement that centred on the band Crass. Westwood remains perhaps the most iconic female punk artist because she helped to define the 'look' of the early British scene with fashions that juxtaposed and defiled signifiers of mainstream culture and fashion. Along with her partner Malcolm McLaren, Westwood catered to punks from her clothing shop, SEX (later renamed Seditionaries) located at 430 King's Road, London. Westwood's stature in British punk art was matched by Jamie Reid, whose famous ransom-note lettering graced the cover of the Sex Pistols' *Never Mind the Bollocks* (Virgin 1977) and whose work inspired many punk artists who mimicked his aesthetic in promotional posters and fanzines for a variety of bands. Westwood's clothing featured some of Reid's imagery, including his portrait of the Queen, and his work inspired Westwood and McLaren to create such works as the infamous 'Destroy', 'Two Cowboys' and 'Cambridge Rapist' t-shirts that were sold in their King's Road boutique. Finally, another collage artist whose work was featured on the cover of an album by a female-fronted band was Russell Mills, who created one of his earliest cut-and-paste pieces for the cover of Penetration's debut album, *Moving Targets* (Virgin 1978). This cover is an amalgam of small images drawn from such sources as historical events (e.g. wartime air sorties, Hiroshima and the 1977 execution of Gary Gilmore), scientific experiments (X-rays, eye surgery and a microscopic image of sperm) and potentially calamitous events (a flock of birds flying towards a jet engine, Lee Harvey Oswald in the moments before his assassination and a man on a golf course during an electrical storm). Following his early collaboration with Penetration, Mills would go on to create album cover artwork for such recording artists as Brian Eno, Robert Fripp, Japan, David Sylvian, Michael Nyman and Nine Inch Nails. Finally, a discussion of punk artwork would not be complete without reference to the graphic designer Barney Bubbles, who joined the punk scene after a long artistic collaboration with the British progressive rock band Hawkwind. Known for his use of bright colours and geometric forms and for occasional references to psychedelic art, cubism or constructivism, Bubbles created artwork for various acts who signed to punk's Stiff Records label. In the case of punk, he became known for his work with The Damned, Elvis Costello and The Adverts, for whom he designed the sleeve for their debut single, 'One Chord Wonders' (*Crossing the Red Sea*, Bright 1978), from a close-up photograph of the face of their female bassist, Gaye Advert (discussed below).[6]

Photographs and photocopies

Photography was an important component of punk iconography, and photographs appear on album covers and concert posters, in fanzines and in music magazines. Punk photography frequently documented spontaneous moments from within the scene, like photographs of bands during live performances or shots of the audience that captured the energy of punk. In other cases, punk photographs were staged in locations that were chosen to expose the grime and urban decay that surrounded punks in the mid-1970s. The class status embodied by the punks depicted in these images finds its correlate in the techniques adopted and adapted by punk photographers, who sometimes tore, folded, cut or cheaply photocopied their photographs to add to the sense of their disposability and to the lack of social position held by those captured in the frame. When female punks were their subjects, photographs sometimes exposed the vulnerability of women in the scene by surrounding them with violent imagery or by staging an act of brutality directed towards that subject. One example of the brutalization of a female punk appears on the sleeve of Siouxsie and the Banshees' debut single, 'Hong Kong Garden' (Polydor 1978), the cover of which I will discuss later in this chapter. In other cases, punk photography captures expressions of anger, defiance and aggression in its female subjects, and although these expressions are ubiquitous in punk photography, the emotions that they represent cut against the grain of traditional notions of female subservience. In punk photography, female subjects defy these conventions with facial expressions or bodily stances that dare their viewer to take notice of their presence and that simultaneously refuse sexual objectification. The image of Siouxsie Sioux in live performance that appears on the cover of this book serves as an example.

Many of the photographic images that appear on punk album covers or in promotional materials like concert posters or album inserts resemble amateur snapshots, even in cases where a professional photographer has been involved in the creation of the image. The pretence that these photographs have been taken on the spur of the moment by an 'amateur' photographer is heightened in some cases by the crudeness of their presentation. Punk photographs are often torn, over- or under-exposed, blurry or overly shadowed to give the impression that they are spontaneous and possibly taken with a cheap, disposable camera (despite the quality of the equipment that was often used by punk's photographers and the expertise that they brought to their art).[7] Original photographs are often photocopied in punk, both for their use as album cover artwork and for their mass reproduction on posters and album inserts. The grainy images that result add to the 'do-it-yourself' appearance of punk photography and differentiate punk images from their 'fine art' photographic counterparts. Punk photography provides images that range from individual or group shots of punk musicians, or what I will hereafter call 'portraiture', to shots of subjects or situations that involve no direct visual reference to the musicians for whom they were designed, or what I will call 'pictorial' photographs. A third category of punk photography is 'photomontage', which can be defined as the cut-and-paste creation of an image or visual landscape from a variety of different photographic sources. Album cover portraits or sleeves and posters that feature photographs of musicians are an important component of punk's promotional artwork, since viewers were often introduced to, and forged relationships with, the members of a band through their depiction in photographs. The names, song titles and lyrics that serve as one aspect of punk's narrative were enhanced for the listener by images that helped them to interpret the meanings inherent in punks' various uses of words or text. For the listener who might have had no opportunity to experience punk first-hand at a club or at a concert, photography also helped to define what punk looked like. However, the downside of photography, as Sontag (1977) noted in her early study of the medium, is that 'it turns people into objects that can be symbolically possessed'.[8] Ironically, while punk photography documented a do-it-yourself approach to fashion that favoured uniqueness and inventiveness, it also conspired in the creation of a punk 'template' that would later come to define visual signifiers of punk for consumers from outside the subculture who aspired to 'look punk'.

Punk portraiture often placed its human subjects, or what we might call its 'referents', in realistic environments like crumbling urban landscapes or shabby domestic spaces. Backdrops to portraits that are taken outdoors range from cement streetscapes to scenes of urban decay whose abandoned structures accentuate the sense of social alienation that can be attributed by the viewer to the subjects who inhabit the frame. Indoor landscapes sometimes capture the squalor of the personal spaces inhabited by those who lived in squats or council flats or the run-down environments of punk clubs. Punk fanzines from the time, like *Sniffin' Glue* and *Ripped and Torn*, provide many examples of visual landscapes in punk photography.[9] In many photographic images, referents express resentment towards, or resignation to, the squalid surroundings in which they appear to live with facial expressions that convey such emotions as anger, contempt and despair. Punk subjects embody their anger in angular or aggressive stances or express their hopelessness by slumping in chairs or by leaning casually against walls within the frame. Adding to the bleakness of the lives and landscapes that they seek to capture, punk photography tends to be monochromatic, using a greyscale palette to present images or portraits of punks in ways that the literary theorist Pinkus (1996) describes as 'saturated with melancholia and loss'.[10] Greyscale photography has the effect of dehumanizing its subjects by erasing the colours that distinguish their hair, eyes and complexion and by rendering a degree 'sameness' between those who inhabit an environment that is similarly composed of gradations of grey. Further, in a world where colour photography was possible, the deliberate use of greyscale gives the viewer a sense of detachment from an image that no longer represents a 'present' or the 'presence' of its subjects. This effect is heightened by the frequent use of photocopied photographs in punk promotional artwork, which lend a sense of the 'unreal' to the portraits and scenes that they depict. Perhaps most importantly, greyscale punk photography erases the distinction between referents and their environment. By denying colour to their subjects and by placing them into an urban background into which they disappear, greyscale punk photography seems to signal to the viewer that its human subjects are as inconsequential as the spaces they inhabit. Colour therefore signifies power, and its opposite, the lack of colour, represents powerlessness. Consistent with this interpretation, the lyrics of Delta 5's third single, 'Colour' (Rough Trade 1980), recount a situation in which its protagonist, a seemingly monochromatic female subject, demands recognition with a lyric that states, 'I'm in colour, too, I don't just come in black-and-white!' As if to prove the point, the protagonist threatens to engage in self-harm to demonstrate that she bleeds in red like everybody else.

While the greyscale palette in punk photography clearly signifies working-class invisibility, the way that gendered referents are represented in greyscale punk photographs reveals a stark difference in the way that the categories of class and gender intersect as sites of resistance in punk art. In greyscale portraiture of male punks, group shots of bands are common, while it is unusual to see a lone male artist singled out from his band for particular photographic attention.[11] A typical example is the cover of The Clash's eponymous 1977 debut album, where the band appears as a group in a greyscale photograph taken outside their Camden Town rehearsal studio by the American photographer Kate Simon.[12] The photograph is a grainy image that appears to have been photocopied from an original photo, with ragged margins and seemingly glued onto a green background. Each member of the band stares blankly and directly into the camera. A contrasting image, produced by Caroline Coon for the sleeve of their 1977 single 'White Riot' (*The Clash*, CBS 1977), captures the band members facing a wall with their arms extended and their legs spread as if they await a pat-down. Taken from behind, the shot conceals their identities from view and its scene of victimization invites any working-class viewer who has been harassed by the police to identify with the three 'anonymous' suspects portrayed in the image. Like many male punk group portraits, these two shots depict the band as marginalized working-class men who inhabit run-down urban spaces and whose class makes them a potential target for unwarranted police attention and brutality (consistent with the 'sus' laws that were often abused by the police in Britain in the 1970s). More importantly, because each is identifiable as male and working-class, no particular subject stands out, suggesting that these subjects unify against a common oppressor. Group photographs of female or mixed-gender punk bands, by contrast, are comparatively rare on punk album covers, and when such photographs are used as album cover artwork, they tend to isolate the female band member(s) as their principal focus of attention by placing the woman in the centre of the frame or by blurring the male members of the band. Isolated by the camera, the female subject is singled out by a photographic gaze that 'points at' or 'targets' her. At the same time, this isolation also forces the viewer to notice the female subject who, by virtue of class *and* gender, might otherwise pass unnoticed. The sleeve of The Adverts' second and final studio album, *Cast of Thousands* (RCA 1979), illustrates this point with a group photograph of the band in which Gaye Advert appears in the foreground of the shot while her male band mates stand closely behind her. Their faces are blurred behind what appears to be a milky film while Gaye's face is clearly exposed. In other cases, male members of the band disappear completely from photographic view. The sleeve for X-Ray Spex's single 'Oh Bondage Up Yours!' (Virgin 1977), for example, features a photocopied greyscale photograph of the face of the band's lead singer, Poly Styrene, as she stares over the shoulder of the photographer with her mouth open as if she is speaking or singing. The rest of her band is absent in the frame. Similarly, The Adverts' single 'One Chord Wonders' (Stiff 1977) is packaged in a sleeve that is decorated with an iconic greyscale photograph of Gaye Advert, who is chosen to represent her band even though it was fronted by the singer and songwriter Tim ('T.V.') Smith and comprised of two other male musicians, Howard Pickup and Laurie Driver.[13] As the bassist, Gaye seems like an unlikely choice for the photograph, since most bands are more strongly identified with their lead singer. (Consider, for example, that the 'face' of a mainstream band like the Rolling Stones has typically been Mick Jagger, and not the band's various bassists – Bill Wyman or Darryl Jones.) The pixilated portrait of Gaye, created by Barney Bubbles, appears to be enlarged and photocopied from its original source, and it blurs the details of its subject's face and draws particular emphasis to eyes and lips that appear like dark blotches or smears against an otherwise ghostly complexion. Notably, the subject stares expressionless into the camera, as if judging or challenging a viewer who might have expected her to assume a more submissive, sensual or seductive posture consistent with more typical media portrayals of women. Close-up facial portraiture in punk art allows its female subjects to 'stare down' certain gender stereotypes that prescribe tokens of feminine beauty. Further, when the face of a subject fills the frame of a photograph, as it does in the sleeve for 'One Chord Wonders', the viewer is forced to confront the expressions of the subject directly and without access to such visual distractions as the body of that subject, the presence of other subjects in the frame or the surroundings that serve as the background for the image.

The medium of greyscale photography is also used to generate artwork in which no band member is featured but, instead, in which a particular scene is inhabited by an anonymous subject. These 'anonymous' photographs tend to locate their subjects in situations that offend or shock their viewer, and often comprise images borrowed from sources like pornography, crime scene photography, pulp fiction, photo-journalism or historical photographs of violence and warfare. In other cases, the photograph represents an action performed by an unidentified (and sometimes an unidentifiable) subject. Because no band member is present in the frame, the meaning of an anonymous image is often context-dependent, requiring the viewer to read the image in relation to the gender of band that it represents and against other images in the visual field of punk. In cases of borrowed images, meaning also arises from the original context from which the image derives. For example, the meaning of an image like the crime-scene photograph of a female victim of the Boston Strangler that appears on the sleeve of The Stranglers' single 'Nice 'n' Sleazy' (United Artists 1978) creates an intertextual relationship between the name of the band, the meaning of the image and the title of the song. The juxtaposition of the signifiers 'Boston Strangler' and 'The Stranglers' suggests a connection between the two, and thereby hints at the possibility that the band's male members (and, by extension, men) are violent, predatory and prone to murder. The portrayal of a female victim on the cover of this single reinforces the hegemonic status of the male performer, since a parallel example of male victimization by a supposed female predator does not exist in the catalogue of punk album-cover photography. When women portray *themselves* as victims, by contrast, the meaning of the image is starkly different. The greyscale artwork that decorates the sleeve of Siouxsie and the Banshees' debut single 'Hong Kong Garden', for example, examines violence from the victim's point of view when it shows a faceless female clothed in a white sack-like dress that is belted around her waist.[14] Her head and face are encased and obscured by a cloth sack that she struggles to remove. Denied her identity, the figure potentially represents any (or every) woman who faces the claustrophobia of sexism and its attendant threat of victimization (a theme that is echoed in the lyrics of such Banshees songs as 'Suburban Relapse' or 'Carcass'). The image can therefore be read as a commentary on the vulnerability of those who are rendered invisible because of their subordinated gender and class.

Although greyscale photography was perhaps more common in punk artwork than its colour counterpart, when colour *was* used, the effect was to bring the viewer into a closer relationship with human subjects who appeared more 'real' or 'present' in the photograph. In the monochromatic landscape of punk, colour therefore becomes a strategy used for the purposes of viewer identification. For female punks who sought to confront their viewer with difficult truths about the experiences of working-class women, colour was also a way to dramatize and emphasize the 'reality' of subjects who might otherwise seem dehumanized by the greyscale palette. Perhaps the most famous example of colour photography in female punk is the image that appears on the cover The Slits' debut album *Cut* (Island 1979). Taken by the photographer Pennie Smith outside Ridge Farm, in Surrey, where the band recorded the album, the picture introduces its viewer to three members of the band who, in full colour, are stripped to the waist and covered in mud. While female nudity was certainly common in mainstream album-cover artwork, particularly as a marketing tool for music geared towards the male consumer, the female form was typically idealized and hyper-sexualized in its conventional use. Oversized breasts and buttocks were typical of the sexual fantasies created for the covers of mainstream albums. In the case of *Cut*, female nudity is used very differently, perhaps to represent the appearance of the 'typical girl' about whom the band sings because it portrays a more natural version of the female form devoid of cosmetic or surgical enhancement. The image provides a more candid view of the female body, but despite its nudity, it seems distinctly non-erotic and, instead, uses its female subjects to challenge the pornographic images common in mainstream album cover artwork. Viv Albertine recalls in her memoir that the band aimed to have 'a warrior stance [and] not try and be all seductive'.[15] Resistance to the gender stereotype that relegates the female to the role of a sexual plaything is heightened by the interplay between the image and the themes explored in the musical tracks of the album, in which the band satirically describes what constitutes a 'Typical Girl' and critiques 'Love und Romance'. With faces that convey aloofness and disinterest in the camera (reminiscent of Gaye Advert's blank facial expression on the sleeve for 'One Chord Wonders'), and bodies that strike a seemingly defiant pose, these subjects invite no sexual response from their viewers, but their nakedness nonetheless commands attention. Instead, the use of mud to cover the female figures in the photograph implies a pagan femininity that recalls tokens of fertility like the Venus of Willendorf. We might speculate that if the image had been rendered in greyscale, the association with the clay Willendorf figure might have been minimized by a palette that would have erased the distinction between flesh tones and mud.[16]

Smith's iconic photograph of The Slits has no male counterpart in punk, perhaps because males are seldom portrayed as the objects of sexual desire in popular culture and are therefore not compelled to resist sexual objectification. Instead, the use of colour in punk photography allows male punks to enhance their anger and aggression, and, by proxy, their victimization of women, with colours that evoke violence or blood. The Stranglers' debut album, *Rattus Norvegicus* (United Artists 1977), for example, shows the band in the entryway of what appears to be an English country house. Two members of the band stand at the foreground of the image in a dimly lit entrance hallway, while the others appear in the background in a room that emanates a reddish light. The inside-outside dichotomy that is represented by the image, the picture of the doorway that frames the background subjects and the red light might be understood as a metaphor for intercourse, consistent with the sexual themes that resonate through the songs that comprise the album. Like criminals or delinquents who belong elsewhere, the leather-clad, working-class referents of the photograph have broken into a house where they are not welcome. In other colour photographs, sexual violence reads blatantly on the surface of the image. Signifiers of male sexual fantasy are unambiguously represented on the cover of Generation X's *Valley of the Dolls* (Chrysalis 1979), for example, which features an image that evokes pulp fiction. In the cover image, an unconscious woman can be seen through a door that is slightly ajar. A black-and-white poster of the band is featured prominently on the outside of the door. Photographed in colour (as opposed to the greyscale poster of the band), the woman is dressed in dishevelled lingerie and she is lit by a lamp that has fallen beside her and that casts a reddish glow over her inert body. The poster suggests a typical gendering of popular music roles that presents males as musicians and females as groupies, but the overall image also creates a scene of sexual violence inflicted on the woman in the frame. In the images created for *Rattus Norvegicus* and *Valley of the Dolls*, the colour red becomes a point of interest not only because it shines a particular glow on the individuals who populate the images but because of its associations with blood. Photographs such as these also demonstrate the ubiquity of violence against women, irrespective of class.

Another technique that is common in punk colour photography is the use of Day-Glo clothing or hair dyes to set human subjects apart from the drab urban landscapes in which they are typically placed. As one punk artist noted, 'a lot of people who were doing punk were also going to art school, so a whole shock wave of art came along with the music. It was like the '50s when Abstract Expressionism accompanied free jazz. Punk art was sloppy with a lot of Day-Glo colors'.[17] The Day-Glo colour scheme finds few correspondents in nature and therefore gave punks who clothed, dyed or adorned themselves with these colours a sense of artificiality or constructedness. Like the distinction between monochrome and colour photography, Day-Glo colours helped to draw the eye towards a particular aspect of an image, and while the use of Day-Glo cuts across gender lines in punk, male and female punks used these colours to highlight different things. In the case of male punk, Day-Glo was used to resist the navy-blue conservatism of such middle-class fashion items as the suit and tie. Some male punks seem to revel in attire that was simultaneously coded 'middle-class', like ties and suit jackets, and 'non-traditional', like garish or clashing colours. Photographs of The Damned's Captain Sensible in a non-traditional suit comprised of a fuzzy pink mohair jacket and canary yellow pants illustrate the use of the Day-Glo as a statement against middle-class masculinity. His outfit is recognizable as a suit, but parodies conventions of male dress with its outrageous colours and furry texture. By contrast, Day-Glo was often used by female punks to accentuate, and thereby ridicule, the artifice of cosmetics and hair dyes that held women captive to a manufactured standard of feminine beauty. The mask of cosmetics behind which women were conventionally expected to conceal their supposed flaws became grotesque in the hands of female punks who replaced the so-called 'natural' and 'tasteful' colours of make-up and dyes with hot pinks, electric greens, shocking yellows and other lurid colours. In punk photography, X-Ray Spex became known for their use of Day-Glo as a language of resistance both with their frequent allusions to colour in song lyrics (notably, 'The Day the World Turned Day-glo') and with the use of lurid colours on their promotional materials, much of which was designed for the band by their lead singer, Poly Styrene. The cover of their debut album, *Germ Free Adolescents* (EMI 1978), illustrates their use of Day-Glo as a marker of artificiality.[18] On this cover, the members of the band, dressed in combinations of pink, yellow, green, red and black, are confined in individual test-tubes, where they appear to be preserved in formaldehyde. The artwork was particularly timely, coinciding with the birth of the first test-tube baby, Louise Joy Brown, in Manchester in July 1978. Read against the current events with which it coexisted at the time, the image seems to serve as a commentary on the struggle between nature and science, or between human beings as 'natural' and 'constructed'. As a confining space in which each figure appears, the test-tube also represents societal constraints that delineate the behaviours of those who exist within that space. This reading is supported by the expressions of angst performed by the confined figures who seem to struggle against the walls of their test-tubes in an attempt to break free from the artificiality imposed upon them by an unseen (and presumably male) scientist.

The photographic landscape of punk articulates a language of anger and defiance in its characterizations of punk musicians or in its depictions of the treatment of anonymous human subjects. Typically coded as male, these emotions are less surprising when enacted by male punks to challenge class oppression. For female punks, however, the same emotions emerge out of the intersection of class and gender as coexisting sites of female oppression. On the one hand, portrayals of females as victims ('Hong Kong Garden') help to point out the problems faced by working-class women whose victimization might otherwise go unnoticed. On the other hand, defiant females (Gaye Advert or Siouxsie Sioux) also populate the visual landscape as subjects who resist victimization. The narrative thread of female invisibility and victimization continues in the non-realistic images that emerged out of the practice of collage, which is another important component of punk art.

Punk photomontage and Dadaism

While portraiture and pictorial photography provided seemingly 'realistic' or 'lifelike' depictions of poverty, violence and victimization, cut-and-paste artwork was another mode of expression used by punk artists. The purpose of cut-and-paste in punk artwork was to create dystopian and disturbing visual narratives from seemingly benign images that were appropriated from popular magazines, advertising, photojournalism and visual documentations of historical events. In some cases, the 'cut-and-paste' procedure produced abstract collages, where pre-existing photographic images and 'found' objects (like bus tokens, tram schedules or concert tickets) were glued together to evoke a junkyard of discarded items drawn from everyday urban life. As two special types of collage, punk 'photomontage' constructed its critique of capitalist society exclusively from photographs, while 'photocollage' incorporated borrowed lettering or text.

The artistic process known as décollage, which was also common in punk art, is the antithesis of collage and involves the laceration of an existing image either to reveal that something (or nothing) is hidden underneath or to create a space for the insertion of another image. For the sake of ease, these four artistic practices will be called 'cut-and-paste' and will only be differentiated as needed in the ensuing discussion.

The physical actions involved in 'cut-and-paste' were appealing to punk artists who viewed the art form as a violent reaction to the social norms depicted in the photographic or textual sources from which they derived the fragments for their artworks. The music journalist and punk artist Jon Savage, for example, explains that for artists who created new images from the juxtaposition of visual scraps and fragments of text cut from magazines and newspapers, 'the knife offered a certain visceral control: it was a process at once violent and peaceful, which allowed the subconscious to come through'.[19] This explanation of punk's creative process is similar to descriptions of the artistic process employed by the early Dadaist Hannah Höch, who helped to establish photomontage as a mode of artistic expression and who equated the scissors that she 'used to cut through the traditionally masculine domains of politics and public life' with the kitchen knife, which she understood as a symbol of female domesticity.[20] For Savage, the process of cutting-and-pasting allowed punk artists to cut away the cultural debris that pollutes a given image in order to expose its underlying symbolic meanings, while for Höch, the procedure was a symbolic act of castration whereby the grip of male hegemony is cut away to allow for the expressions of those who exist on the periphery.

The various procedures associated with cut-and-paste artwork were not unique to punk and are described by Teal Triggs (2006) as 'a language of graphic resistance … [that] emerged from [punk's] position in a continuous timeline of self-conscious Dadaist and Situationist International "art" practices'.[21] Early proponents of cut-and-paste, like such Dadaist visual artists as Raoul Hausmann and Höch, used the process to protest the First World War, and social critique thereafter became intrinsic to the artwork that coalesces under the term. As a mode of visual critique, the work of early Dadaists, and later, the surrealists, provided a template for such cut-and-paste punk artists as Jamie Reid, Linder Sterling and Gee Vaucher, who spearheaded the use of décollage, photomontage and photocollage in punk artwork. Cut-and-paste procedures in punk range from the simple juxtaposition of two or three unrelated images or fragments of text to the more complex constructions of entirely new images or landscapes from numerous fragments plundered from a variety of different photographic sources.

The visual experience of cut-and-paste artwork, described by the art-historian Mary Ann Caws (1997) as 'the act of seeing one thing through another', allows its viewer to experience several visual narratives simultaneously.[22] The cut-and-paste artist folds together the signifiers of the society that she aims to critique and eliminates the temporal and physical distance that separates these signifiers in order to expose underlying meanings or to posit alternative meanings for, and from, familiar images. As a tool for social critique, cut-and-paste involves a process commonly known as *détournement*, through which photographs and advertisements that reflect the perspectives of hegemonic social groups are juxtaposed in a way that will expose social bias and prejudice. The cut-out of a plump, live chicken that appears in the foreground of the post-apocalyptic scene of urban chaos created by Gee Vaucher for the cover of Crass' debut album *The Feeding of the 5000* (Crass Records 1979), for example, suggests a farm or a source of food in an environment where food seems to be at a premium.[23] The chicken is a nostalgic image of rural life that makes Vaucher's surreal depiction of urban decay more stark and desolate by contrast. Visual fragments, like Vaucher's chicken, signify in cut-and-paste artwork because they allude to the meanings of their progenitor text and because they combine in ways that allow new meanings and visual narratives to emerge within their new context. Cut-and-paste artwork distorts reality with 'photographic manipulation [that] disrupts the notion of a "rational self" as represented in the synchronous presence of images'.[24] The viewer of Vaucher's chicken is caught in a kind of schizophrenia in which she struggles to decode the familiar image and to account for its relationship to its new cut-and-paste environment. While Vaucher's chicken might seem like a benign part of the rural scene from which it was likely appropriated, its appearance as the sole animal in a post-apocalyptic scene dominated by human subjects suggests a scarcity of food and thereby marks the image as a token of starvation (both physical and, given the biblical title of the album, also spiritual). Like the fish and bread that were meant to feed five thousand people in the Biblical parable, the chicken is the only source of food in the scene constructed by Vaucher. Once the chicken is gone, the viewer is left to assume that humans will be forced to eat one another. Read this way, the chicken represents the last vestige of a 'civilized' society that has eroded within the frame of the photo-montage.

Other, and perhaps more familiar, examples of *détournement* appear in Jamie Reid's infamous punk artwork.[25] Reid's contributions to the covers and sleeves of the Sex Pistols' recordings have become iconic images in the visual landscape of punk, although his work tends to tackle the issue of class bias and to ignore gender bias. Icons of British culture, like the Union Jack and the monarchy, were favoured by Reid as images for *détournement*. Perhaps his most famous image is his 1977 'portrait' of Queen Elizabeth II, which is based on Cecil Beaton's Silver Jubilee photograph of the monarch and which features a safety-pin that has been glued over her mouth to give the impression of a punk-style piercing. In some instances, the image is altered with swastikas that are glued over the irises of her eyes. In other versions, like that used for the sleeve of the Sex Pistols' 1977 single 'God Save the Queen', the Queen's eyes and mouth are covered by ransom-note lettering that has been cut out of various magazines to spell out the title of the song and the name of the band. Hebdige (1979) provides an early reading of this image when he argues that the Queen's face was disfigured by 'black bars used in pulp detective magazines to conceal identity (i.e., they connote crime or scandal)'.[26] As a symbol of a social class from which most Britons are excluded and a class to which membership is determined by birth but not necessarily by merit, the monarch is defaced by Reid in order to expose the authoritarianism of the British class system. Hebdige argues that the swastika, in particular, is used to challenge the authority of the monarch, since 'conventionally, as far as the British were concerned, the swastika signified "enemy"'.[27] The notion that Britons are held captive by a leader who refuses to cede power is reinforced by the ransom-note lettering that is glued over the face of the monarch in certain punk iterations of her portrait. The lettering also democratizes the artwork by providing a text that could be constructed by anyone with a pair of scissors and a newspaper.

While Reid's artwork sought to resist classism, the issue of sexism was central to two female artists, Gee Vaucher and Linder Sterling, who used punk's cut-and-paste methods to create images and visual landscapes that challenged gender norms. Their work draws an aesthetic and philosophical lineage to Höch's interwar photomontages, which used

> the images of modern femininity, especially the sensational 'New Woman,' to question the complicated relationship between the sexes in post-World War I Germany. With her bobbed hair, sleek new fashions, and increasingly frequent appearance on the streets and in the workplace, this New Woman emerged in Europe in the 1920s as a symbol for all that was fashionable and up-to-date in the metropolis. In many of her photomontages, Höch juxtaposes these sporty, active women with modern technology and domestic appliances, creating ironic

statements on the ambiguities and deep conflicts that accompanied the new female presence in the public realm.[28]

A typical example of Höch's use of photomontage is the 1919 work entitled *Da-Dandy*, which explores the theme of male ambivalence towards the 'New Woman' whose independence was at once appealing and threatening to male hegemony. The image comprises a set of fragmentary images of the New Woman that have been glued together to form the silhouette of a male face. His profile is outlined in red, and the women who comprise his silhouette appear to stare invitingly or adoringly at the camera, and through it, at the viewer. On the one hand, the *trompe–l'oeil* effect of *Da-Dandy* reinforces a binarism between the genders by forcing the viewer to switch between the two images that comprise an ambiguous figure. On the other hand, the image also problematizes the issue of female emancipation in its suggestion that a singular man has a multiplicity of options of potential female partners, while women must vie against each other for the attention of the singular man. The Dada scholars Dietmar Elger and Uta Grosenick (2004) explain that '"Da-Dandy" appears to have his head full of nothing but women' who he perceives as sexual objects but not as individuals.[29]

Like Höch, Linder Sterling's visual collages seek to challenge contemporary views about gender norms and sexuality, although while Höch constructs her critique from images of the New Woman, Sterling's imagery derives largely from the combination of pornographic and domestic images. The cover that she created for the Buzzcocks single 'Orgasm Addict' (United Artists 1977) is perhaps her most famous image and is typical of the work that she produced in the mid- and late-1970s for a fanzine that was devoted largely to the promotion of the Buzzcocks called *The Secret Public*.[30] Sterling's cover depicts a nude, blue-toned female torso that is sprawled against a lemon-yellow background.[31] Her identity is obscured by a cut-out image of an iron that is pasted over her head while two oversized, grinning female mouths are pasted over her breasts. The image folds together tokens of female servitude, both fetishizing the iron in a pornographic context and domesticating female sexuality as servile and submissive to the male viewer of the pornographic image on which Sterling's work is based. Sterling's one-time collaborator Jon Savage, with whom she worked on *The Secret Public* from 1978 to 1981, explains that, in its conflation of sex and domestic servitude, Sterling's imagery is meant to call attention to what she perceives as 'the dismemberment of women by conventional attitudes to gender and sexuality'.[32] The symbolic amputations and substitutions that are characteristic of Sterling's work recall surrealist depictions of women in which the female body as a site for mapping out the relationships between body and culture … was deconstructed (through dismemberment or violation) or connected with nature, art or machinery under the dynamic gaze of the surrealist (predominantly male) artist. Even when they questioned preconceived images of sexuality, most surrealists conceived the woman's body as a collective space of visual consumption. In other words, women were visual constructs or images of the aesthetic and cultural transformations proposed by surrealists.[33]

Taken in this context, Sterling's image also challenges the surrealist male gaze because it offers an ironic take on surrealist depictions of women.

The Dadaist visual artist Gee Vaucher, who contributed album artwork to such bands as Crass and Poison Girls, took the process of cut-and-paste a step further when she created highly detailed surrealist landscapes from photographic clippings often drawn from multiple sources. The visual busyness of her artwork often arises from dozens of unrelated images that vie for the attention of the viewer and thereby mimics the frenetic pace of the urban life that Vaucher seeks to critique. Consistent with the anarchist views expressed by the bands for which she designed her artwork, Vaucher's work challenges its viewers to look closely at objects that are ugly, offensive and even repulsive, and to accept these as part of the modern, urban landscapes in which we exist. Although some of her artwork appears to be gender-neutral in its portrayal of these landscapes, Vaucher tended to embed visual references to domesticity or pornography in many of her works as a way to critique gender norms. Further, her artwork appropriates many of its images from advertising and turns these images against idealized depictions of such social spaces as the home, the suburban neighbourhood or the workplace. The greyscale image that she constructed for Crass' debut album *The Feeding of the 5000*, to which I have already alluded, depicts a post-apocalyptic suburban neighbourhood whose half-destroyed houses are variously missing doors, roofs and windows. A menacing haze hangs above the scene and suggests an impending storm or, more likely, a radioactive cloud. In the centre of the frame, in a courtyard surrounded by ruined houses, a set of figures warms their hands over a burning corpse as a small boy sifts through the dirt beneath them. The middle figure holds a flag that bears the logo of the band. To the left of the crowd, a barefoot woman in a dark dress appears to be severely burnt, while three wartime soldiers lurk behind her and make their way towards one of the houses in the background. Off to the side, a bikini-clad woman clings to the legs of soldier who wields a gun and looks towards a chicken that walks across the courtyard in the foreground of the frame. In one of the houses, two people can barely be seen through a missing window as they watch television. Oblivious to the carnage, a pristine young boy reads from a Dr Seuss book in the lower right corner of the image while his doting mother stands behind him in a kind of modern-day Madonna-and-child configuration. Above the entire scene, another pristine child jumps sky-high as if playing on an invisible trampoline that sends him out of the orbit of the carnage that lies beneath. A message in white stencil-lettering surrounds the image and provides not only the name of the album but also a caution to 'pay no more than £2.00' for the recording and the phrase 'Anarchy and Peace'. Perhaps the most important phrase on the cover of the album appears along the bottom frame to suggest that the viewer is privy to 'The Second Sitting' of the biblical feast referenced in the title, although no such meal exists in the original parable. The feast of fish and bread described in the biblical story is often interpreted as a metaphor for eternal life, immortality or resurrection, but in this collage, neither fish nor bread appears. Rather, the viewer bears witness to an assumed 'Second Sitting' that reaffirms human mortality. According to Gee Vaucher, stencils were used by Crass as a way to offset the challenging messages written by the members of the band with a visual sense of order and harmony. Vaucher explains that 'every month, we would decide who was going to spray what [London] underground line and head out in pairs to graffiti on all the sexist and violent advertising with a very neatly placed message. The stencil sprays always looked very neat and acceptable even if what they were saying didn't.'[34]

The cover of *The Feeding of the 5000* provides many intriguing and puzzling visual stimuli and the overt biblical reference of the title invites the viewer to consider that the work might be more closely aligned with the Book of Revelation. The Four Horsemen of the Apocalypse are referenced throughout Vaucher's image, and most clearly by the horses that are painted on the side of a Mini Cooper that is parked in the centre of the courtyard. As symbols of conquest, war, famine and death, each of the horsemen finds his representation in the collage. Conquest is clearly represented by the bikini-clad figure who grasps the legs of a soldier to the right of the Mini Cooper. While war is ubiquitous in the scene, it is referenced specifically by the wartime soldiers who appear at the far left of the image. Famine is suggested by the lone chicken that appears in the foreground of the image and by the crumbling Tesco supermarket logo that appears in the far distance and out of reach of the courtyard. Finally, Death is represented not only by the set of bones that lie in a heap beneath the three grieving male figures who stand beside the Mini Cooper but it also appears in the guise of burnt female figure who stands half-clad in a torn stylish dress in front of the wartime soldiers. With the exception of the figure of the adoring mother who appears in the foreground and on the far right of the frame, most of the females who appear in Vaucher's image contribute to its apocalyptic reading. The doting mother contrasts sharply with other figures in the image, because of the comparative whiteness of her skin and the neatness of her dress. As a figure who fixates on her child despite the carnage that surrounds her, she represents the alleged oblivion experienced by those who acquiesce to idealized motherhood and who find themselves engulfed in housework at the expense of a critical engagement with the world.

The ambiguity of the meanings of signifiers that comprise a cut-and-paste image is a theme that is also explored in various punk songs, where lyrics sometimes express confusion about place and identity. The theme of ambiguity is particularly evident in songs like Siouxsie and the Banshees' 'Jigsaw Feeling' (*The Scream*, Polydor 1978), whose protagonist states that 'one day I'm feeling total, the next I'm split in two', or 'Christine' (*The Scream*, Polydor 1978), which underscores the crisis of identity in punk artwork with lyrics that provide a surrealist account of a subject who believes that 'now she's in purple, now she's a turtle, disintegrating'. X-Ray Spex is also known for songs that describe the schizophrenia felt by women, in particular, in a modern society that requires them to conceal their 'natural' faces behind a façade of make-up that constitutes their 'social' faces. The song 'Identity' (*Germfree Adolescents*, EMI 1978), for example, evokes a crisis of self and perhaps a sense of self-loathing by women who are told their 'natural' faces are not good enough, with a lyric that asks 'when you look in the mirror do you smash it quick?'

Typography

On album covers and in punk fanzines, typography serves as a form of graphic language whose meanings are encoded in the visual appearance of a chosen typeface and in its relationship to the text that it expresses or to any images with which it coexists. Graphic designers who work extensively with text are keenly aware of the visual impact of text upon the consumer of the products that they help to design or to market. The colour and size of a font can determine the attention paid to a given product as it vies against other fonts, and the products that they represent, in a consumer landscape that is filled with text. In his research on expressive typology and meaning, Stuart Mealing (2003) notes that type itself is protean, its production involving the specification of a number of variables. Choice of typefaces (from many thousands), weight, size, color, kerning, leading and layout are the most obvious and the possibility of customizing or inventing new typefaces also exists. It will be obvious that some of these parameters might be defined by the procedure used – a typewriter, for instance, prescribing the way that many of them are set and a display surface defining the maximum available size. The interaction between these variables is what distinguishes at a glance an up market broadsheet newspaper from a populist tabloid.[35]

In the case of punk, typeface is an important source of meaning for individual albums, fanzines and the genre more broadly. Punk's do-it-yourself aesthetic relied upon two dominant modes of typographic design that express both defilement or vandalism and simplicity or naïveté. As Hebidge notes, punk labelled band names and album titles either with 'graffiti which was translated into a flowing "spray can" script, [or] the ransom note in which individual letters cut from a variety of sources (newspapers, etc.) in different type faces were pasted together to form an anonymous message'.[36] In other instances, punk titles and text eschewed expensive or elaborate printing and graphic design in favour of handwritten or typewritten texts that looked spontaneous and home-made, as they often were. Noteworthy examples of 'do-it-yourself' typography appear in punk fanzines like Mark Perry's *Sniffin' Glue* (1976–7) and Tony Drayton's *Ripped and Torn* (1976–9), where text was 'used as [it] was written with grammatical and punctuation corrections made visible with crossing outs. This stressed the immediacy of its production and of the information, but also the transparency of the design and journalistic process itself'.[37] The class implications of graffiti, cut-and-paste lettering, error-ridden typing and handwritten text are clear, since each of these represents a mode of visual expression that requires no formal training and is accessible to all. Despite its working-class associations, however, punk typography is used very differently in the packaging of male and female punk.

Punk's trademark ransom-note and typewriter typography were uncommon modes of visual expression in female punk, and tend, instead, to appear on the album covers of male punk bands. Ransom-note lettering, for example, is closely identified with the Sex Pistols' debut album, for which the font was designed by Jamie Reid. Male punk was also closely associated with graffiti lettering, as illustrated by The Jam's debut album, *In the City* (Polydor 1977), where the name of band has been spray-painted above the three band members as they stand against a tiled wall. Ransom notes and graffiti emerge out of acts of violence and defilement: the former arises from the act of cutting and the latter involves the act of spraying. Symbolically, the ransom note also evokes a sense of forced imprisonment and the power differential that this implies. The prisoner, in this case, is presumably the working-class male who is held captive to his financial circumstances by those who hold economic and political power.

Female punk, by contrast, was more closely linked to handwritten text, which provides a sense of intimacy, and which suggests a writer who, by virtue of class, has no access to a typewriter. It is curious that the typewriter, which was then so strongly associated with the female role of the secretary, is virtually absent in female punk lettering. Its absence suggests a strategy of resistance to more 'typical' visual modes of female correspondence, like the font that signifies 'a typewriter'. The Raincoats eponymous album, *The Raincoats* (Rough Trade 1979), eschews typeface and provides its title in uneven, handwritten grey script. Beneath the title, a cartoon depiction of a children's choir highlights the childishness of this script. Similarly, the cover of Delta 5's *See the Whirl* (PRE 1981) features cameos of the members of the band that are glued into the crudely drawn blocks of a hop-scotch course. The name of the band is scribbled in the upper left corner of the image. Handwriting also appears on the sleeves of various female punk singles, like Siouxsie and the Banshees' 'The Staircase (Mystery)' (Polydor 1979), which sets a threatening greyscale image against a shaky script in pink-, blue- and yellow-coloured pencil. The allusion to such writing implements as pencils or crayons in certain punk scripts implies the fleetingness of messages that can be erased on a whim or that will fade over time. Perhaps more importantly, their appearance also suggests childishness and vulnerability, particularly when they are juxtaposed against such images as a child's choir or an outdoor game or when they coexist with images that evoke danger and inspire fear in their viewer. Given the strong association of handwritten text with female punk, and its comparative absence in promotional materials associated with male punks, we might conclude that this form of typography is meant to represent the infantilization of women in a society that demands their dependence on males. Additionally, the avoidance of typewriter script also implies a resistance to female subservience to male bosses within the workplace.

Typography was also used to portray 'the outsider' on punk album covers. Artwork for The Clash's second album, *Give 'Em Enough Rope* (CBS 1978), for example, repurposes a historic postcard based on a historical photograph by Adrian Atwater entitled 'End of the Trail'. The original image depicts two vultures who feast on a dead cowboy. Repurposed for the cover for The Clash's album, the image is enhanced by American artist Gene Greif, who brightens the background colours, reduces the figures to greyscale and inserts the figure of a Japanese horseman who looks down upon the rotting Western corpse. The juxtaposition of 'Western' and 'non-Western' characters in the image, and the association of death with the former, serves as a comment on the decline of Western society. In the image, only the Asian 'other', like his working-class counterpart, is privy to the decay (and these two figures are drawn together by the greyscale palette that represents them). To draw attention to 'the outsider', the banner at the top of the image (in the UK release) announces the album title in a mock-Asian typeface.[38] A similar font is used by Siouxsie and the Banshees on the sleeve of the single 'Hong Kong Garden', but the implication of its use in this case is decidedly different. Here, the typeface is associated with a female figure whose actual ethnicity is concealed behind a hood. The song title and mock-Asian typeface work together with the gender of the figure to depict the 'outsider' status of the female.

While typeface may go unnoticed as a contributor to the meanings that we associate with the images on album covers, inner sleeves and in fanzines, this important component of any promotional image can contribute another layer of meaning to the photographs or artwork on which it is imposed. Typeface announces bands and album titles, and punk typefaces clearly distinguish between the do-it-yourself use of the typewriter (and its potential to represent such 'errors' as typos, misspellings and grammatical errors) and the do-it-yourself eschewal of the typewriter (and its substitution with hand-written text). The preponderance of the latter in female punk suggests a scenario in which males are given access to machinery that is denied to females. But the 'typewriter', as an apparatus typically associated with secretarial work, curiously emasculates its male user, while its avoidance by female punks can be seen as a resistance to jobs that are more conventionally coded as female.

Fashion

Punk fashion drew its inspiration from two principal sources, each of which reflected, and was reflected in, a particular aesthetic portrayed in punk visual art. The first source was BDSM, which reproduced the violent and nihilist images of punk visual art in fashion. Black leather or PVC, rubber, chains, studs, safety-pins and dog-collars echoed the victimization depicted in such images as the sleeve of 'Hong Kong Garden' or Vaucher's post-apocalyptic artwork and described in the violent narratives of songs like the Au Pairs' 'Repetition' (*Playing with a Different Sex*, Human 1981) (discussed in Chapter 2), Siouxsie and the Banshees' 'Carcass' (*The Scream*, Polydor 1978), or Sick Things' 'Bondage Boy' (*The Legendary Sick Things*, Chaos Records 1983). The second source of punk fashion was thrift-shop clothing, whose items were often mismatched on their wearer, ripped or torn, pinned together, splattered with paint, sprayed with graffiti and slogans, or adorned with seemingly hand-drawn or screen-printed images. This approach to fashion echoed the photomontage and décollage practices of punk visual art through its juxtaposition of unrelated items of clothing that pointed to different origins and that were often torn to expose undergarments or bare flesh. Karina Eileraas (1997) argues that, in its use of fetish wear and second-hand clothing, 'punk imagined the body as a quasi-Hobbesian state, ruled by uncontrollable urges for sex and violence; [its] imagery employed the body's uncontrollability as a means of waging a symbolic war against the status quo'.[39]

Punk's fashion designers, many of whom opened boutiques on or near London's King's Road in the mid-1970s, drew a strong connection between punk music and the fashions adopted by its fans. Malcolm McLaren explained that 'fashion seemed to be the place where music and art came together … Creating my own clothes was like jumping into the music end of painting. The shop [SEX, which later became Seditionaries] became a natural extension of my studio. I was very anti-careerist and, in my head, I was promoting failure'.[40] Inspired by Westwood and McLaren's King's Road shop, John Krevine and Steph Raynor opened the boutique 'Acme Attractions' in the basement of 135 King's Road, where they sold retro mod and rock 'n' roll-inspired fashions that evoked what Paul Gorman (2001) described as a 'flick-knife gang attitude'.[41] While SEX and Acme Attractions catered to street-level punks, 'confrontational dressing' found in its haute-couture counterpart in the fashion designs of Zandra Rhodes, whose shop on London's Fulham Road (opened in 1968) 'rejected images suggesting breeding and wealth – elegance, symmetry, and harmony – and instead showed clothing with seams turned inside out, ripped dresses, tattered hems, pinned-on sleeves, and T-shirts with political messages'.[42]

The 'promotion of failure' and the 'rejection of images suggesting wealth' were not the sole purview of punk fashion designers, and as some punks have noted, there is an essential contradiction in the notion that punks would look to designers to construct punk's 'do-it-yourself' look. While Rhodes and

Westwood may have sought to subvert the concept of 'designer clothing' within the industry in which they worked, most punks constructed their individual 'looks' from recycled clothing and objects found in the urban landscape that surrounded them. The singer Ari Up, who was notorious for her torn clothing and who inverted the conventional underwear/outerwear dichotomy by sporting panties over her leather pants, observed that

> for the boys to do punk was just about acceptable, but because we were all female, it was different. At the time women usually wore mini-skirts with nice tights and high heels, and it was terrible for us to wear them with Doc Martens and torn up tights and torn up shirts. We would wear clothes out in the open instead of beneath the clothes where they belonged – I wore Silver Jubilee underwear over my pants, and the way people reacted! It just became systematically a hunt for the rest of the outside world. It was like they wished it was the Middle Ages so they could have burned us at the stake![43]

Ari Up's stage persona was unique because of her inventive use of clothing, but some observers have noted that the do-it-yourself ethos of punk quickly fell victim to mass-marketing when designers intervened in the scene. As one observer notes,

> slipping into Punk clothing that was pretorn by the parents of the movement, Malcolm McLaren and Vivienne Westwood, is like putting on the mask of faciality: one becomes the victimization of fashion. In contrast, Lydon [known at the time as Johnny Rotten] claims that he wore his own clothes, or better, that his clothes grew organically from his Punk body like moss.[44]

The thrift-shop aesthetic to which this observation about Lydon alludes arose in punk not only out of financial necessity but also as a way to critique the inherent classism of an industry that seemed to cater exclusively to those who have money. In her influential study of the sociology of fashion Kaja Silverman (1986) notes that

> although the fashion industry operates through replication and mass production, making variants of the same garments available to every class, a temporal lag always separates the moment at which such a garment is available to a select few from the moment at which it is generally disseminated. This temporal lag guarantees that by the time most people have access to a given 'look,' it will no longer be 'really' fashionable, and so asserts class difference even in the face of the most far-reaching sartorial homogenization.[45]

Punk thrift-shop fashion, by contrast, was immediate and available to everyone regardless of their socio-economic status, since the design of punk's 'look' was the charge not only of up-and-coming or established fashion designers but also of individual punks who manufactured their 'look' from the clothing that was immediately available and most affordable.

The thrift-shop 'look' was adopted almost universally across the visual field of punk fashion, where garments and adornments were shared across genders to an extent that was atypical in mainstream fashion. The seemingly self-styled cropped haircut, torn clothing and safety-pin accoutrements were adopted equally by male and female punks as codes of 'confrontation'. Further, the liberal application of facial make-up was not gender-specific, and its use to create an anaemic complexion that was enhanced by overemphasized eyes or lips added to punk's 'performance of ugliness'. The lead singer of The Damned, Dave Vanian, likely wore as much make-up as his female counterpart, Siouxsie Sioux, both of whom strove for a washed-out, almost grey-scale complexion that appears never to have been exposed to sunlight, with darkened eyes to emphasize the paleness of their skin. Further, the artwork that appeared on Westwood's infamous t-shirts, which were sported by punks of both genders, helped to satirize conservative gender roles and their meanings were often meant to be read against the gender of their wearer. For example, the t-shirt design known infamously as 'Tits', which features a life-sized greyscale photograph of nude female breasts, was worn by men and women alike, although it was popularized by the Sex Pistols' guitarist, Steve Jones, who was photographed many times while wearing the item. As Jon Savage (1992) noted in his study of the band, the effect of the t-shirt on a male wearer like Jones 'was both androgynous and, in the double-take it forced upon you, distinctly unsettling'.[46] The placement of breasts on the torso of a man was clearly meant to challenge the machismo of 1970s popular culture and once again reaffirms the sense of working-class emasculation that runs throughout punk. Barbara Ehrenreich has noted that in film, machismo was on full display through 1970s popular culture, where it took centre stage in such blockbuster hits as *Saturday Night Fever, Rocky (I and II)* or *Bloodbrothers*. She contends that, in each of these films, 'violence and machismo, along with male bonding and obsessive determination, are allocated to the working-class. Maturity and self-mastery are allocated to the middle-class. The masculine dialectic between machismo and maturity is externalized; class struggle is internalized'.[47] Each of these films instructs its male viewer that to succeed (as a dancer, a boxer, a professional or a lover), he must abandon the attitudes of his working-class origins and recreate himself in the image of the 'new man', who is marked as middle-class, successful and more caring and nurturing in his personal relationships. The photographic image of breasts on the chest of a working-class male is unsettling precisely because it disrupts and lampoons this narrative with a counternarrative of the emasculation of the working-class.

The appearance of female anatomy on the male wearer of the 'Tits' t-shirt also blurs gendered identity, not only reinforcing the subordination of working-class males to their middle-class counterparts but also suggesting an ambivalence about gendered roles within the working-class, itself. Punk fashion was notable for its adoption of such signifiers of 'sexual deviance' as bondage wear, masks, dog-collars and rubber clothing, all of which evoked the 'pathology' of sado-masochism. Female punks embraced the dominatrix imagery, in particular, and adorned themselves with 'the straps, the suspenders, the shiny PVC that make up the "bad girl" image … [but which] were intended to deceive: punk women clearly were not good girls, but it was far from clear who was to profit (or indeed suffer) from their badness'.[48] I would suggest that the dominatrix imagery pointed unequivocally to a victim embodied as the male masochist (whose subservience and emasculation is echoed by the male wearer of the 'Tits' t-shirt). In Gilles Deleuze's formulation of sado-masochism, outlined in 'Le Froid et le Cruel', masochism is gendered as male, consistent with its representation in Sacher-Masoch's *Venus in Furs*, while sadism is gendered as female.[49] The male masochist negotiates a space between the ideal of the dominant mother and the reality of male patriarchy. For the masochist, the mother resides at the centre of his sexual fantasy, and through his subordination to her, he cedes his masculinity and assumes the submissiveness typically performed by the female. Silverman (1993) explains that 'the male masochist not only prefers the masquerade of womanliness to the parade of virility, he also articulates both his conscious and unconscious desires from a feminine position'.[50] By reversing the locus of power and dominance, the female sadist thereby becomes identified with the dominant position (male, middle-class). But while emasculation is signified by BDSM, the sexual practices to which punk bondage-wear alludes also have implications for female punks. Caroline Evans and Minna Thornton (1991) argue that

> bondage dress allowed women to express the crudest will to sexual power, or, indeed, to sexual victimization, while preserving a central ambiguity. Punk girls
> – and they were girls – engaged *en masse* in the forbidden activity of confusing

sexual messages: they looked like prostitutes but were not. They were women but were not 'feminine', 'tarty' but not tarts. This was an exercise of power, not in the literal sense of what could be done, but on the level of representation, of what could be signified.[51]

Perhaps more than any other signifier discussed in this chapter, bondage wear was ambiguous for female wearers because it both simultaneously invited the gaze and resisted that gaze: on the one hand, the use of fetish wear as an element of everyday attire drew the attention of viewers who would expect the costume to remain closeted away in private spaces where the wearer can engage freely in the 'deviant' sexual practices represented by her clothing, while, on the other, women who dressed in bondage attire defied their conventional gender roles by presenting in a way that was frightening and threatening to male hegemony. Symbolically speaking, the punk dominatrix therefore inverts the power structures within which the working-class woman is imprisoned, and she wields power over her expressions of gender and over class hierarchies with a 'look' that is sexual but that also traditionally conveys control.

Closing thoughts on 'being seen' in female punk

In my closing thoughts, I return to X-Ray Spex's description of females as objects to be seen and not heard, which I referenced at the end of the second chapter in relation to punk as text and which I have appropriated as the title of this chapter. The statement resonates loudly with the aspect of image in punk, which plays with the concept of the male gaze by problematizing the object to which it is drawn. The notion of 'beauty', in particular, becomes a point of departure for a counternarrative of 'ugliness', whose performance is manifest in punk clothing and ornamentation and in the images that emerge from visual art collage and décollage, both of which are designed to command or demand the gaze. The assumption is that the eye will be drawn to the 'ugliness' of punk because it provides a stark contrast with the standards of 'beauty' that define mainstream (middle-class) femininity. At the same time, female punks also use their bodies to challenge sexual stereotypes, either by adopting the façade and behaviours of their (male) oppressors or by exaggerating the artificiality and constructedness of the mainstream female archetype. Against a backdrop of feminine ideals like those presented in the media, female punk redefines what it means to 'be seen'. While 'being seen' is an important component of punk iconography, we will see in the next chapter that, in the absence of a large catalogue of video documentation of the punk scene, punk's still imagery and artwork also helped (and continues to help) to frame the songs that were performed by punk.

Notes

1   Mikhail Bakhtin, *Rabelais and His World* (Bloomington, IN: Indiana University Press, 1984). For an application of the 'carnival' concept to popular music, see Lee Barron and Ian Inglis, '(Re)Constructing the Carnival: Continuity and Change in Contemporary British Popular Music', *International Review of Aesthetics and Sociology of Music* 33/1 (2002), 95–112.

2   Karina Eileraas, 'Witches, Bitches & Fluids: Girl Bands Performing Ugliness as Resistance', *The Drama Review* 41/3 (1997), 122–39.

3   See Karen Fournier, 'Nazi Signifiers and the Narrative of Class Warfare in British Punk', in *Beyond 'No Future': Cultures of German Punk*, eds. Mirko Hall, Seth Howes, and Cyrus Shahan (New York: Bloomsbury, 2016), 91–108.

4   One notable exception is The Stranglers, who have often been criticized for the misogyny of their lyrics and who famously hired strippers to perform alongside them at an open-air concert at Battersea Park in 1978, during which one member of the band also removed his clothing.

5   Sterling's collage work originally appeared the one-off fanzine *The Secret Public*, which she co-authored with Jon Savage and published in January 1978. She has released a thirty-year retrospective of her work, entitled Linder Sterling, *Linder: Works 1976–2006* (Zurich: JRP-Ringier, 2006).

6   A retrospective of Bubbles' work has been edited by Paul Gorman and published as *Reasons to Be Cheerful: The Life and Work of Barney Bubbles* (London: Adelita, 2008).

7   For example, Pennie Smith took her famous shot of Paul Simonon with a Pentax ESII: https://thenoisyshutter.com/2024/01/17/classic-camera-review-pentax-spotmatic-es-ii/.

8   Susan Sontag, *On Photography* (New York: Farrar, Straus, and Giroux, 1977), 14.

9   For one of the most comprehensive study of British punk fanzines, see Matthew Worley, *Zerox Machines: Punk, Post-Punk and Fanzines in Britain, 1976–88* (Chicago, IL: University of Chicago Press, 2024). Examples of punk's DIY photography can be found in Tony Drayton, *Ripped and Torn: 1976–1979* (London: Ecstatic Peace Library, 2018), Teal Triggs, *Fanzines: The DIY Revolution* (San Francisco, CA: Chronicle Books, 2010), and Mark Perry, *Sniffin' Glue: The Essential Punk Accessory*, (London: Sanctuary, 2000).

10 Karen Pinkus, 'Self-Representation in Futurism and Punk', *South Central Review* 13/2–3 (1996), 180.

11 A notable exception, and perhaps the most famous punk photograph of the period, appears on the cover of The Clash's 1979 *London Calling* album, where a greyscale photograph by Pennie Smith shows the bassist Paul Simonon in concert as he smashes his instrument on the stage. Designed by Ray Lowry, the sleeve is framed by text that spells out the name of album in an oversized pink and green font that is borrowed from Elvis Presley's 1956 eponymous debut album. For those who are aware of the source of the text, the borrowing draws the two photographs into a dialogue that posits the later image as a violent act of opposition to the history represented in the photograph of Elvis that appears on the cover of the earlier album.

12 Other examples include The Jam's singles 'The Modern World' (*This is the Modern World*, Polydor 1977) and 'Down in the Tube Station at Midnight' (*All Mod Cons*, Polydor 1978), The Damned's single 'Neat, Neat, Neat' (Stiff 1977) The Strangler's *Black and White* album (United Artists 1978).

13 An image of the sleeve for 'One Chord Wonders' is available on the Discogs website: https://www.discogs.com/release/668913-The-Adverts-One-Chord-Wonders-Quick-Step.

14 An image of the sleeve for 'Hong Kong Gardens' is available on Wikipedia: https://en.wikipedia.org/wiki/Hong_Kong_Garden_(song).

15 Viv Albertine, *Clothes. Clothes. Clothes. Music. Music. Music. Boys. Boys. Boys* (London: Faber & Faber, 2014).

16 An image of the cover of the Slits' debut album, *Cut*, is available on Wikipedia: https://en.wikipedia.org/wiki/Cut_(The_Slits_album).

17 Robert Williams and Carlo McCormick, 'Cartoon Surrealism', *Grand Street* 52 (1995), 57.

18 An image of the cover of X-Ray Spex's debut album, *Germ Free Adolescents*, can be found on Wikipedia: https://en.wikipedia.org/wiki/Germfree_Adolescents.

19 Jon Savage, 'The Secret Public', in *Linder: Works 1976–2006*, eds. Linder Sterling and Lionel Bovier (Zurich: JRP | Ringier, 2006), 12.

20 Kristin Makholm, 'Strange Beauty: Hannah Höch and the Photomontage', *The Museum of Modern Art* 24 (1997), 21.

21 Teal Triggs, 'Scissors and Glue: Punk Fanzines and the Creation of a DIY Aesthetic', *Journal of Design History* 19/1 (2006), 72.

22 Mary Ann Caws, *The Surrealist Look* (Cambridge, MA: MIT Press, 1997), 13.

23 An image of the cover of Crass' debut album, *The Feeding of the 5000*, can be found on Wikipedia: https://en.wikipedia.org/wiki/The_Feeding_of_the_5000_(album),

24 Marta Sierra, 'Oblique Views: Artistic Doubling, Ironic Mirroring and Photomontage in the Works of Norah Lange and Norah Borges', *Revista Canadiense de Estudios Hispánicos* 29/3 (2005), 564.

25 Retrospectives of Reid's work include: Jamie Reid, *Rogue Materials*, London: L-13 Light Industrial Workshop, 2021 and Jamie Reid and Jon Savage, *Up They Rise: The Incomplete Works of Jamie Reid* (London: Faber & Faber, 1987).

26 Dick Hebdige, *Subculture: The Meaning of Style* (London: Routledge, 1979), 112.

27 Hebdige, 116.

28 Makholm, 21–2.

29 Dietmar Elger and Uta Grosenick, *Dadaism* (Cologne: Taschen, 2004), 42.

30 An image of the sleeve of the Buzzcock's single, 'Orgasm Addict', can be found on Wikipedia: https://en.wikipedia.org/wiki/Orgasm_Addict.

31 The lettering and backdrop of the image was designed by Malcolm Garrett, who has since become one of the most influential graphic designers in Britain.

32 Savage quoted in Sterling 2006, 12.

33 Sierra, 570.

34 Gee Vaucher quoted in Josh MacPhee and Erik Reuland (eds), *Realizing the Impossible: Art against Authority*, (Edinburgh: AK Press, 2007), 73.

35 Stuart Mealing, 'Value-Added Text: Where Graphic Design Meets Paralinguistics', *Visible Language* 37/1 (2003), 48.

36 Hebdige, 112.

37 Triggs, 72.

38 In its American release, 'Give Em Enough Rope' (Epic 1978) features non-stylized, block-letter typeface.

39 Karina Eileraas, 'Witches, Bitches & Fluids: Girl Bands Performing Ugliness as Resistance', *The Drama Review* 41/3 (1997), 123.

40 Malcolm McLaren quoted in Paul Gorman, *The Look: Adventures in Pop and Rock Fashion* (London: Sanctuary, 2001), 116.

41 Gorman, 123.

42 Ruth Rubinstein, 'Review: Valerie Steele, *Women of Fashion: Twentieth Century Designers*', *Women's Art Journal* 15/1 (1994), 43.

43 Ari Up quoted in John Robb, *Punk Rock: An Oral History*, (San Francisco, CA: PM Press, 2012), 320.

44 Pinkus, 183.

45 Kaja Silverman, 'Fragments of a Fashionable Discourse', in *Studies in Entertainment: Critical Approaches to Mass Culture*, ed. Tania Modledski (Bloomington, IN: Indiana University Press, 1986), 148.

46 Jon Savage, *England's Dreaming: Anarchy, Sex Pistols, Punk Rock, and Beyond* (New York: St. Martin's Press, 1992), 284.

47 Peter Biskind and Barbara Ehrenreich, 'Machismo and Hollywood's Working Class', in *American Media and Mass Culture: Left Perspectives*, ed. Donald Lazere (Berkeley, CA: University of California Press, 1987), 202.

48 Caroline Evans and Minna Thornton, 'Fashion, Representation, Femininity', *Feminist Review* 38 (1991), 58.

49 Gilles Deleuze, 'Coldness and Cruelty' (1967), in *Masochism*, trans. Jean McNeil (New York: Zone Books, 1991), 9–142.

50 Kaja Silverman, 'Masochism and Male Subjectivity', in *Male Trouble*, ed. Constance Penley and Sharon Willis (Minneapolis, MN: University of Minnesota Press, 1993), 60.

51 Evans and Thornton, 58.

4

'Don't create, don't rebel': Music

From a musical standpoint, punk famously positioned itself in opposition to mainstream popular music, and punks argued that many popular musicians had compromised their ethical values by the 1970s for the sake of making money. Punk heaped particular scorn on the 'hippy' counterculture of the 1960s whose musical spokesmen accrued great wealth despite their supposed advocacy for the underclasses. No longer 'outsiders' who critiqued social imbalances and inequities, mainstream rock musicians of the 1970s had lost touch with their rebellious roots, according to punk observers, and were no longer the 'authentic' voices of protest. Instead, punks argued, 1960s counterculture had become absorbed into hegemonic culture, whose appropriation, mass-production and marketing of the hippy image and its music had diluted or perverted its original meanings. Further, punks also believed that in packaging popular culture for mass consumption, the music industry had canonized a small cadre of voices who would be authorized to speak through popular music, and silenced all the rest. The end result, at least in punk's reading of popular music history, was that the industry both created and reinforced a distance between the performer, as the purported creator of popular culture, and the audience, as the passive recipient of a culture in whose creation they played little part. The antipathy felt by punks towards the music that was popular with mainstream consumers in the 1970s (like progressive rock and disco) arose from their consensus that these genres merely reinforced the power differential between performers and listeners because disco, on the one hand, required access to expensive electronic equipment and recording studios, while progressive rock, on the other, obstructed participation because of the excessive performance and compositional demands that it placed upon musicians. Punk, by contrast, sought to present itself as an alternative in which anyone could participate regardless of musical training or access to the expensive musical accoutrements typically associated with a rock ensemble. To bridge the 'gap' that had allegedly sprung up (or, perhaps, that was manufactured) between the listener and the musician in mainstream popular music, punk democratized access to the field of cultural production by stripping away the excesses of popular music. Punk retraced a path back to an earlier time of late-1950s and early-1960s 'rock 'n' roll', during a time when ensembles were comprised of instruments that were easily obtained and popular songs were constructed from established song forms and comparatively simple harmonies. As Lawrence Grossberg (1990) has argued,

> when [punk] looked inside itself, it did not find nothing: it found the emptiness of the 'blank generation' of postmodern youth. Even as it seemed to celebrate anarchy and the pure negativity of its deconstruction (the insanity, dissonance, its threatening difference), even as it projected a potentially expansive pluralism of apparatuses and styles (a pluralism that could arise only after punk celebrated its own death), it reencapsulated rock and roll within a surprisingly circumscribed range of sounds, styles and attitudes.[1]

Pete Dale (2020) corroborates that the nihilistic, 'rip it up and start again' description of punk misses its many historical connections to folk, with which punk shares not only its activism but also its DIY ethos and its sense of collective music-making.[2]

Certain normative practices emerge from punk's reencapsulation of past practices that can help to define punk as a musical genre. For example, punk bands typically comprised the four-piece line-up (of vocals, lead and bass guitar, and drums) that was commonplace in 1960s rock 'n' roll. With only a few exceptions, punk abandoned the keyboard instruments that were common in progressive rock and shunned the synthesized sounds that characterized disco.[3] The principle of democratization that characterized punk's approach to music-making extended to the roles played by each performer in a given band. Punk songs rarely featured extensive or elaborate instrumental solos that would cast the spotlight on one member of the band and, instead, tended to give equal weighting to the musical contributions made by each member of the ensemble. When they did occur, punk solos were often perfunctory and stripped down to reiterate the melodic lines sung in the surrounding verses rather than to offer improvised melodies designed to showcase the musical expertise of the soloist. Further, like the rock 'n' roll precursors that it imagined and attempted to emulate, punk was performed in spaces that were appropriate to smaller bands, and the intimate clubs from which punk emerged (like London's 100 Club, The Roxy or The Marquee) put the audience in close proximity to punk bands in a way that echoed the club culture of early American rock and roll, folk and British pub rock. The physical immediacy of punk helped to break the barriers that typically separated musicians from their fans. Punk's performance venues enabled fans to climb onto the stage, where they could dance or perform alongside the musicians, and these venues also allowed musicians to dive into the audience, following the transgressive performance practice that was popularized in the early 1970s by Iggy Pop.

From a musical perspective, many of punk's compositional norms also pointed to an earlier time in the history of popular music-making. Punk retained conventional popular-music song structures that traced their lineage through the 1950s and 1960s to Tin Pan Alley, and the vast proportion of songs in the genre feature either a verse-chorus (ABAB …), strophic (AAAA …) or 32-bar (AABA) song form.[4] While a comprehensive list of examples of each of these forms in punk would be too vast to provide here, a couple of examples can be used to illustrate. The verse-chorus song structure, for example, is reflected in The Clash's 'Career Opportunities' (*The Clash*, CBS 1977) and The Slits' 'Typical Girls' (*Cut*, Island Records 1979), while Au Pairs' 'Diet' (*Playing with a Different Sex*, Human Records 1981) provides an example of strophic form. Punk also revived the 32-bar form that had been largely abandoned by the 1970s in favour of the standard verse-chorus format.[5] This song form traces its roots to early twentieth-century American popular song and is illustrated in such rock 'n' roll classics as Jerry Lee Lewis' 'Great Balls of Fire' (Sun Records 1957) and Buddy Holly's 'That'll be the Day' (Decca 1957), and such early Beatles tunes as 'We Can Work It Out' (Capitol/Parlophone 1965) and 'Yesterday' (Capitol/ Parlophone 1965). The 32-bar form was used in punk because of the kinds of poetic narratives that its formal structure can support. In her study of narrative strategies in country music, Jocelyn Neal (2007) defines the elements of a popular song in terms of what they add to a narrative. She characterizes the verse as 'a section of a song with a fixed melodic and harmonic identity and whose text advances the basic plot [by using] new texts that further advance the storyline' and the chorus as 'a section of a song whose text reflects statically on the main point of the song, supported by fixed melody and harmony'.[6] In the verse-chorus format, plot advancement within the verses is confined by the recurrence of the chorus, since the story narrated in the verses is always interrupted by the choruses. The advantage of the verse-chorus structure, however, is that the recurring lyrics of the chorus are easily recalled by a listener and can therefore serve as the 'hook' that compels the listener to purchase the song. In the case of the strophic song, the absence of the chorus allows the narrative to wander without restriction, although the recurring melodic and harmonic content of the verses can make it difficult to differentiate between verses. Each verse sounds the same from a musical point of view, in spite of whatever twists might take place in the plot of the song from one verse to the next. The 32-bar structure, by contrast, circumvents the repetition that marks verse-chorus structure and the undifferentiated verse structure of strophic form. This formal design allows the storyline to unfold naturally as the song proceeds, offering the opportunity to focus on a particular aspect of the narrative in the contrasting 'B' (or 'middle-eight') section. It is highly likely that the format was revived in punk specifically because of this narrative potential. In a 32-bar song like the Sex Pistols' songs 'God Save the Queen' (*Never Mind the Bollocks*, Virgin 1977), for example, the 'A' sections are used to construct a pointed critique of the monarchy while the contrasting 'B' redirects the narrative towards the listener, for whom it offers guidance about how to resist the social oppression described in the other sections of the song ('don't be told what you want' and so on). A similar narrative strategy is used in Buzzcocks' single 'Orgasm Addict' (United Artists 1977), where the 'A' sections are used to describe the root cause and the various symptoms of compulsive sexual behaviours, while the 'B' section provides a humorous list of the various sexual partners with whom the protagonist has been involved (among whom include 'school kids', 'women with no body hair', 'winos' and 'international heads of state'). From a structural point of view, then, punk is somewhat conservative in its use of existing song forms from the early days of rock 'n' roll and Tin Pan Alley.

The formal conservatism of punk is echoed in its harmonic language, which tends to be straightforward and economical, consistent with punk's quest to democratize access to musical performance. As the punk fanzine *Sideburns* famously suggested, punk allegedly required that its participants master merely three chords before they could 'form a band'. The comment was used in its original context to challenge the comparative value placed on 'musical expertise' over 'musical inexperience' so that the latter would become favoured over the former in punk. (Of course, mainstream readings of the credo tend to fixate on the meanings latent in these instructions, among other things, rather than to examine whether punk music was, indeed, 'inexpert'. As the music proves, the credo is contradicted by the strong musicianship that is often on display in the genre, even in songs that were built upon a small selection of chords.) From a harmonic point of view, the credo points to the relatively conservative palette that characterizes the musical language of punk, many songs of which retained the traditional I-IV-V chord structure or some variant thereof. Examples include such songs as The Clash's 'Career Opportunities' and The Raincoats' 'Fairytale in the Supermarket' or such variants as The Clash's 'London's Burning' (I-II-IV-V) or The Strangler's 'London Lady' (I-VII-IV-V) and 'Oh Bondage Up Yours!' (whose verses and choruses focus on I and IV, respectively, and therefore strip away the third chord or the resolution to V). Despite the common appearance of the I-IV-V progression in punk, it is not ubiquitous enough to be considered normative. In some cases, songs are founded on other three-chord patterns (as in Siouxsie and the Banshees' 'Suburban Relapse', which features a recurring I-II-$\flat$VI progression) or on harmonic patterns that involve more than three chords (like The Adverts' 'One Chord Wonders', which is built on the recurring progression I-VII-VI-V). Commonly, songs that exhibit a verse-chorus or 32-bar structure will use different chord progressions to differentiate 'A' or verse sections from 'B' or chorus sections. The A sections of 'God Save the Queen', for example, are built upon the recurring progression I-IV-III-IV in A Major, while the B section, in E major, is based upon a different chord progression: I-V-VII-I. Similarly, in the verse-chorus design of The Clash's 'Career Opportunities', the verses unfold over a I-IV-V progression, while the choruses swap the second and third chords and embellish the result with the submediant harmony: I-V-VI-IV.

As Grossman and Dale have suggested, punk can be viewed as a musical 'reencapsulation of rock and roll' and an extension of folk because of its return to the guitar-based ensemble typical of these earlier genres, its use of existing song forms and its conventional harmonic language. What Grossberg's comment fails to explain, however, is how the angst of the 'blank generation' of postmodern youth came to express itself within what he describes as punk's 'circumscribed range of sounds'. The conservatism of punk's structural and harmonic framework provides a foil for punk's voices, many of which rejected traditional notions about 'what it means to sing' and instead tended to waver or glide between indeterminate pitches, or to shriek, yell and imitate the inflections of speech. From a male perspective, these vocal practices allowed for the expression of such emotions as anger or contempt, as my discussion of the voices of Johnny Rotten and Sid Vicious in the next section of this chapter will illustrate. For female punks, by contrast, the same vocal practices allowed women to challenge normative femininities that were inscribed into the voice and to resist gender biases that either silenced female voices or limited the ways in which women were allowed to speak. Female punk singers answered these biases in various ways, as the ensuing discussion will demonstrate. On the one hand, vocalists like Gina Birch (The Raincoats) or Poly Styrene (X-Ray Spex) parodied the stereotypical 'feminine' voice with seemingly untamed (or untameable) vocal lines that soared and shrieked into high registers. One contemporary observer of The Raincoats observed that 'at times, delicate male ears complained of strident or shrill notes, but these were the sounds of liberation. One of the Raincoats' greatest strengths has been their willingness to *risk* their voices, to push them beyond the limit in their attempts to reshape the parameters of female pop singing'.[7] Poly Styrene's voice has been similarly described, particularly as it was featured in her most memorable song, 'Oh Bondage Up Yours!' (Virgin 1977). Gillian Gaar (2002) observes that the song begins with 'a veritable battle cry as Styrene shrieked the title with glee'.[8] Haddon (2019) notes that, in cases like Birch and Styrene, 'the aesthetic and performative language of amateurism offered an important space of play for women whose musical voices and bodies had hitherto, and in other genres, been so stringently policed'.[9] On the other hand, vocalists like Siouxsie Sioux opted to sing in a more 'natural' and 'melodic' mid-register but to parody gender stereotypes with gliding vocal lines that evoke hysteria or with the 'earth-shaking moans and wails' that simultaneously point to sexual pleasure or the vocal response to pain.[10] The importance of the voice as a vehicle through which to express resistance to gender stereotypes is underscored by the title of Siouxsie and the Banshees' debut album, *The Scream* (Polydor 1978). In her study of female voices in punk, Jayna Brown (2011) explains that 'screams [are used in punk to] disrupt in several directions: they interrupt a masculinist claim to dissidence as they disrupt the very ground of dissonance'.[11]

Pathologizing the female punk voice

One important facet of punk rock is the role played by its many voices, each of whose timbral quality contributes meanings to the musical text by inviting the listener to identify with, and perhaps even attempt to mimic, the singing subject. The voice is the point of connection between the punk singer and the listener, the latter of whom can 'perform' alongside the former without recourse to an instrument other than their larynx. The ability to generate sound from the larynx reaffirms the human bond that connects the singer to the listener and, in the case of punk, underwrites the do-it-yourself ethos that encourages participation from anyone who wants to sing. Moreover, the listener can often identify the singer from the timbral quality of his or her voice, even in the physical absence of that singer, since 'the voice stands for the subject more directly than other instrument. Indeed, so tied to the body is the voice that even when disembodied we easily identify it as belonging to a particular subject'.[12] Richard Middleton (1999) has similarly argued that the voice is 'a key marker of identity, representing a person and (usually) carrying the machinery of (always gendered) subject-positions embedded in language'.[13] The voice not only helps to identify the individual subject for a listener but also, as Middleton suggests, points to certain social categories that define the individual. Middleton identifies gender as one category that is expressed in the voice, but we can also add class to his definition of the voice, particularly in cases where class distinctions reveal themselves in different accents or dialects.

For those familiar with the voices that speak through punk, the subject-position of individual singers can be ascertained from the unique flavour or texture of the vocal sounds that each singer produces, or the voice's 'grain'.[14] The distinctive characteristics of Johnny Rotten's voice, as a quintessential example within the scene, have been the subject of study in Dave Laing's foundational work on punk, where it is noted that Lydon's satirical mimicry of the affectations of the upper-class British accent (in particular its rolled *r*'s and the insertion of extra '*er*' embellishments at the end of certain words) is viewed as a critique of class oppression and characterized by Laing as 'a vocal representation of suffering'.[15] Laing suggests that when Lydon appropriates certain traits that he perceives in the upper-class accent and draws these vocal sounds into an otherwise working-class British discourse, his locutionary acts draw attention to the class that Lydon embodies in his performances. Sean Albiez (2003) concurs with Laing's observations when he claims that 'the *voice*, in all senses, of Johnny Rotten seemed unique and it was this that was the focus of the emotive and assaultive performances of the Sex Pistols'.[16] A similar reading of the voice can be applied to Sid Vicious' legendary re-creation of Sinatra's classic song, 'My Way', which begins with a pointed parody of the affectations of the trained singing voice.[17] Vicious' opening gambit, in which he executes an exaggerated vibrato in a register that clearly falls outside his natural range while his instrumental accompaniment satirizes a string orchestra, quickly gives way to a guitar-based 'punk' rendition and thereby juxtaposes what Vicious lampoons as the 'manufactured' voices of those who recorded the song before him (like Sinatra and Elvis) against his own, more 'sincere', working-class vocal delivery of the text. As in spoken language, accent becomes a marker of class in punk singing, and the 'otherness' of the working-class accent is heightened in punk by the impersonations that we see in the performances cited here.

As this discussion suggests, the meanings that a performer might embed within a song, or that a listener might subsequently ascribe to the song, often lie beyond the content of its poetic text. The lyrics of 'My Way', for example, might remain recognizable in Vicious' cover but they also assume a new set of meanings because of certain performance decisions made by Vicious in his rendition of the song. To explain how meanings might derive from the performance of a text, rather than from its semantic content, a study of vocal timbre following scholars like Roland Barthes (1977) and Victoria Malawey (2020) suggests that the meanings that we attribute to the lyrics of songs like 'My Way' or 'God Save the Queen' become subordinated to the meanings that can be deduced from their vocal delivery. This approach asks the listener to consider why Vicious opts to warble his way through the opening of his rendition of 'My Way' or why Lydon inflects certain words as he does, rather than to focus exclusively on the content of the song lyrics as the principal source of the meaning of a song. As we listen to a given song, Roland Barthes urges us to focus on what he describes, following Julia Kristeva, as the *geno-song*, or the aspect of a song whose meanings lie in 'that apex (or that depth) of production where the melody really works at the language – not at what it says, but the voluptuousness of its sounds-signifiers, of its letters' (in other words, its performance).[18] Barthes also urges us to resist the temptation to focus exclusively on what he calls, again after Kristeva, the *pheno-song*, or the part of the song that 'covers all the phenomena, all the features which belong to the structure of the language being sung' (in other words, its lyrics).[19] While the singing voice points to a particular identity, as Middleton suggests in terms of its relationship to gender (and, as I have suggested, also in terms of its relationship to class), it also alludes to the emotional states expressed by the performer through such strategies as vocal inflection, pronunciation, articulation, tessitura, vocal extension, tempo and the techniques associated with breathing, to name just a few.

One of the many meanings that can be attributed to the voice emerges from a consideration of its position relative to others in what Pierre Bourdieu (1984) has called the 'field of cultural production'. From Bourdieu's writings about the relationship between 'taste' and class, we can argue that aspects of the voice (like its 'grain') help to identify subjects within a given field of potential speakers and to differentiate those subjects in terms of their comparative access to power within that field. One observation that emerges from Bourdieu's writings about 'taste' is that hegemonic groups within a field of cultural production will define a 'normative voice' against which all others will be measured. This voice will reflect the perspective (i.e. the 'tastes') of the dominant group for whom it speaks. Bourdieu argues that since 'aesthetic choices belong to the set of ethical choices that constitute a lifestyle', an individual who aspires to power within the field of cultural production must embrace the 'tastes' and 'lifestyle' of the dominant group as these express themselves through, among other things, the 'normative voice'.[20] This suggests that dominant voices within the field of cultural production will authorize the voices of certain identities to speak and will force others to remain silent. Participation (or non-participation) in cultural production might therefore be determined by vocal identifiers like regional or class accents or the gendered timbre of the individual's voice, all of which mark the subject position of a given speaker relative to an authorized voice and enable the pathologizing of 'other' voices as a justification for their containment or erasure. The implication is that participation in the field of cultural production by 'non-normative' voices (like those that mark a subordinate class or gender) will always be delimited by a dominant group that will establish strict limits on what subjugated voices can say, when and whether they can speak, and how they must perform their speech acts. Against established codes of behaviour and expression that contain the performance of class, Lydon's voice in 'God Save the Queen' or Vicious' voice in 'My Way' become read as violations of these codes. From the perspective of the *geno-song*, we can argue that Lydon and Vicious perform like they do in order to break the silence imposed upon them by those whose voices they mimic. At the same time, and on the surface of the music (or its *pheno-song*), these artists co-opt specific musical objects that represent a social space into which they are not supposed to intrude. For Vicious, this is the space of the musical 'superstar' whose sleek performances become markers of 'taste' for a particular audience of musical 'connoisseurs' (or members of the dominant class). For Lydon, this is the space inhabited by the aristocracy whose anthem confirms their commitment to a world order in which their 'tastes' and 'lifestyles' are viewed as ideal and are therefore never subject to critique. The hostile reception of 'God Save the Queen' in Britain at the time of its release illustrates the extent to which Lydon and his band breached the boundaries meant to contain and suppress the sentiments of punk's working-class constituency: the song was silenced by a BBC ban levied on 31 May 1977 and its title was subsequently concealed behind a thick black line on the UK Singles Chart on 11 June 1977 because it was deemed to be in 'poor' taste, particularly during the Queen's Silver Jubilee.

While Bourdieu's thesis does not involve gender per se, we can extrapolate his observations about 'taste' (and the 'normative voice' preferred by the dominant class) to the participation of women in the field of cultural production. The censorship faced by working-class male voices was also faced by female voices, which were 'othered' both within and beyond the dominant class. As Leslie Dunn and Nancy Jones (1997) argue, the 'voice' has been of particular interest to feminists because it represents

> a wide range of aspirations: cultural agency, political enfranchisement, sexual autonomy, and expressive freedom, all of which have been historically denied to women. In this context, 'voice' has become a metaphor for textual authority, and alludes to the efforts of women to reclaim their own experiences through writing ('having a voice') or to the specific qualities of their literary and cultural self-expression ('in a different voice').[21]

The extent to which the male voice was viewed as normative within the dominant class in the mid-1970s was reflected in the comparative absence of female voices in such arenas of power as politics, the media and academia, to cite just three. In the mid-1970s, female voices were notably absent on BBC radio news programmes and were underrepresented in television news, both venues of which were dominated by men. The American anchor Barbara Walters, who was one of the first female news anchors to break the gendered sound barrier, has spoken at length about her struggles against what she described as 'voice prohibition' in her career as an American television news anchor.[22] A British counterpart to Walters who faced similar 'voice prohibition' was Margaret Thatcher, who is known to have hired a vocal coach to lower the pitch of her otherwise 'shrill' voice and thereby increase her legitimacy as a politician both within the Houses of Parliament and among potential voters.[23] Unlike Walters and Thatcher, who fought for a voice within a dominant class in whose dialect they already spoke (albeit in a register that needed to be tamed), the working-class female voice was doubly contained both because of its subordinate gender and its subordinate class. Despite the obstacles that she faced, Thatcher was able to rise to power in spite of her gender because she spoke like others who comprise the 'educated' ruling class (i.e. her voice was authoritative because she used what is commonly known as the 'BBC pronunciation' of the 'Queen's English'). The voices of working-class women could never aspire to be heard in the public sphere not only because of their gendered timbre but also because their speech patterns did not reflect the 'tastes' of the dominant class.

Dunn and Jones suggest that women who violate the submissive, quiet or non-speaking roles assigned to them by males in the dominant class have historically been pathologized as delusional, immoral or mentally unstable. They point, in particular, to such mythical female transgressors as the siren, the madwoman and the prostitute as historical female archetypes whose 'unruly sexuality and disturbing vocalizations' were perceived by mainstream culture as threats to the civilized social order that it sought to promote and protect.[24] These female archetypes were singled out for vilification not only because of what and how they spoke but because of the dangers posed to those who listened. In their literary characterizations, the siren's voice promises death to any man who is exposed to it, the madwoman's voice displays an animalistic character that is antithetic to conventional notions of femininity, and the prostitute's voice represents aspects of carnality and female sexuality that are typically viewed as obscene in mainstream culture. In their literary depictions, behaviours that flaunt or celebrate female power and sexuality are dismissed as 'deviant' because of the dangers that they pose to male sexual dominance. Through these stories, women are told that, in a society that aspires to maintain 'civility', they will be punished and silenced if they opt to embrace the behaviours and vocalizations of these female transgressors.

The literary connections forged between the voice of a subject and her state of mind find clinical 'confirmation' in Freudian psychotherapy, where an analysis of the utterances of disturbed (often female) patients became central to the 'talking cure' that was developed in the nineteenth century to relieve the symptoms of hysteria in women. As one feminist critic explains,

> Freud forged his landmark 'sexual thesis' investigating hysteria, an illness considered especially acute among women … [by] rejecting the commonplace diagnosis as either neurological disease or willful malingering [and declaring] hysteria as a sexual disturbance. … [a diagnosis of the disease] culminates in a prescription for psychoanalysis, the 'talking cure', whereby the patient comes to terms with the 'primal experience' of early childhood that presumably sparked the fateful repression of sexual desire.[25]

Freud's case histories, for example, famously focused on his female patients (specifically Frau Emily N., Miss Lucy R., Katharina, Fräulein Elisabeth von R. and Dora) and those of his colleague Joseph Breuer (like Anna O.) as exemplars of the hysteric.[26] Historically, nervous maladies suffered by men were rarely the subject of discussion in psychoanalytic literature, where male patients who presented with psychological symptoms 'were either handled very privately … or were formally diagnosed with non-derogatory diagnoses, such as "nerve exhaustion" and "neurasthenia"' to ensure that their masculinity was not thrown into question because of the symptoms that they exhibited.[27] As a treatment for hysteria in female patients, Freud and his followers employed free association as a way to unlock the psyche and to reveal the root causes of an illness that they characterized as hysteria. Accordingly,

> the patient says everything, however trivial or unpleasant, that comes to mind … [and] in this way, one's actions or the language of the body is squeezed into words. Instead, for instance, of getting locked out of one's home repeatedly or having a cramp in one's neck for which there is no physical explanation, one hears the chain of associations that leads to one having lost the key or to finding out what or who is a pain in the neck.[28]

On the one hand, the approach urged practitioners to examine the meanings latent in *what* a patient says (an aspect of an utterance that finds its parallel in the music-analytical dimension of the *pheno-song*). On the other hand, free-associative talk-therapy also encouraged the therapist to examine *how* a patient communicates (or that aspect of an utterance that finds a closer parallel in the music-analytical dimension of the *geno-song*). Since the performance of language was believed by some Freudians to reflect the mental state of its speaker, therapists looked for evidence of mental illness in such overt verbal symptoms as aphasia, confusion, yelling, stuttering, involuntary verbal tics, moaning and glossolalia, and in more subtle verbal cues like vocal inflection, breathing patterns, volume, pitch, timbre and the pace of verbal delivery. The physical gestures associated with verbal communication were also subject to scrutiny in talk therapy as they contributed meanings to the performance of speech. In attempting to catalogue the variety of cues through which a patient might 'speak', Freud's acolyte, Theodor Reik, developed a technique for talk therapy that has interesting possibilities for musical analysis when he suggested the Nietzschean concept of the 'the third ear' as a psychoanalytical approach that would enable a therapist to posit a diagnosis from an observation of verbal and corporeal cues enacted in the physical performance of speech by a patient of psychotherapy. The content of 'talk' became secondary to its performance in Reik's theory, outlined in the treatise *Listening with the Third Ear* (written in 1948, only three decades before punk), which argues that 'it is not the words that are spoken by the voice that are of importance, but what [the voice] tells us of the speaker. Its tone comes to be more important than what it tells'.[29] Consistent with Freud's own writings and reflective of the decade in which it was written, his theory also assumes a gendered reading of the application of 'the third ear' in clinical diagnoses that imply a doctor-listener who is male and a patient-speaker who is typically female. This power imbalance was maintained through the 1970s, when talk therapy was replaced by anti-depressants. Jonathan Metzl (2003) has argued that 'the visual construction of *patienthood* [in advertisements for anti-depressants] implicitly connects a woman's sanity with her marital status. Manipulations of perspective are also used to paint women's illnesses as threats to a specific notion of *doctorhood*, defined by convention as male'.[30] The gendering of mental illness is a theme that is reinforced in popular culture, where female characters suffer from 'psychosomatic symptoms' as they plan for a wedding that never seems to materialize (as in 'Adelaide's Lament' from the 1950 musical *Guys and Dolls*) or find themselves trapped in domestic lives that are so painfully dull that they need to be tranquilized (as in The Rolling Stones' 1966 hit 'Mother's Little Helper').

In female punk, the voice was often used to resist its pathologizing in mainstream culture, where a woman who speaks when she should be silent or who speaks in a way that is deemed unacceptable risks being dismissed as mentally ill. The supposed dangers inherent in the voices of female transgressors are brought to the fore in female punk narratives, where the constraints imposed upon women by the hegemonic male notion of feminine 'civility' are challenged by characters who display the 'non-normative' or 'asocial' behaviours associated with such archetypes as the siren, the madwoman and the prostitute. Female punks re-enact (and parody) the gendering of patienthood when they embody and vocalize the mental anguish and distress associated both with the physical and emotional victimization that is meted out by their male partners and with the isolation and claustrophobia that they experience within their suburban kitchens and nurseries. They also challenge the silence imposed upon the working-class female voice with songs that encourage the transgressor to speak, often in the guise of the madwoman (or the hysteric housewife) or the prostitute (or the sexual libertine). As Karina Eileraas (1997) argues, one of the legacies of female punk is its use of 'the ugly voice as a tool for cathartic expression; a means to articulate the "self" while acknowledging it as a site of fiction, contest, incoherence, social inscription, and performativity. Girl bands use their voices as weapons', thereby reinforcing the danger that is believed to be embodied in the voice of the female transgressor.[31]

Listening to punk with the 'third ear'

Given female punk's apparent interest in playing with such roles as the patient or the female transgressor as a strategy of resistance to class and gender oppression, it follows that analytical theories about musical embodiment prove to be fertile resources for the analysis of the 'grain of the voice' in female punk. From a music-analytical standpoint, one parallel to Reik's 'third ear' psychoanalytic approach lies in the theory of kinaesthetic empathy, which was proposed by Andrew Mead (1999) to describe an intuitive approach to the analysis of musical performance. Mead defines his term as 'an identification with the embodiment of a sound', and in a passage that is particularly useful for a study of female punk voices, he explains that 'one of the visceral thrills of hearing a singer comes from the intimate knowledge of making sounds with our voices that we share as human beings. We are transported in part by what it must be like to make such a sound'.[32] Mead argues that a canny listener (like a canny psychoanalyst) will perceive sound as the product of a particular set of physiological actions whose performance carries certain meanings, and will map her experience of these actions onto the sounds that she perceives. The listener of a given voice can imagine what it feels like to sing in a register or at a tempo that seems 'natural' and that allows the singer to breathe 'naturally'. Elizabeth Le Guin (2005) argues that, in performance, 'comfort is the ideal state. It does not expand or contract, nor seek to become greater to alleviate itself'.[33] If a song forces the performer's voice into an unnaturally high or low register, the listener can imagine the physiological demands placed upon the larynx as it strains to produce pitches that lie beyond its comfortable range. Similarly, if the tempo of a song appears to reel out of control, the listener can imagine the stress imposed upon a performer who struggles to keep up with the pace of the music that accompanies her song. The listener can also empathize with a singer who is asked to sustain pitches seemingly beyond the capacity of the average breath or to catch short breaths through a passage filled with staccato articulations: both of these situations mimic the laboured breathing associated with hyperventilation. Through kinaesthetic empathy, the stress placed upon the body by these kinds of performance demands can be experienced vicariously by the listener, who can map the physiological response of the singer's body onto a variety of emotional states to which this stress might allude. The use of unnatural registers, fast tempi and irregular breathing, along with such other possible vocal techniques as shouting or screaming, excessive or pointed use of loud or soft dynamics, vocal glissando, singing 'off-key' and the mimicry of speech (or *Sprechstimme*), carry extra-musical references that point to such emotions as fear, confusion, agitation, psychosomatic pain and other mental states consistent with 'hysteria'.

One significant difference between the application of Reik's psychoanalytic 'third ear' to a speaking subject and a music-analytic approach to the voice that relies upon 'kinaesthetic empathy' in its interpretation of a singing subject is the surrounding context within which the voice performs. In the case of psychoanalysis, the therapist encounters merely the voice, presumably in the quiet surroundings of his office, as he interacts with a female patient behind closed doors. The voice is foregrounded in a context where silence serves as its background. In music, by contrast, the voice is rarely unaccompanied, but speaks instead with or against a musical background that often shapes a listener's perception of what the voice says or how the voice speaks. The voice is superimposed upon a harmonic and rhythmic framework that contributes to its performance either by determining its pitch content and rhythmic pulse or by providing a framework that contradicts the voice. A music-analytical 'third ear' must therefore consider the relationship between a vocal foreground and its musical background as the latter contributes to the meanings that might be ascribed to the former.

Most theories of musical embodiment, of which Mead's and Le Guin's are but two examples, are based upon the observation of live performances and assume that any reading of a musical work will be informed what is heard *and* what is seen. Fisher and Lochhead (2002) explain that

> the performers' body moves when making music, and those movements provide a strong visual cue to how individuals carry out a performative enactment of musical meaning. For listeners … watching a performance instead of merely listening to it contributes not only to music's entertainment value but also to a better understanding of its meaning: the interaction of the visual and aural components creates the richest possible musical experience. In situations where listeners apprehend musical sound through the non-visual medium of recordings, performative enactment of musical meaning relies on a prior backdrop of experience that allows listeners to imaginatively engage the physical activities that went into its performance.[34]

Their comment is consistent with Reik's theories, which urge the psychoanalyst to diagnose a patient on the basis of verbal and physical cues enacted in the performance of language. In the case of a genre that predates the MTV music video, like punk, little evidence of the physical aspect of performances survives and the analyst is left to create a 'third ear' reading of a performance based largely on the kinaesthetic trace. Some embodiment theorists maintain that the lack of visual corroboration does not impede a reading of the *geno-song*, since 'music, unlike painting, film, performance art, theater, and dance, is not necessarily dependent upon sight … [instead] music's most radical feature is its disruption of vision's authority'.[35] The listener can hear the difference between comfort and stress as it is embodied in the voice of a singer, whether or not the listener can see that singer's corporeal response to the demands of the performance. By extension, distress can be read in the voice of a singer through cues that require no visual engagement. In the case of punk, the lack of video confirmation for any reading that might emerge from the performance of a given song is mitigated by the richness of punk's visual field, as described in the preceding chapter. We can argue that documentary evidence like punk portraiture and still photographs from concerts helps to inform our empathic response to a given performance by framing performances in terms of their performing subjects.

Punk that was created and performed by women tended to play out its resistance to gender norms through its embodiment of a set of transgressive feminine figures whose voices express the 'disturbing vocalizations' of 'out-of-control' and 'uncontrollable' female hysterics. Punk performances are replete with vocalizations of emotions that women were not conventionally allowed to express (like desire, regret, anguish or anger) and the female characters who populated punk songs often found an outlet for these pent-up emotions in such 'non-normative' behaviours as sorcery, criminality, seduction, nymphomania or sadism. Corresponding roughly to Dunn and Jones' archetypes, the female characters who are represented most often in female punk songs serve to 'give a voice' to the silent female who exists on the periphery and whose voice is erased because it fails to conform to the 'tastes' of the dominant culture. The purpose here is not to map these archetypes onto working-class women but, rather, to point out how these familiar female exemplars were used by women in the British punk scene to expose the sexism and classism that were a daily part of their lives.

In what follows, examples of several female punk archetypes will be examined to show how women in the scene mobilized behaviours that were conventionally stigmatized as symptomatic of hysteria as a means of social critique. Female punk inverts the diagnosis of 'hysteria', reading 'bad' behaviour as a normal reaction to the various circumstances within which women are confined and thereby reading 'good' behaviour as complicit in the subjugation of women. Each female archetype in punk acts out her 'bad behaviour' in vocal performances that are consistent with the alleged symptoms of hysteria. At the same time, the voices in female punk tend to resist the musical settings into which they are placed, often foregrounding pitches that are dissonant against the underlying harmonies or gliding on indeterminate pitches that similarly rub against the chord patterns with which they coexist. Rhythm, tempo and articulation are also explored in female punk for their ability to convey the distress seemingly experienced by the characters described in punk songs. Interestingly, each of these musical features paints an aural picture of the 'hysteric' that is often contradicted by the visual imagery that surrounds female punk. The anguished or rebellious cries of the imprisoned housewives depicted in songs like 'Suburban Relapse' (Siouxsie and the Banshees, *The Scream*, Polydor 1978) or 'Diet' (Au Pairs, *Playing with a Different Sex*, Human 1981), for example, gain further meaning in performance because they are juxtaposed against images of the dominatrix (like that embodied in an early persona adopted by Siouxsie Sioux), the androgyne (as a typical 'look' for punks of both genders) or the female who simply refuses to accept conventional standards of feminine beauty. The 'ugliness' embraced by female punks became reflected in voices that challenged the interpretations imposed upon women by a 'third ear' that was typically marked as male.

As an object of parody in female punk, the 'hysteric' assumes many guises that range from mythic creatures like the banshee to such everyday characters as the rebellious housewife and mother, the petty thief and the sexual libertine. Each of these characters challenges gender norms in a unique way (whether they lash out at their husbands, steal from the grocery store or initiate a sexual encounter that they are subsequently seen to enjoy), although what they hold in common is a tendency to express their defiance openly in voices that are loud, abrasive and unapologetic. While various aspects of female transgression are catalogued in punk lyrics, the emotional states associated with transgression are captured in the performance of these lyrics. The true nature of these transgressors reveals itself both in *what* the lyrics of a song might imply about a subject and *how* those lyrics are delivered either by a singer who performs in the guise of the subject or who merely observes her from a distance. The dramatic possibilities that emerge from interactions between the voice and its poetic text are numerous, each of which can contribute to our understanding of a given song. This aspect of our interpretation of song most closely resembles Reik's 'third ear' approach. We can also assert that an emotionally charged text that clashes with its mode of delivery (e.g. a violent scene that is described by a singer in a measured voice) might suggest resignation, whereas a different performance of the same text (e.g. in a voice that shrieks or hyperventilates in response to a violent attack) would suggest defiance by comparison. On the other hand, a seemingly benign text that inspires an emotional performance (e.g. a domestic scene that is described in a voice that shrieks or hyperventilates) might imply defiance, while a different performance of the same text (e.g. in a voice that is sweet or pleasant) might imply submission or compliance.

Unlike the voices to which Reik turned his 'third ear', the singing voice also exists within a musical framework that can alter the way that it is interpreted. In punk, the framework acts as a kind of background for the text, and is typically comprised of short, repetitive chord progressions that serve as the harmonic basis of a given song and that delineate its formal subdivisions. We can theorize that a voice that is dissonant against a given harmonic framework might be heard to emphasize or dramatize negative emotions or to display its resistance to the musical 'norms' represented by the chord progression with which it coexists. Further, a voice that resists melodic repetition, in spite of the cyclic nature of the chord progression on which it is superimposed, can be seen to 'clash' with its musical surroundings and thereby posit itself as a site of resistance to musical 'norms'. By contrast, a voice that is consonant with a given framework or that repeats its melodic materials in a way that parallels the harmonic foundation of a given song might evoke for its listener the passivity, acceptance or submission of the subject that it represents. This is not to suggest that every song will delineate clear character types. A voice might alternate within a song between states of agreement with, and divergence from, the harmonic framework, and might thereby strike the ear as indecisive, hesitant or even fearful to 'strike out on its own' against the norms represented by the framework.

While interpretations of the voice that performs a text against a musical background approximate a 'third ear' approach to psychoanalysis, the relationship between a poetic text and its musical setting also contributes meanings to a song, as many musicological studies will attest. If 'conflict' can be taken as the basis of resistance (and 'unity', conversely, as the basis of compliance), a similar narrative can play itself out in arenas that involve the voice only peripherally. The meanings implicit in song lyrics, like the voice that sings the poetic text of a song, may or may not correspond with the character of its musical accompaniment, and each of these options presents a different kind of narrative that might add to our interpretation of the 'grain' of the female punk voice. A song whose lyrics and music convey the same kind of emotion (say, a text that describes a fearful event that is accompanied by ominous music) will convey different meanings in comparison to a song whose poetic text seems to be contradicted by the music that surrounds it (like a song about a fearful event is set to calm music).

In the analyses that follow, meanings will be attributed to the voice from the performative decisions made by each singer as each reflects a certain corporeal state, whereby comfort is seen as an ideal physical state against which physical stress can be read as non-normative. The notion that physical stress represents a distress that can be experienced kinaesthetically by the listener is extended in the analyses to acknowledge other parameters that are operative in the performance of a song. As a marker of distress, 'stress' is extrapolated to the relationships between lyrics and their performance, the performing voice and its musical context, and between lyrics and their accompaniment. The objective is to demonstrate how hysteria, as a physical manifestation of emotional distress, expresses itself through the interaction of voice, text and music.

'Hysteric' archetypes in punk

The Banshee

Siouxsie and The Banshees' 'Pure' offers a unique possibility to deploy the 'third ear' in musical analysis in a context where lyrics have been removed and the listener is invited to respond merely to the sound of the voice. The song launches the group's debut album, *The Scream* (Polydor 1978), and is a short ambient track that seems almost introductory in the context of an album whose subsequent songs feature poetic texts that describe various facets of female life. 'Pure' eschews conventional song structures, provides no discernible harmonic progression and plays with a tempo that slowly increases from fifty-two beats per minute at the beginning of the song to a climax of eighty-four beats per minute by the middle of the song, after which the tempo ebbs. Adding to the instability of the tempo of the song, the guitars are noteworthy for their liberal use of glides and dissonant intervals, notable among which is the interval of tritone as a hallmark of the bass guitar. Finally, the keynote of the song is ambiguous for the first third of track, as the bass guitar slowly ascends from A_2 to rest on the keynote, G_3, in measure 13.[36] The voice enters for the first time in this measure and subsequently meanders around G_3 as it migrates unpredictably between the left and right stereo channels (see Figure 1):

Figure 1 Vocal tracks, closing measures of 'Pure'.
(Siouxsie and the Banshees, *The Scream*, Polydor 1978) (mm. 24–31) (Author's transcription)

In the absence of a consistent harmonic and rhythmic framework against which to measure the distress of the voice, a 'third ear' interpretation of Siouxsie's vocal tracks relies on other factors. Specifically, the voice is foregrounded in the mix, where it can be heard to glide upwards by the interval of the seventh, octave or ninth, before descending to rest on G_4 in each of its iterations. These vocalizations alternately evoke a sigh or the wail of the banshee to which band's name refers, both vocalizations of which are historically interpreted as symptomatic of 'hysteria'. In his historical study of the 'illness', Andrew Scull (2009) has argued that women who engaged in neurotic and crazed behaviours, like those suggested by the vocalizations of Siouxsie's banshee in 'Pure', were typically linked to 'the supernatural – to bewitchment, or to possession by devils' and thereby singled out for punishment that was designed to silence them, often forever.[37] By launching her album with the wail of the banshee, Siouxsie's performance places this transgressor at the centre of a set of ensuing narratives comprising *The Scream* that explore various facets of female oppression.

The rebellious housewife

On the ninth track of *The Scream*, Siouxsie's banshee speaks through the character of a rebellious housewife who feels imprisoned in her suburban environment and who dreams of freedom. The band's iconic portrayal of domestic misery, 'Suburban Relapse', opens with a series of sharp, jarring guitar chords that call to mind the famous shower scene in Hitchcock's *Psycho*. In a 2009 BBC interview, Siouxsie later claimed that the reference to Bernard

Herrmann's score was intentional because of its immediate association with violence and mental illness.[38] Like the image of the knife as it tears through the shower curtain, the opening chords rise and fall repeatedly throughout the introduction of the song and the listener senses that the attack becomes more frenzied as the bass guitar and drums are added to the mix. From an emotional standpoint, the intertextual reference sets up the opening lyric, in which a female subject is heard to apologize for lashing out against the constraints of her married life. The associations to Hitchcock's film invite the listener to imagine the subject's fantasy, in which she emerges half-crazed from the kitchen to stab her husband repeatedly as he naps on the couch. Like Norman Bates, this housewife can see no alternative to murder in her quest to rid herself of the source of a psychosis that, in her case, is brought about by her unwillingness to live according to social norms. For Bates, however, the fear of his own sexuality drives him to identify with a dead mother who counsels him to murder a subject who represents that fear. As one observer has remarked, '*Psycho* is not about feminine sexuality and division, but rather concerns masculinity and the desire to reunite with the lost maternal-subject.'[39] The married female subject of 'Suburban Relapse', by contrast, is driven by the alienation of her suburban imprisonment to recall, and perhaps aspire to reunite with, her former unmarried self. Given the psychosis that she experiences from within the confines of her kitchen, we might alternately read the text of 'Suburban Relapse' as an internal monologue, similar to the lines delivered by Bates in the voice of his mother at the end of the film. While descent into psychosis manifests itself on the body of Norman Bates, however, the housewife's angst is expressed through a steady accelerando that drives unremittingly towards the climax of the piece, which occurs just before the coda. During the coda, the song is marked by an increased use of vocal glissandi and the gradual fragmentation of the song's lyrics, which become repeated hysterically in the song's closing measures.

From a musical standpoint, the 'identity crisis' experienced by the anguished female subject of 'Suburban Relapse' is presaged in the jarring guitar chords that launch the narrative and its reference to *Psycho*. Initially, these chords obscure the keynote of the song. The upper voices of the opening chord sequence oscillate between the tritone components E_5 and $A\sharp_4$ and thereby infer a resolution to B_4 that can be confirmed by functional analysis: the opening passage alternates between a supertonic chord and a dominant chord, both of which can be conceived in terms of b-minor:[40]

                    Punk and Disorderly

Figure 2 Intro, 'Suburban Relapse'.
(Siouxsie and the Banshees, *The Scream*, Polydor 1978) (mm. 1–4) (Author's transcription)

However, this reading is complicated by the appearance, in measure 3, of G_3 in the bass (see Figure 2), which is introduced by its dominant, D_3, in the preceding measure and ornamented by its leading-tone, $F\sharp_3$. Any thought that we might be in g-minor, or b-minor for that matter, is dispelled when the guitar chords are fleshed out and transposed in measure 5. At this point, the upper voices oscillate between the pitches G_5 and $C\sharp_5$ (see Figure 3):

Figure 3 'Suburban Relapse'.
(Siouxsie and the Banshees, *The Scream*, Polydor 1978) (mm. 5–8) (Author's transcription)

This tritone suggests a resolution to D_5, which is finally established as the key-note in measure 11 and which therefore forces the reinterpretation of the bass note, G, as a subdominant and the opening allusion to b-minor as the relative key.

While any confusion about the identity of the key is rectified by measure 11, the listener continues to be thrown off by various factors that conceal the modality of the song. The chord progression that underpins the song from measure 11 until the reappearance of the opening '*Psycho*' guitar chords in measure 113 repeats a progression that is launched by the tonic chord (D), proceeds through the supertonic (E), and comes to rest on the flattened submediant chord (B♭), used here as a substitute for the more conventional dominant harmony. The tritone, E_5 to $A\sharp_4$, that launched the song has been transferred to the bass guitar, where it is enharmonically respelled as E to B♭, the latter pitch of which serves as the root of the flattened submediant (see Figure 4):

Figure 4 Chord progression, 'Suburban Relapse'.
(Siouxsie and the Banshees, *The Scream*, Polydor 1978) (Author's transcription)

The enharmonic change from A♯ (in Figures 2 and 3) to B♭ (in Figure 4) is significant because it renders the modal identity of D indistinct. On the one hand, the supertonic chord (E) points to D major (since it contains a B♮), while, on the other hand, the submediant chord (B♭) points to its parallel minor. Only at dramatic moments in the text, for example when the subject admits that her 'string snapped' or that she experiences a 'suburban relapse' does the major-key modality of D become clear, although its confirmation is momentary and fleeting, as if the subject of the song, seeing a glimpse of herself, is plunged once again into psychosis. Moreover, the juxtaposition of the major tonic triad (D) and its submediant triad (B♭) actually adds to the identity crisis expressed in the song, since the former contains an F♯ that is neutralized by the F♮ of the latter. The voice exploits this relationship with melodic lines that ascend from the tonic pitch, D, to waver and glide between an ambiguous mediant that is variously inflected as F or F♯. By measure 113, the subject appears to have worn herself out, as the tempo drops markedly and the recurring chordal passage is abandoned in favour of a reprise of the opening reference to the Hitchcock film. With the keynote of D firmly established in the ear, the opening passage is interpreted in its reiteration at the closing of the piece as a prolongation of the relative minor, B. The vocal line itself comes to rest on this pitch in measure 119, but as if to reiterate the modal ambiguity of the piece, the pitch is harmonized with a B major chord. The third of this chord, D♯₅, is then transferred to the vocal line, where it initiates, as the final glissando of the song, a sliding descent to the key-note D. From a melodic point of view, the song could have concluded there, but the supporting harmony provides no closure to the song. Instead of a more conventional conclusion on the tonic harmony, this key-note pitch becomes part of an unstable diminished triad on G♯, which seems to demand a resolution to A, but which is left hanging unresolved at the end of the song. Siouxsie and the Banshees deploy such vocal strategies as glides, indeterminate tonalities and modalities, and tempo fluctuations to embody the hysteria that is described in the poetic text of the song and the identity crises depicted in its music. The emotional distress and confusion experienced by the singer are also reflected in the musical accompaniment, whose chord progression sets up an expectation of the dominant (both in the underlying chord progression and at the end of the song) that it ultimately fails to deliver.

In other punk narratives about the life of the suburban housewife, rebellion manifests in entirely different ways. For example, The Raincoats portray a housewife in 'Fairytale in the Supermarket' who indulges in tea breaks and romance novels as a way to build an imaginary (or 'fairytale') life and thereby relieve the boredom of her everyday domestic routines. The song is built on a conventional I-IV-V-I foundation in the key of E, against which a female voice is heard to clash with pitches that rarely derive from her underlying harmonic support. Like its counterpart in 'Suburban Relapse', the female voice of 'Fairytale in the Supermarket' glides and wavers through its melodic line, although while Siouxsie uses indeterminate pitches to evoke uncertainty and to convey hysteria, the vocal line performed by her character is nonetheless governed by the song's underlying chord progression, as if contained by a situation from which she cannot escape. Moreover, her melody repeats and is singable, and tends to inflect pitch components of the song's underlying harmonies in order to problematize the modality of the song. By contrast, the female narrator of 'Fairytale in the Supermarket' intones a melody whose pitches and gliding tones seem to exist independent of, and frequently clash with, the song's cyclic I-IV-V-I chord progression. This voice's refusal to accept the melodic limitations imposed upon it by the harmonic framework around it serves as another mode of resistance in punk, and the dissonant tone with which the voice sings in the guise of a day-dreaming housewife might be said to represent another facet of hysteria, as an 'illness' whose symptoms present as vocalizations that disrupt an expected norm. The housewife described by The Raincoats uses her non-normative voice to construct an alternate reality that coexists, but rarely intersects, with the everyday reality embodied by her musical accompaniment. On first encounter, Ana da Silva's jarring vocal performance might be dismissed as naïve and untrained, consistent with punk's 'do-it-yourself' approach to music-making. Lucy O'Brien (2002) offers this interpretation when she suggests The Raincoats' 'lack of musical expertise make them inventive' – a point that is echoed in Mimi Haddon's (2019) argument about 'amateurism' in punk.[41] Despite this commonly held view of the band, I believe that da Silva's seeming 'ineptitude' was a deliberate vocal strategy whose spontaneous 'bends and turns' deliver a vocal line that 'fractures the musical surface, drawing the listener in without providing an opportunity for identification', as Caroline O'Meara (2003) suggests in her study of the band.[42] 'Fairytale in the Supermarket' up-ends the conventional relationship between a singer whose melodic line typically invites the listener to participate in her own 'performance' of the lyrics and an accompaniment that conventionally resides in the background of the mix. By contrast, the bass guitar in 'Fairytale' provides the song's most hummable and memorable melody, which becomes foregrounded as a kind of signature tune for the song in the absence of a vocal line with which the listener might identify.

Despite its apparent lack of musical coherence and the seeming prominence of the bass guitar, the voice nonetheless 'draws the listener in' because it is so unexpected both in the context of popular music and in the context of punk. Da Silva's performance aesthetic invites various readings of the housewife that she embodies in the song. First, the exaggerated inflections of her voice seem to parody the stereotypical female voice as it delivers lines like 'it makes no difference', 'I don't know', or 'don't ask me anything' with a nagging, child-like whine evoking a subject who refuses to acknowledge or address the reality of her domestic situation. At the same time, these lyrics imply that this housewife wants to be left alone to imagine new possibilities for her life, and this demand for a release from the domestic space described as a supermarket is reiterated in the relationship between the voice and the harmonic structure of the song against which it rubs or abrades. The independence of the voice from an accompaniment that would conventionally constrain it is perhaps the most significant aspect of this song. Unlike Siouxsie's captive housewife, the female singer of 'Fairytale in the Supermarket' intones her text with little attention to the harmonic structure with which it intersects only occasionally, and seemingly by chance.

In its resistance to the harmonic framework of the song, da Silva's voice suggests a character who will not be controlled or contained by the norms laid out by the lowest voice in the song, played by the 'masculine voice' of the bass guitar whose melody outlines the song's harmonic structure. Rather, this housewife seeks her escape from these norms in her imagination, as the lyrics of the song suggest.

Interestingly, while da Silva's voice resists interaction with the harmonies presented by the bass guitar, it is surprisingly sympathetic with the violin whose appearance in The Raincoats' ensemble is unusual in punk (perhaps with the notable exceptions of Urban Blitz, who played violin in The Doctors of Madness, or Billy Currie, who was the violist in Ultravox). Played by the

Figure 5 Opening lyrics, 'Fairytale in the Supermarket'.
(The Raincoats, *The Raincoats*, Rough Trade 1979) (mm. 6–9) (Author's transcription)

classically trained Vicki Aspinall, the violin engages in a dialogue with the voice in 'Fairytale in the Supermarket', where it provides a countermelody to da Silva's vocals in the verses of the song. From a narrative perspective, we might view the violin as the housewife's alter ego, with whom she shares a common performance aesthetic and, towards the end of the song, a common vocal line. Like the voice that it mimics, the violin resists active participation in the song right from the start, and opts, in the opening verse, to sustain a single pitch, E_5, through the duration of the verse (see Figure 5). The pitch rings piercingly above the texture of the song and the vocal line that lies beneath, and its ethereal effect recalls the haunting voice of the banshee in Siouxsie and the Banshee's 'Pure'. By the second verse, the violin consents to participation in the song, but is used uncharacteristically as a rhythmic instrument. Now embedded within the texture of the song, the violin problematizes the verse with an off-kilter rhythm that constantly interrupts the vocal line and that oscillates persistently between a quarter-note on B_4 and an eighth-note on A_4, unfolded over a section that switches between a two-measure block in 4/4 time and a one-measure interruption in 6/4 time. The rhythmic pattern performed by the violin belies the melodic simplicity of its two-note melody, and thereby illustrates that the 'naivete' of the band is a pretence: the pattern, which begins with the pitch B_4 on the downbeat of a measure in 4/4 time, is displaced by the appearance of the 6/4 meter and must proceed through twenty-four beats before it returns to the original downbeat in its opening quadruple meter. At the end of that verse, the violin breaks out of this two-note pattern and enters into a true dialogue with da Silva's gliding vocal line, which it interrupts and imitates at regular intervals with a recurring melody in 6/4 time that slides upwards from A_4 to a climax on E_5 and then glides downwards to rest briefly on $C\sharp_5$ before it finally descends to E_4. Played against the dominant harmony, C♯ strikes the ear as a particularly dissonant point of repose, but contributes to the false sense of 'amateurishness' in the violin part by emphasizing a pitch that seems out of tune in relation to the prevailing harmony. (The listener might be inclined to ask if the violinist *meant* to play D, but missed.) As a substitute for the voice of the housewife, the violin demands to be heard both because of its unusual timbre in the context of punk and because it adopts the performance aesthetic of the transgressive female voice in 'Fairytale in the Supermarket'.

Unlike the defiant housewife depicted in 'Suburban Relapse' or the housewife who constructs an alternate reality in 'Fairytale in the Supermarket', some housewives contain their emotions more successfully in punk songs and only hint at the distress that they experience. The housewife depicted by Lesley Woods in Au Pairs 'Diet' is one example, although the listener quickly recognizes that her passivity is medically induced. In a near monotone, the voice of this housewife describes her domestic life with a melody constructed from two pitches, B_4 and A_4. The implication in the small range of pitches that comprise her melody, delivered in a clipped and emotionless voice, is that the housewife is expected to speak very little and to be restrained in her vocal delivery. The limitations imposed upon her voice contrast sharply with the instrumental tracks, whose funk-inspired bass line suggests a celebration to which the housewife is not invited. Her detachment from the other elements of the song is reinforced by her relationship to the song's key of E-minor, whose tonic pitch she only sings once. For the majority of the song, Woods' voice oscillates between the dominant and subdominant pitches, but at the moment when it is revealed that a housewife 'needs to be tranquilized' in order to accept her domestic circumstances, the clipped voice drops away, ascending to sustain the tonic pitch E_5. As the highest vocal pitch in the piece, and held over several measures in a song whose voice sustains very little, this climax pitch draws attention to a voice that finally seems enraged by the narrative of suburban containment that it describes.

The rebellious housewife figure is represented variously in punk through musical depictions of madness and hysteria ('Suburban Relapse'), refusal to participate in a predetermined suburban narrative ('Fairytale in the Supermarket') and occasional glimpses of the 'real' woman behind the tranquilized façade ('Diet'). For other female archetypes, punk offers different oppositional strategies that similarly play themselves out in the voice and in its relationship to the musical text with which it coexists.

The anti-consumer

The female transgressors depicted in many of the songs written and performed by X-Ray Spex operate outside of the personal spaces that are typically coded as female (the suburban home, the kitchen or the supermarket) and instead present themselves as critics of a 'consumer society' that constructed an idealized female identity and that rejected female non-conformists. The anti-consumer archetype often vocalizes her resistance to female ideals in loud and angry tones that are atypical for the 'demure' conventional female, and that would likely be dismissed as symptomatic of hysteria by the 'third ear' interpreter. Poly Styrene, X-Ray Spex's lead singer, explained that a driving force behind many of the band's songs was her refusal to exist 'in bondage to material life. In other words, [our music] was a call for liberation. It was like saying: "Bondage? – forget it! I am not going to be bound by the laws of consumerism or bound by my own senses".[43] Because they were written by one of the scene's few performers of colour, Poly Styrene's lyrics can also be interpreted as a comment upon the racism that she experienced as a Black woman. Jayna Brown argues that, in songs like 'Oh Bondage Up Yours!', 'Poly Styrene linked pithy critiques of slavery, authoritarianism, patriarchy, and plastic'.[44] Her comments are perhaps reflected best in the lyrics of the band's most famous song, 'Oh Bondage Up Yours!', which framed their anti-consumerist mandate and which also established Styrene as one of the most defiant singers of the punk era. Unlike other songs that parody 'hysteria' in the behaviours of other types of transgressive females, songs like 'Oh Bondage' turn the diagnosis back towards its source, and suggest that the malady known as 'hysteria' is actually symptomatic of a sickness defined broadly as 'consumerism'. Since women were expected to defer to those who constructed and marketed the female image, according to the band, then it followed that women would experience (and therefore express) the unhappiness, frustration and emptiness experienced within the consumer society more acutely than men.

In 'Oh Bondage', the voice offers strategies for resistance to feminine ideals that differ from those offered by Siouxsie, Ana da Silva and Lesley Woods, given the song's immediate association with 'otherness' through its choice of pitch materials. With the exception of a few important pitches in the vocal and saxophone tracks, the song is almost entirely pentatonic, and draws its pitches from the minor pentatonic on D (i.e. the scale represented as D-F-G-A-C-D). As a source scale, the pentatonic is a staple in popular music, and is occasionally used in punk to represent the Asian 'other' (e.g. in Siouxsie and the Banshees' debut single, 'Hong Kong Garden'). In 'Oh Bondage', the scale helps to frame a conception of 'otherness' that arises from its association with childhood songs, many of which are pentatonic. This association is consistent with the lyrics of the song, in which Poly Styrene describes, and mimics the voice of, a 'little girl' whose behavioural constraints are listed and described in the infamous barb that launches the musical assault of the song's introduction. The idea expressed here, elaborated in the remainder of the song, and used as a theme in many of the other songs that appear on the band's album, *Germ Free Adolescents*, is that a consumer society that fetishizes the beautiful, silent woman (who is 'seen and not heard') denies her the possibility to participate in the construction of her own identity. We might argue that the minor pentatonic, with its musical allusions to childhood songs, represents this infantilization of women.

Despite the pentatonic setting of the song, Poly Styrene's vocal line struggles to break free and to wander into the diatonic realm. Like the housewives depicted by Siouxsie Sioux and described by Ana da Silva, Styrene's 'character' rubs against the musical grain of the pentatonic instrumental tracks that surround her and attempt to confine her. Lauraine Leblanc (1999) argues that Styrene 'transformed a seemingly masochistic plea into an indictment of consumer culture, denouncing the blind impulses of the mainstream shopper. In depicting herself as both an agent and resister of her submission, she created a parody of both positions, juxtaposing them powerfully against each other'.[45] The duality to which Leblanc alludes is apparent in the pitch materials that comprise the vocal lines of the verse and the chorus of 'Oh Bondage'. While the melodic line of the verses derives its two pitches, D_5 and C_5, from the pentatonic scale, Styrene's vocal line veers towards the diatonic minor scale on D during a chorus whose melody moves from F_5 to D_5 and comes to rest on E_5 before the pattern begins again. As a pitch that is foreign to the source scale, E_5 introduces the interval of the semitone (E-F) into a musical texture that is otherwise dominated by whole steps and minor thirds. This 'foreign' pitch emphasizes the character's resistance to the 'bondage' of consumer culture because it is placed strategically on phrases that challenge the status quo: namely, on the lyrics 'no more' and 'up yours'. But more surprisingly, and perhaps most memorably, the final iteration of the chorus pattern ($F_5 - D_5 - E_5$) propels Styrene's voice into the stratosphere, where it comes to rest on the leading-tone, C♯$_6$. Here, the singer reinforces her resistance in a final outburst of the phrase 'no more', with a shrieking tessitura that displays her resentment and that suggests an unwilling participant in the act of societal bondage (see Figure 6):

Figure 6 Vocal line, 'Oh Bondage Up Yours!'.
(X-Ray Spex, Virgin 1977) (mm. 43–46) (Author's transcription)

Each chorus ends in this surprising way, with the exception of the final chorus, which provides an open-ended and abrupt conclusion to the song on an unresolved dominant chord and the vocal pitch E$_5$. Like 'Suburban Relapse', this song undercuts its conclusion, leaving its listener to wonder whether the protagonist has managed to break free from the confines of her circumstances.

Any discussion of the song must acknowledge that, at the time of the release of 'Oh Bondage', the band had two strong frontwomen. The second, Lora Logic (Susan Whitby), provided the iconic alto-sax track for the single. Like the violin that appears in The Raincoats' 'Fairytale in the Supermarket', this atypical punk instrument is strongly associated with the voice of the female singer, whose melodic line it mimics during its solos. It substitutes for, or supplements, Poly Styrene's voice in the same way that Vicki Aspinall's violin interacts with Ana da Silva's voice, and these atypical instruments help to reinforce the 'otherness' of these female transgressors as they exist and perform in a genre that is dominated by the sound of the guitar.

Another band whose songs address consumer culture was The Slits, whose 1979 debut album *Cut* features several songs that are memorable for their critique of conspicuous consumption. Perhaps their most famous, 'Typical Girls', satirizes media portrayals of the 'perfect' female and challenges the invisibility imposed upon women who fall short of the manufactured ideal. Brian Cogan (2012) argues that the song 'epitomizes the Slits central message as they rail against women who "don't create, don't rebel".[46] In a typical verse-chorus song structure, the narrative of 'Typical Girls' lists various characteristics that define normative female behaviour, such as 'buying magazines', 'falling under spells', and 'worrying about spots, fat, and natural smells'. Although the list strikes its listener as ridiculous, it nonetheless reflects a certain reality in the media, where teenaged women tended to be portrayed as self-obsessed and boy-crazy while their adult counterparts were seen to settle happily into marital bliss and motherhood. The opening lyric of the song, superimposed on a hypnotic accompaniment that repeats throughout the introduction, soars above the guitar line with a pointed directive to females who aspire to conventionality (Figure 7).

Figure 7 Intro to 'Typical Girls'.
(The Slits, *Cut*, Island 1979) (mm. 4–7) (Author's transcription)

The predictability of the 'typical girl' is subsequently represented throughout the song by the association of those lyrics with a pair of recurring motives. Descriptors of the 'typical girl' that precede each iteration of these motives, by contrast, are subject to various rhythmic and pitch permutations to accommodate the differing characteristics listed in the changing text. While the title lyric remains constant in its musical depiction, the descriptors associated with the 'typical girl' are often the site of musical parody, particularly in instances where the band's lead singer, Ari Up (herself atypical as she performed with dreadlocked hair and sported her undergarments over her outerwear), emphasizes certain words with glides and tremolos as if to expose how ridiculous gender stereotypes actually are. Her voice deploys these vocal effects for dramatic purposes. In Figure 8, for example, the listener can visualize Ari Up's vibrating throat as she struggles with the words 'magazine' and 'feel'. Ari Up's performance might strike the listener as the vocal counterpart to a knowing wink to someone who is 'in' on her joke, but it can also be read as an embodiment of the unease felt by her character as she describes gender stereotypes that are not characteristic of her brand of femininity.

Figure 8 Vocal effects, 'Typical Girls'.
(The Slits, *Cut*, Island 1979) (mm. 57–62) (Author's transcription)

A view of the female experience 'on the street' is created by The Slits in the song entitled 'Shoplifting', whose protagonist is the antithesis of the 'typical girl' parodied in the previous song. Forced to steal in order to eat, this protagonist finds herself in a supermarket where her financial circumstances require her to resist the passive role of the consumer in favour of the more active role of the shoplifter. She is the anti-consumer because she cannot engage in a sanctioned commercial transaction and is forced to steal food and 'do a runner' under the watchful eye of the security camera. Like Siouxsie's housewife, the woman represented in 'Shoplifting' acts out within a space that is typically coded as female (the grocery store), so that as she contravenes the rules of the consumer society, she also violates the conventions associated with her gender. 'Shoplifting' shows many characteristics of the reggae style for which the band is known: notably, its placement of harmonies on the off-beats and the prominent role of the bass guitar in the infectious two-bar riff that repeats throughout most of the song. The genre is a curious choice for the band, since reggae was more commonly associated with male performers (notable at the time, Bob Marley, whose music was introduced to British punks by the disc jockey Don Letts). The reggae rhythms add to the excitement surrounding the illegal activities described in the lyrics of 'Shoplifting' and also allow its singer to engage in various vocal techniques associated with reggae, like tremolo, in order to evoke a character who is both nervous and out of control. In 'Shoplifting', Ari's voice whispers and giggles through the planning of the crime, and her character is breathy and confessional as she describes the moment at which the crime is committed. In the planning stages of the crime, the voice oscillates between the pitches E_4 and D_4, but once the crime has been committed and the thief begins to worry about whether she will be caught, her voice rises to a climax on F_5 as she runs for the exit and onto the high street. We can hear the singer scream and hyperventilate as she attempts to make her escape, and through our own experiences with these vocal gestures, we can empathize with her terror and excitement. Following this dramatic climax in the text, and the climax in the vocal line, Ari's voice slides downwards from a melodic peak on F_5 to land on E_4, and as her vocal line slips down into the lower register, it appears to fade from our ear as if to represent the getaway. We hear the thief disappear into the distance while the accompaniment ascends by chromatic step from A_4 to reach its apex on E_5 (see Figure 9). If we consider this section of the song to represent a race to the pitch E, the shrieking female voice gets there first and the accompaniment (like the security guard who chases the song's protagonist) lags several measures behind her. As if to reinforce this message in the lyrics of the song, Ari's relief is depicted in the closing moments of the song (not reproduced in the ensuing example) when she admits, in *sotto voce* and in a way that is contravenes 'feminine' modesty, that she has soiled her underwear.

Figure 9 Voice-against-accompaniment race to E in 'Shoplifting'. (The Slits, *Cut*, Island 1979) (mm. 68*ff*) (Author's transcription)

The rebellious housewife portrayed by Siouxsie Sioux acts out her resistance to female subjugation within the private spaces of the kitchen and the nursery, and daydreams about how life 'could have been' if she had opted against marriage and motherhood. The Slit's version of the anti-consumer, by contrast, acts out in public spaces like the high street and the grocery store, where she resists the gendering of consumerism by refusing the goods that are marketed to her or by stealing them. This version of the anti-consumer also suggests that theft is sometimes the only option for a consumer who needs to eat but who cannot afford food. The transgressors cited here who embody the anti-consumer play out their defiance in ways that differ from those cited as examples of rebellious housewives. The anti-consumer embodied by Poly Styrene, for example, refuses the pentatonic framework within which she is embedded, and breaks free on a shrill note that derives from the diatonic collection. The performance embodied by Ari Up, by contrast, suggests a subject who recognizes that her transgressive behaviours might be punished by those in authority (in this case, the police), and conveys fear to the empathic listener through such performative means as giggles, conspiratorial whispers and hyperventilation.

The sexual libertine

The sexual libertine represented a third type of female transgressor in punk whose willingness to speak openly about sex is typically viewed as non-normative, and perhaps even obscene, by a culture that demanded that females play passive roles in their romantic and sexual relationships. Historically, the androcentric view of the male as the locus of sexual power was designed not only to subjugate women but also to protect a man's sense of self-worth. A quote cited in Ch. 2 is equally applicable here: 'to deny women native erotic desires was to safeguard a man's sexual adequacy. However he performed, it would be good enough. She would not – would she? – ask for more'.[47] In female punk, male self-worth was a favourite subject of critique and satire, particularly in songs where male sexual performance was portrayed as inadequate to the demands of female sexual satisfaction. The topic of sexuality is central to many of the songs on the Au Pairs' debut album, *Playing with a Different Sex*, where the listener can find candid descriptions of non-traditional relationships (e.g. the story of an open relationship in the song 'We're So Cool') and female orgasm (a taboo topic that is vividly described in the song 'Come Again'). These topics invite different kinds of musical embodiment by their performers. The musical representation of female orgasm, for example, can play itself out in such musical devices as an ascending melodic line, a vocal line that repeats a melodic motive, a vocal articulation that suggests a hyperventilating subject, or an increase in rhythmic activity, while a thwarted orgasm can be represented by a sudden interruption in any of these music gestures. Among the many punk songs that place female sexuality in the spotlight, Au Pairs' 'Come Again' offers perhaps the most candid description of female sexual expectations. The song can be described as an account of a tepid sexual encounter recounted from the perspective of an unsatisfied female participant who ultimately fakes it so that she might be allowed to sleep, and it focuses its attention on an inexperienced or hapless male lover who seems incapable of satisfying his partner. Unlike many female punk songs, 'Come Again' allows the male voice to be heard, and the 'grain' of his voice is surprising in a sonic landscape that is otherwise dominated by the female voice. His character, performed by the singer Paul Foad, is central to the song and the insecurity that he expresses in the lyrics of the song contributes to its narrative of female sexual empowerment. The instructions provided by the female singer during the sexual act described in the song also lampoon misunderstandings about female biology and sexual response by uninformed male sexual partners.

Despite the participation of the male singer in 'Come Again', the verses of the song, set over the reiterated tonic pitch, E, are sung by a lone female voice (Lesley Woods) who intones her text on the pitch B_3 in a register that is lower than most of the other female voices described here. Diverging only occasionally from this pitch as the verses unfold, Woods' voice states the song's lyrics clearly, deliberately and mechanically, as if she is detached from the activity described in the song and preoccupied with the instructions that she conveys to her male partner. As Figure 10 demonstrates, the voice departs from B_3 only when it rises to pose questions in the text ('is it real?' 'are you feeling it?' and 'is your finger aching?'), and these inflections imitate those of the speaking voice. For the most part, however, the voice is insistent and repetitive, as if to mimic the manual stimulation described in the text of the song and to represent a disenchanted subject who cannot seem to reach a climax.

Figure 10 Typical vocal line, 'Come Again'.
(Au Pairs, *Playing with a Different Sex*, Human 1981) (mm. 46–49) (Author's transcription)

In the choruses, Wood's voice breaks from the monotony of the verses to rise from $C\sharp_4$ to E_4, to represent the expectation of sexual gratification. The accompaniment echoes this ascent and abandons the pedal on E that dominates the verses in place of a reiterated gesture on the subdominant, A. The anticipation embodied in this melodic ascent is contradicted by the text, however, which expresses the protagonist's 'frustration', 'aggravation' and 'annoyance' as she fails to reach orgasm: her melodic line only rises by the interval of a fourth in each chorus, after which it drops sharply to its original pitch, B_3. Further, the chord progression initiated by the verse (E) and continued in the chorus (A) fails to bring about the expected dominant chord (B). Instead, the chorus leads back in the next verse to E, and as the song oscillates between the tonic and the subdominant, it frustrates the listener's expectation for the dominant chord and, by extension, the singer's quest for sexual satisfaction. The musical relationship between the female voice and that of her male partner is particularly interesting in this song, since the male part imitates the vocal line of his female partner, even though it is clearly differentiated by vocal timbre. Like his partner, the male in this narrative intones his text on the pitch B_3, but his character differs from hers because his voice never strays from this pitch. This suggests that the male climax is not the objective of this sexual encounter. Moreover, the staccato delivery of his repeated text ('am I doing it right, doing it right…?' and so on) portrays an anxious and clueless lover.

A different kind of sexual relationship is described in Au Pair's 'We're So Cool', which explores the insecurities felt by the participants in an open relationship. While this theme might not lend itself as readily to musical embodiment because it does not involve the body as directly as the events described in 'Come Again', it nonetheless engenders emotions, particularly in participants who seem more accustomed to a conventional partnership, as one of the song's characters appears to be. A song about non-monogamy invites such reactions as jealousy, possessiveness, insecurity and paranoia (not to mention the defensiveness that these responses can provoke in the accused), each of which can lend itself to musical depiction. The narrative of 'We're So Cool' explores these facets of non-monogamy from the perspective of one participant in an open relationship. The song, sung by Lesley Woods, recounts her male partner's insecurities ('I know I'm the main man in your life') as he grapples to accept the sexual relationships that she pursues outside of their open relationship. The song is largely devoid of any markers of anxiety or insecurity, and, instead, Wood's voice seems to celebrate the sexual liberation that she enjoys in her open relationship with a dance-inspired melody that outlines b-minor triad in each verse. Derived from the natural form of the minor, the melody of the verse is anchored by the dominant ($F\sharp_4$) and the subtonic (A_3), the latter of which comes to rest on the tonic (B_3) only at the conclusion of each verse, when the speaker reassures his partner that he is not jealous. However, the possessiveness implicit in the text of each verse exposes itself in the choruses of the song, where two voices are heard to reiterate the sentiment 'you're mine' against a melodic line that outlines the tonic triad, the relative major, D. At this point, Woods is joined by Paul Foad, whose voice expresses the male jealousy to which Woods merely alludes in the verses. The move to the D triad in the chorus, and its superimposition on a foundation that reinforces the tonic of b-minor, is hardly surprising, given that this is merely the mediant of the home key. What *is* jarring, however, is the abrupt change from the lyrical melody of the verses to the monotonous repetition of D_4 in the chorus. The narrative effect is threefold. First, the declamatory style of the chorus contrasts sharply with the more melodic character of the verses, and the change in vocal delivery suggests that the text of the chorus is designed to strip away the melodic excesses of the verses in order to reveal the true sentiments of its (male) speaker. Second, because he is silent in the verses, the male appears unwilling to celebrate the openness of his relationship. Instead, the listener might deduce from his sudden appearance in the chorus that he aims to thwart this arrangement by imposing a more 'conservative' melody upon his female partner. Finally, as the vocal line abandons the b-minor triad in favour of the D-major triad against an accompaniment that remains in b-minor, the male character distances himself in the chorus from the lifestyle celebrated by his female partner in the verses. Read as a battle between opposing partners for control in the non-traditional relationship that it describes, 'We're So Cool' provides no resolution to the conundrum that it raises. Instead, as Figure 11 shows, the outro extends the chorus with multiple reiterations of the same text, ultimately leading to an open-ended conclusion.

As the accompaniment drops away, and the b-minor harmonic support evaporates, the song ends mid-sentence on the mediant pitch, and in doing so raises several questions. The abrupt conclusion of the song leaves its narrative open and suggests that the discussion between the two characters about the nature of their relationship comes to no satisfying conclusion in the song. Perhaps the relationship itself has ended abruptly. Alternately, since the text concludes without the expected iteration of 'mine', the open-ended lyric raises questions about ownership within the relationship and implies that each character is left to decide his or her fate (and is therefore invited to consider how they might frame their relationship to the partner with whom they share the closing lyric).

Unlike her counterparts in the housewife and consumer, both of whom rail against the situations in which they are contained, the sexual libertine described in these examples poses a threat because she is *not* contained. Her sexuality is freely expressed and discussed in these songs, and the demands that she

Figure 11 Concluding measures, 'We're So Cool'.
(Au Pairs, *Playing with a Different Sex*, Human 1981) (Author's transcription)

makes upon the male character with whom she interacts poses challenges to the hegemony of the male role within the bedroom. These songs relocate sexual power into the hands of their female characters, who use various vocal strategies to express their sexual dissatisfaction or their refusal to conform to the roles prescribed for them within their intimate relationships.

Closing thoughts on 'being heard' in female punk

Historically, females who exhibited non-normative behaviours or who engaged in activities that were not socially sanctioned tended to be diagnosed as mentally unstable or hysterical by psychotherapists who looked to unlock the source of these misbehaviours through talk therapy. The idea that the mental state of a patient is reflected in the inflections of her voice as she recounts episodes in her life invites comparison to the singing voice in punk, where female 'illness' and the gender stereotypes that ensue become sources of parody that are acted out in various vocal performances. In the songs examined here, caricatures of female hysterics make themselves evident both in the performance decisions made by the individual singers and in the various relationships between the female voice and the music with which it coexists in a given song. On the one hand, punk vocal techniques like glides, screams, tremolos, speech-like declamations and 'out of tune' melodic lines coalesce to satirize the 'hysteric' who chafes against the confines of domesticity, who resists her role as the mindless consumer or who makes demands of her partner in the bedroom. In each of these cases, the 'grain' of the female voice refuses the conventions of normative singing, and reaches instead into the realm of speech and other types of vocalization both to enact a particular emotional state and to dramatize certain events described in the poetic text of a given song. The emotions conveyed through the female punk voice (some which include anger, fear, frustration and insecurity) play upon the listener's empathy in order to make themselves understood. A scream like that enacted by Poly Styrene or a vocal glissando like those performed by Ari Up or Siouxsie Sioux, for example, signifies both from our identification with the physical effort required to produce the sound and from our prior experiences with these sounds as we might have used them to express particular emotional states. On the other hand, the female voice also conveys meaning through its association with the music that surrounds it in any given song. In these cases, the singer plays less with the vocal grain of her voice than with its relationship to its sonic environment, where it rubs against its surroundings in a quest to express resistance to an underlying harmonic structure. In other cases, the voice cedes its 'normal' melodic role to another instrument, and opts instead to imitate or dramatize speech. Unlike the techniques associated solely with the voice, these relational techniques exhibit resistance in a way that requires a closer look at the sonic environment inhabited by the voice. In these cases, listener empathy therefore arises less from an identification with the physical efforts involved in the production of a particular sound than from a reaction to the seeming misfit between the voice and its accompaniment.

While these vocal strategies are not unique to punk (since rock is full of examples of shrieking voices, vocal glissandi and tremolo), the emotions associated with many of these approaches tended to be marked as male in the rock arena in the 1970s. Shrieks and yells, for example, were often used to convey emotions that were typically denied to women, like anger and aggression. Similarly, punk's liberal use and tactical deployment of glissandi and tremolo tended to 'trouble' the singing voice, a role in popular music that has been traditionally associated with women. Further, declamatory vocal lines or voices that imitate speech similarly challenge the conventions associated with singing, both approaches of which are used liberally in punk. While many of punk's vocal strategies were also common in other forms of popular music, they were used perhaps less often and less intentionally than they were in punk songs like 'Pure' or 'Fairytale in the Supermarket'. Taken together, these performance strategies help to mark the punk female voice as different from her male punk counterpart or her mainstream female counterpart as a vehicle through which female stereotypes are questioned and parodied.

Notes

1   Lawrence Grossberg, 'Is There Rock after Punk?' in *On Record: Rock, Pop, and the Written Word*, eds. Simon Frith and Andrew Goodwin (New York: Pantheon Books, 1990), 118.

2   Pete Dale, 'Punk as Folk: Continuities and Tensions in the UK and Beyond', in *The Oxford Handbook of Punk Rock*, eds. George McKay and Gina Arnold (New York: Oxford University Press, 2020), online.

3   One notable exception is the use of Hammond organ by The Stranglers, which defined the band's sound and made it unique in punk's otherwise guitar-based sonic landscape. From a sonic perspective, a parallel might be drawn between this band and The Doors.

4   While the term 'Tin Pan Alley' is typically understood as an early twentieth-century song-writing and music-publishing phenomenon that is associated with New York City, Britain also had its own variant, centred largely on Denmark Street, at the edge of London's West End. Coincidentally, the Sex Pistols rented a practice studio at No. 6 Denmark, fifty years after the Tin Pan Alley period.

5   One exception to this is country music, where the AABA form continued to be used through the period. See Jocelyn Neal, 'Narrative Paradigms, Musical Signifiers, and Form in Country Music', *Music Theory Spectrum* 29/1 (2007), 41–72.

6   Neal, 45.

7   Graham Lock, 'The Raincoats: Moving', *New Musical Express*, 4 February 1984.

8	Gillian Gaar, *She's a Rebel: The History of Women in Rock & Roll* (New York: Seal, 2002), 200.

9	Mimi Haddon, 'Not Playing Properly: Amateurism as Generic Choice in Three Postpunk Case Studies: The Slits, Lora Logic, and the Raincoats', *Women and Music: A Journal of Gender and Culture* 23 (2019), 183.

10	Karina Eileraas, 'Witches, Bitches & Fluids: Girl Bands Performing Ugliness as Resistance', *The Drama Review* 41/3 (1997), 126.

11	Jayna Brown, '"Brown Girl in the Ring": Poly Styrene, Annabelle Lwin, and the Politics of Anger', *Journal of Popular Music Studies* 23/4 (2011), 458–59.

12	Grant Olwage, 'The Class and Colour of Tone: Essay on the Social History of Vocal Timbre', *Ethnomusicology Forum* 13/2 (2004), 206.

13	Richard Middleton, *Voicing the Popular: On the Subjects of Popular Music* (New York: Routledge, 1999), 92–3.

14	Roland Barthes, *Image Music Text*, trans. Stephen Heath (New York: Hill and Wang, 1977), 179*ff.*

15	Dave Laing, *One Chord Wonders: Power and Meaning in Punk Rock* (Milton Keynes: Open University Press, 1985), 58.

16	Sean Albiez, 'Know History!: John Lydon, Cultural Capital and the Prog/Punk Dialectic', *Popular Music* 22/3 (2003), 364.

17	For an excellent analysis of Sid Vicious' cover of 'My Way', see Evan Ware, 'Food for Thought: Sid Vicious's Cannibalization of Frank Sinatra's "My Way"', in *Hardcore, Punk, and Other Junk: Aggressive Sounds in Contemporary Music*, eds. Eric James Abbey and Colin Helb (Lanham, MD: Lexington Books, 2014), 1–20.

18	Barthes, 184.

19	Barthes, 184.

20	Pierre Bourdieu, *Distinction: A Social Critique of the Judgement of Taste* (Cambridge, MA: Harvard University Press, 1984), 283.

21	Leslie Dunn and Nancy Jones, *Embodied Voices: Representing Female Vocality in Western Culture* (Cambridge: Cambridge University Press, 1997), 1.

22	Marlene Sanders and Marcia Rock, *Waiting for Prime Time: The Women of Television News* (Urbana, IL: University of Illinois Press, 1994).

23	J. Maxwell Atkinson, *Our Masters' Voices: The Language and Body Language of Politics* (London: Methuen, 1984). Through comparisons of early (pre-Prime Ministerial) and later (Prime Ministerial) interviews, Atkinson notes that Thatcher's voice dropped in pitch by 46 Hz.

24	Dunn and Jones, 7.

25	Mari Jo Buhl, *Feminism and Its Discontents: A Century of Struggle with Psychoanalysis* (Cambridge, MA: Harvard University Press, 1998), 29–30.

26 Sigmund Freud and Joseph Breuer, *Studies in Hysteria* (originally published in 1893), trans. Nicola Luckhurst (New York: Penguin Books, 2004). Case studies of these five women comprise the second section of the study (see pages 25–181).

27 Mark S. Micale, *Hysterical Men: The Hidden History of Male Nervous Illness* (Cambridge, MA: Harvard University Press, 2008), 7.

28 Juliet Mitchell, ed. *The Selected Melanie Klein* (New York: Penguin, 1986), 11.

29 Theodor Reik, *Listening with the Third Ear* (New York: Grove Press, 1948), 136.

30 Jonathan Michel Metzl, *Prozac on the Couch: Prescribing Gender in the Era of Wonder Drugs* (Durham, NC: Duke University Press, 2003), 129.

31 Karina Eileraas, 'Witches, Bitches & Fluids: Girl Bands Performing Ugliness as Resistance', *The Drama Review* 41/3 (1997), 125.

32 Andrew Mead, 'Bodily Hearing: Physiological Metaphors and Musical Understanding', *Journal of Music Theory* 43/1 (1999), 10–11.

33 Elizabeth Le Guin, *Boccherini's Body: An Essay in Carnal Musicology* (Berkeley, CA: University of California Press, 2005), 9.

34 George Fisher and Judy Lochhead, 'Analyzing from the Body', *Theory and Practice: The Journal of the Music Theory Society of New York State* 27 (2002), 47.

35 Tracy McMullen, 'Corpo-Realities: Keepin' It Real in "Music and Embodiment" Scholarship', *Current Musicology* 82 (2006), 63.

36 This study uses scientific pitch notation, where middle-C is represented as C_4, the C below as C_3, the C above as C_5 and so forth.

37 Andrew Scull, *Hysteria: The Biography* (London: Oxford University Press, 2009), 15.

38 Siouxsie Sioux cites Bernard Herrmann's score for Hitchcock's *Psycho* not only as an inspiration for these opening chords but also for the single 'The Staircase (Mystery)'. 'The Movie That Changed by Life: Episode 3', aired 31 July 2009 on BBC2.

39 Robert Samuels, *Hitchcock's Bi-Textuality: Lacan, Feminisms, and Queer Theory* (Albany, NY: State University of New York Press, 1998), 138.

40 In her analysis of the work, Linda Kouvaras interprets this opening gesture in D, as a move from ii (a diminished chord on E) to III (a major chord on F♯). I am inclined to disagree with the reading, particularly in view of the A♯, which points more strongly to B as its resolution in the opening measures. See Linda Kouvaras, 'Two Domestic Prison Scenarios', in *Music Research: New Directions for a New Century*, eds. Michael Ewans, Rosalin Halton, and John Phillips (London: Cambridge Scholars, 2004), 215–29.

41 Lucy O'Brien, *She-Bop: The Definitive History of Women in Rock, Pop and Soul, II* (London: Continuum, 2002), 147.

42 Caroline O'Meara, 'The Raincoats: Breaking Down Punk Rock's Masculinities', *Popular Music* 22/3 (2003), 308.

43 Poly Styrene quoted in Jon Savage, *England's Dreaming: Sex Pistols, Punk Rock, and Beyond* (New York: St. Martin's Press, 1992), 327.

44 Jayna Brown "'Brown Girl in the Ring": Poly Styrene, Annabella Lwin, and the Politics of Anger', *Journal of Popular Music Studies* 23/4 (2011), 456.

45 Lauraine Leblanc, *Pretty in Punk: Girls' Gender Resistance in a Boys' Subculture* (New Brunswick, NJ: Rutgers University Press, 1999), 46.

46 Brian Cogan, 'Typical Girls?: Fuck Off You Wanker! Re-evaluating the Slits and Gender Relations in Early British Punk and Post-Punk', *Women's Studies* 41/2 (2012), 131.

47 Peter Gay, *The Education of the Senses (Volume 1) The Bourgeois Experience: Victoria to Freud* (New York: Oxford University Press, 1984), 197.

Epilogue: 'Nostalgia for an age yet to come': Memoirs

Many of the artefacts examined in the preceding chapters were created in response to an idealized femininity that was marketed to women in the 1970s and to restrictive gender norms that relegated women to domestic spaces and that denied them any political or social power. As we have seen, female punk musicians expressed their resistance to sexism in song lyrics that describe the negative experiences of women in a society where they are viewed as subordinate to men and they created a performance aesthetic that demanded the attention that was typically denied to women. Additionally, they used artwork and fashion to resist conventional beauty standards that were meant to appeal to the male gaze. The cut-and-paste aesthetic that featured prominently in punk's visual language represented a blatant, and sometimes violent, response to that gaze when it was used by women. In this chapter, I propose that, while the artefacts examined thus far might respond to a distant historical moment, the women who helped to create the British scene continue to resist their marginalization through the act of autobiography or life narrative. The punk scholar George Grinnell (2024) explains that 'memoirs have become a significant new addition to the canon of punk cultural production that deserves an equal place alongside music, fashion, zines, and other expressions of punk culture'.[1] Personal reflections on punk provide context for some of the subcultural objects that define punk and explain some of the creative impulses and decisions that might have informed them. Further, when stories about punk are told from subordinated gender or racial positions within the punk subculture, then punk memoirs also serve to add missing details to a historical record about punk that has tended to focus on the creative work of men and to consign women to the sidelines in spite of their significant contributions to punk. First-person accounts of punk can challenge the erasure of women or racialized punks from histories about punk and demand the acknowledgement of their contributions to the scene. In this chapter, I will describe how the themes of personal challenges and survival that mark the creative work examined in the previous chapters of this book echo the life experiences of four female punks as described in recent punk life narratives.

Writing wounds through the life narrative

The term 'life narrative' is defined by Sidone Smith and Julia Watson (2010) as a literary genre that dedicates itself to 'self-presentation of all kinds and in diverse media that take the producer's life as their subject, whether written, performative, visual, filmic, or digital'.[2] Regardless of the format that it will take, a life narrative will be created from selected memories drawn from the lived experiences of its narrators. Like photographs in a family album, these memories serve as snapshots of episodes and events in the life of a narrator that are woven together to form the story of an author's life. However, while a life narrative might seem on its surface to recount the memories of an author in the first-person, the story of an author is also the story of those whose lives intersect with the life of the author in a shared social space. The literary theorist G. Thomas Couser (2005) explains that because 'one person's autobiography is inevitably someone else's biography … one cannot write about oneself without representing others'.[3] He argues that to overlook the impact of interpersonal relationships on the life story of a narrator is to interpret only a portion of that narrator's personal history, and he counsels us to consider how interactions and power dynamics between a narrator and other subjects in her life narrative contribute to, and shape, the personal history she will share. Moreover, as a story that takes place within a social group, a life narrative will reflect tacit agreements among members of that group about the stories that can be told within a group and the perspectives that these stories will reflect. Personal details shared by an author in a life narrative about the punk subculture, for example, will reflect the cultural and symbolic capital that defines that group for everyone who aspires to belong within it, including that author. These stories will also uncover social hierarchies and aspects of gatekeeping that delineate the boundaries of group and that define the relationship of the author to the locus of power within that group. In her work on collective memory in life narratives, Aleida Assmann (2010) adds the additional caveat that the stories recounted by a life narrator from within a particular social group will also be informed by life experiences accumulated outside of that group that will shape the perspective of the life narrator. She explains that narrators exist 'in various formats of the first-person plural. They become part of different groups whose "we" they adopt together with the respective "social frames" that imply an implicit structure of shared concerns, values, experiences, and narratives'.[4] The author of a life narrative must therefore be understood not merely as the member of one group but as the sum of the many social groups to which she belongs, each of which will contribute to the stories that she will tell about her life. In the case of punk, Grinnell explains that life narratives represent 'a community-driven mode of reflecting on punk [that will] illustrate and theorize its many and varied effects upon a life. In the end, that means they are almost always about more than punk; they are narratives that consider how punk intersects with one's life and everything outside of punk'.[5] I would argue that the inverse is also true: that life narratives also invite their reader to consider how life outside the punk subculture intersects with and informs a life that is described within punk. While a narrator might identify as a punk in her life narrative, Assman explains that her standpoint within that group will be shaped by experiences that she has gained in social spaces that have little to do with punk but that work together to frame her behaviours within punk. She cites groups like 'the family, the neighbourhood, the peer group, the generation, the nation, and the culture' as co-contributors to the perspectives that will be narrated by an author.[6] I would add that these perspectives will also be informed by an author's identification with broader social groups that coalesce around identity categories like socio-economic class, gender identity, sexuality, race and/or ethnicity and by the author's privilege or subordination within each of these categories. Life narratives about punk will therefore illustrate the web of interlocking identities embodied by their narrators, whose experiences of punk will be inflected by stories of their lives outside punk. For the purposes of this chapter, the ways that the perspectives of life narrators are shaped specifically by gender, class and race will inform the ways that they memorialize punk.

In her influential work on gender and ageing in punk, Abigail Gardner proposes that life narratives that tell stories about punk or post-punk from a female standpoint will 'disrupt the sanctity of the subcultural boy's club and allow us to see what else was happening behind these musical scenes and within these musical subcultures'.[7] She argues that descriptions of gendered experiences in punk will add missing details to existing stories about the subculture by drawing attention to glaring omissions in the mythologies and written histories that have been constructed around punk. Reflecting on the importance of female voices to the stories that we tell about the subculture, J. Jack Halberstam adds that 'without [these voices], punk becomes a rebellion without a cause, a boy's club of heroic art school drop outs and another master narrative in which white guys play all the parts'.[8] When women write about their experiences in punk, they tell stories that lie outside the bounds of the knowledge that has been circumscribed by punk's 'boy's club'. Their stories expose some of the troubling obstacles that made careers in punk more difficult for women than for men. They recount the impact of marginalization, sexism and gender-based violence on women in the punk scene, and they reveal that female punks were often singled out for abuse and threats of violence by outside observers of the scene who were confused or frightened by punk's subversive femininity. They describe the negative impact of punk's expressions of femininity on the acceptance of female punk artists by the music industry, particularly when punk became incorporated into mainstream culture and marketed to everyday consumers who were more inclined to accept 'bad' behaviours from male punks than from their female counterparts. Finally, they illustrate how broader societal expectations surrounding marriage, domesticity, parenthood and ageing were, and remain, more burdensome for women and how these expectations often shortened the lifespans of female punk careers.

As one of the first women to write a life narrative about her time in the British punk scene as a member of The Slits, Viv Albertine provides a useful analytical framework for female punk life narratives with her admission that 'the experiences documented here left an indelible emotional imprint on me; they shaped and scarred me. And I was present at every one. Let others who were there tell their versions if they want to. This is mine'.[9] Albertine's testimony invokes the metaphor of the scar as the indelible imprint, or lingering reminder, of certain psychic wounds that she experienced in her life within and outside punk. The related metaphors of the wound and the scar have been used by literary theorists as a way to define personal challenges and healing, respectively, particularly as they pertain to the expression of trauma inflicted on, or experienced by, female literary characters and life narrators. In her foundational work on trauma and testimony in literature, Cathy Caruth (2004) offers the image of the wound as a synonym for trauma when she describes the latter as 'a wound inflicted not upon the body but upon the mind'.[10] She adds that trauma is

> more than a pathology, or the simple illness of a wounded psyche: it is always the story of a wound that cries out, that addresses us in the attempt to tell us of a reality of truth that is not otherwise available. This truth, its delayed appearance and its belated address, cannot be linked only to what is known, but also to what remains unknown in our very actions and our language.[11]

In this reading, trauma results from the denial or repression of a memory associated with an unsettling or violent event, while the figure of the wound represents the gaps and inconsistencies that will arise in the memory of the survivor as a consequence of this repression. Caruth argues that traumatic memories are repressed largely because the survivor lacks the language needed to express the impact of the wound on her psyche. Instead, she will attempt to process trauma in her dreams or nightmares, while the impact of her psychic wound will manifest itself subconsciously and outwardly in her actions and behaviours. The literary theorist Kathryn Robson embraces Caruth's concept of the wound, but argues against the claim that survivors are not equipped to articulate the impact of trauma. She advises that we must 'take care with the term "unspeakable." Frequently, traumatic events remain unspoken primarily because they are disavowed in particular social contexts and thus there are no available templates, no formulations in which to give voice to these traumatic experiences'.[12] In some cases these events are not shared by a life narrator in the interests of safeguarding the integrity of a social group and preserving its dominant narrative. In other cases, subordinated members of a social group who experience trauma (like women, who are the focus of Robson's research) will sanitize or otherwise alter their stories in order to protect themselves from the potential of backlash from the dominant members of a social group. In Robson's conception of trauma, then, the wound represents both a psychic injury and a gap in historical knowledge that results when a marginalized voice is silenced. Despite the threat of sanctions imposed upon minoritized members of a social group who dare to defy the limits imposed on their freedom to express trauma, Robson notes that some life narrators will nonetheless engage in a subversive practice of storytelling that she describes as 'writing wounds'. Robson explains that 'writing wounds' involves 'breaking out of the silence' and 'exploring, and exploding, the limits of what can be told' within a social group.[13] By writing about wounds and the trauma that they signify, life narrators move towards the healing that is signified by Albertine's scar.

The figure of the wound is woven into punk's cut-and-paste visual landscape, while the sounds of trauma are embodied in the screams and guttural sounds that define the performance aesthetic created by female punks and that demand attention for performers who may otherwise be ignored or silenced. In female life narratives, the wound and the scar, as metaphors of injury and healing, provide a narrative pathway through the life experiences of women in the scene who describe not only the challenges that they faced while in the punk subculture but their attempts to grapple with a life after punk. These stories reveal how women wrestled with their status as gendered outsiders, how they turned to punk because it purported to embrace the outsider and how they ultimately left punk when marriage and motherhood intervened. Told from a distance, these stories also reveal aspects of discomfort in punk that are felt uniquely by women and therefore fill gaps in our knowledge about punk. They add missing details to histories of the scene that have tended for favour a 'boy's club' perspective and they subvert a historical master narrative in which women play supportive roles, when they are represented at all.

Female life narratives about punk: Four case studies

The past decade has witnessed a growing interest in life narratives by women who were associated with punk, and while many of these memoirs have been written by American punks, three women have released narratives about their lives in the British punk scene. These include *Clothes, Clothes, Clothes. Music, Music, Music. Boys, Boys, Boys.* (Viv Albertine, 2014; hereafter *Clothes. Music. Boys.*), *Defying Gravity: Jordan's Story* (Jordan Mooney, 2019) and *Life's a Gamble: Penetration, The Invisible Girls and Other Stories* (Pauline Murray, 2023). A fourth life narrative, *Dayglo: The Poly Styrene Story* (2019), was written posthumously by Poly Styrene's daughter, Celeste Bell, and while this book was not authored by its subject, it nonetheless shares stories about Poly Styrene from her diary entries, letters, poetry, song lyrics and photographs. The memories related in this book are supplemented by live interviews and historical film clips of its subject in the documentary film *Poly Styrene: I Am a Cliché* (2021), which is narrated by Bell. Because of their heavy reliance upon the words of their subject to frame her life story, the biography and documentary stand as examples of life narrative in the broader definition of the term proposed by Smith and Watson, so I will examine them alongside the other three. My purpose in examining these narratives is to expose examples of 'the wound' in both senses of the term. At a granular level, I will highlight the impact on the narrator of her interactions with others in her orbit within the punk subculture. I will explain how the motivations of a small selection of these interactions reflect gender norms that limited women in the scene. On a broader level, each of these life narratives helps to fill a gap, or a 'gaping wound', in our historical knowledge about punk. While each of these stories spans the breadth of their author's life, I will necessarily limit this discussion to the authors' reflections on punk and on events outside punk that played a role in their careers as musicians and artists.

Viv Albertine: *Clothes. Music. Boys.* (2014)

Viv Albertine (b. 1954) opens her life narrative with a reflection on the topic of female masturbation, which she characterizes as the epitome of loneliness even if it releases its female participant from her sexual dependency on men. This curious opening gambit establishes the author's ambivalence towards the 'boys' in her life and towards her own body, both themes of which become important threads in her life narrative. Albertine's ambivalence towards men traces its origins to her relationship with her often-violent father during her childhood in the North London suburb of Muswell Hill. She describes him as the 'big hairy beast' who controlled the behaviours of his two daughters with 'the belt' before he abandoned his family altogether in 1965. As a consequence of his unpredictability and his eventual departure, Albertine was raised largely without a male role model, which prompts her to speculate that 'I don't think I'll ever have a healthy relationship with a man whilst my relationship with [my father] is non-existent'.[14] Her ambivalence towards men also extended to her relationship with her husband, who slowly eroded her self-confidence over the period of eighteen years, from their first encounter in 1990 to their divorce in 2008. In one particularly painful recollection, Albertine shares her husband's response to a flirtation that she imagined with the American actor Vincent Gallo, with whom she had struck up an online friendship. She confessed to her husband that '"I get the feeling he might be coming on to me." He comes back immediately: "Not unless he wants to fuck his mother," and with that, climbs into bed. ... I feel so still. So cold inside. Not shivery cold. *Cold like steel*.'[15] As she considers this relationship in hindsight, Albertine denies her husband any authority in her life by anonymizing and objectifying him as 'The Biker' during their courtship and as 'Husband' during their marriage. A second, and related, thread in Albertine's life narrative is her conflicted relationship with her body as a marker of her gender. She describes her revulsion to the sight of blood, which she interprets as a sign of female weakness, and recalls the feeling that, as a teenager,

> I couldn't bear to live if it mean going through life bleeding every month and being weak and compromised. It was so unfair ... from the first time onwards I was resentful and angry inside, I felt cheated and I knew to the core of my being that life was unfair and boys had it easier than girls. A burning ball of anger and rebelliousness started to grow within me. It's fuelled [*sic*] a lot of my work.[16]

As a signifier of gender in this life narrative, blood also features prominently in Albertine's description of the many miscarriages that thwarted her attempts at motherhood, which would prompt her to proclaim that 'failure has become my middle name'.[17] Blood also recurs as a symptom of her eventual diagnosis of cervical cancer in 1999, soon after giving birth to her only child. She speculates on its origins in the human papilloma virus and implies that ailments that arise from this virus, like cervical cancer, unfairly punish women for the sexual liberation that seems to be more freely enjoyed by men.[18]

This life narrative shows how Albertine's anger about patriarchy and gender 'fuelled a lot of her work' in punk and how her experimentation in music served as an outlet for this rage. Early encounters with popular music through bands like The Beatles and T-Rex inspired her and she recalls that 'listening to T. Rex was one of the first times I actually noticed guitar playing … Girls didn't usually listen out for the guitar solos and riffs, that was a male thing – *wow, that was so fast, wow that was a really obscure scale, wow the way he bends the notes*'.[19] But she notes that, while 'every cell in my body was steeped in music … it never occurred to me that I could be in a band, not in a million years – why would it? Who'd done it before me? There was no one I could identify with. No girls played electric guitar. Especially not ordinary girls like me'.[20] This gendered perspective on music changed when she encountered the music of Patti Smith, whose album *Horses* (Arista 1975) prompted her to purchase her first electric guitar (a 1969 Gibson Les Paul Junior) and, with the encouragement of her then-boyfriend Mick Jones (later of The Clash), to teach herself how to play. She explains that one of her principal aims was to create new sounds with the instrument that would reflect her gendered positionality:

> I don't want to copy any male guitarists. I wouldn't be true to myself if I did that … I keep thinking, 'What would I sound like if I was a guitar sound?' It's so abstract. As I experiment, I find that I like the sound of a string open, ringing away whilst I play a melody on the string next to it. It sounds like bagpipe music or Chinese, oriental and elemental. I try to play like John Cale in the Velvets, I don't realise for ages that he's playing violin and viola, not guitar. I want my guitar to sound like that. I like hypnotic repetition, I like the same riff played over and over again for ages. I like nursery rhymes. I love the top three trebly strings, the higher up the neck the better, and I turn the treble knob on the guitar and on the amp up full.[21]

For scholars of punk, this insider perspective is immensely valuable because it reveals some of the motivations that lie behind the performance aesthetic that Albertine later brought to The Slits when she joined the band in 1977. As a songwriter for the band, she recalls that

Lots of girls' history of music is playground songs; chants, folks songs, and nursery rhymes, passed down through mothers, aunts, older sisters, and friends. I want to incorporate these rhymes into [The Slits] songs … this is one of the ways we can build an identity for ourselves – we're starting from zero, no rules, no role models.[22]

As a lyricist, she adds that

In the past I listened to tracks as a whole, paying most attention to the lyrics … That's how girls listened to songs. Most of the songs I've been exposed to are about romantic love. They're an extension of the fairy tales I read as a little girl … which is shocking when you think about the effect that obsessive listening and repetitive exposure to songs about idealised love must have had on my brain. I've been brainwashed.[23]

Comments about Albertine's approach to performing the guitar and to songwriting resonate with some of the songs examined in the preceding chapters, like the lyrics of 'Typical Girls' (*Cut*, Island 1979), whose 'misfit' protagonist challenges some of the premises of the fairytale romance, or the giggling silliness and fun embodied in a song like 'Shoplifting' (*Cut*, Island 1979). But despite the new musical horizons that Albertine hoped to explore with The Slits, her time in the band was also strained by arguments among its members about what feminism was meant to achieve. She notes that she joined the band because she wanted 'boys to come and see us play and think *I want to be a part of that*. Not *They're pretty* or *I want to fuck them*'.[24] But at the same time, she explains that the freedom that punk appeared to offer to women had its limits. She recalls having raised concerns when the band's drummer, Palmolive, refused to wear a bra on stage, to which the Palmolive responded that

she's a free person and this is who she is, why should she change? That it's more feminist to not wear a bra than wear one. I argue back that although she's right, the impression she gives off whilst playing doesn't match her ideals … most people have never seen a girl drum before and instead of watching her play and thinking she's great, they're fascinated by her boobs bouncing up and down.[25]

Clothes. Music. Boys. also shares insider stories about the dangers faced by women in the British scene who were often targeted on the street when they presented as punk. Albertine remembers how she embraced the often-violent responses to her image as evidence of the impact of punk's statement against conventional femininity:

I've got so used to my life being challenging and fraught with danger that I
don't question it any more. Whether I'm knocking on the door of a hardcore
sex shop, walking through suburban streets being verbally abused and spat on,
or being threatened on the tube, I don't give in. I don't dress normally to have
an easy life.[26]

In Albertine's life narrative, the breakup of The Slits in December 1981 is
attributed to the pregnancy of its lead singer, Ari Up. Faced without the option
of moving forward without her or joining another band, Albertine moved back
home with her parents to recalibrate her life. After an account of motherhood,
marriage, cancer treatment and divorce, Albertine concludes her life narrative
with the uplifting story about her return to music as a soloist in 2009 and, later,
as part of a reformed version of The Slits. *Clothes. Music. Boys.* describes the
positive responses that her reengagement with music engendered as a form
healing from the challenges that she faced in punk and the years of domesticity
that interrupted her career. In hindsight, Albertine's life narrative concludes
with a broad overview of women's contributions to popular music through
punk, and she claims that 'it's only recently that everything and everyone from
back then is starting to be re assessed [sic] and often credited with influencing
what's happening in music today'.[27]

Jordan Mooney: *Defying Gravity* (2019)

Jordan Mooney (née Pamela Rooke, b. 1955, d. 2022) is recognized in Viv
Albertine's life narrative as the quintessential punk whose unique visual style
inspired a legion of punk designers and members of the punk community.
Albertine writes that 'Jordan is a work of art. Her look is so extreme and yet she
isn't scary or threatening at all. She has a soft voice, gentle manner and is calm
and centred. … Her attitudes filter through to all of us. You have to live it [i.e.,
punk].'[28] Although she performed a couple of times with Adam and the Ants,
whom she managed in the early phase of their career, Jordan has become known
principally as one of punk's leading fashion icons. Her memorable appearance
shifted over the course of several years: at the beginning of her association
with punk, she paired a white bouffant with raccoon-eyed makeup; this was
replaced by bondage wear and Mondrian-style makeup; towards the end of her
association with the punk scene, she adopted an even more confrontational look
that was marked by red curly hair, red contact lenses and deathly white pancake
makeup. The filmmaker Derek Jarman worked with Jordan in the feature film

Jubilee (1978) and short films such as *Jordan's Dance* (1977) and *Every Woman for Herself and All for Art* (1977), and he described her look as 'art history as makeup'.[29] Jordan was a muse for Vivienne Westwood's creations, and she wore many of the clothes sold at Westwood's SEX boutique after she was hired there as a sales assistant in 1974. Her position at SEX placed her at the epicentre of the early British punk scene and her life narrative provides accounts of the formative years of such punk artists and bands as the Sex Pistols, Sid Vicious, Siouxsie Sioux, Chrissie Hynde and Adam Ant (with whom she had a romantic relationship). Her observations about these punk figures are both personal and historically important. However, Jordan also recounts how her position at the former SEX store (which had been rebranded as Seditionaries in 1976) came to an abrupt end in June, 1981, when she claims to have been fired by Westwood because of her marriage to the guitarist Kevin Mooney. Jordan also chronicles her stint as the manager of Adam and the Ants, where she met her future husband, and as the manager of Mooney's band, 'Wide Boy Awake', which he formed in 1982 after leaving the Ants. However, Jordan's life narrative also describes how her three-year marriage to Mooney was marked by heroin addiction, which she managed to overcome only after leaving him and relocating to her sister's farm. The experience of working with farm animals led Jordan to train as a veterinary nurse and a professional breeder of Burmese cats.

In *Defying Gravity*, Jordan characterizes her childhood in Seaford, East Sussex, as happy and nurturing. She recalls how her parents identified, and made sacrifices to support, her natural talents in ballet, which lead to years of serious ballet study. The tutu would later become incorporated into Jordan's unique fashion style, and she would perform on pointe shoes in two of Jarman's films: *Jubilee* and *Jordan's Dance*.[30] As the daughter of a veteran of the Second World War, Jordan describes the impact of Britain's wartime attitude of 'make do and mend' on the style for which she became known in punk, which was often created from repurposed, torn and visibly mended clothing. She also explains how her increasing awareness of sexism and gender bias during her teens prompted her to change her name to the more androgynous name 'Jordan' in 1973, which referenced the Great Gatsby character Jordan Baker, who embodied the qualities of a modern, liberated woman. Presenting as Jordan allowed her to be someone who 'defied all the old gender stereotypes and made [her] own transformation into the person [she] wanted to be'.[31] This defiance was expressed largely through fashion, beginning with her job as a sales clerk at Harrod's 'Way-In' boutique in 1973 and, a year later, the SEX boutique. She notes that, at first, she refused to shop at SEX but 'brought my own style to the place, because that's how I wanted it … in those days, you'd never see anyone walking down the road in just a pair of tights like I did'.[32] During her first few months at SEX, Jordan lived with her parents and faced a daily two-hour commute to the King's Road. Given her unusual appearance, she recalls that

> I had many strange experiences on the train from Seaford to London. Sometimes, when I got into the carriage, everybody else would leave. Once, when my outfit comprised a see-through bra and knickers with customized fishnet stockings – I would make patterns by burning holes into them with cigarettes – the police threatened to arrest me. On other occasions, the British rail guard would move me into First Class to separate me from the rest of the passengers.[33]

In a 2019 interview, Jordan reflected on how little social attitudes have changed since her time at SEX, and she speculated that 'if I wear one of Vivienne's "tits" t-shirts, even now, I don't think a lot of people are comfortable with it. A lot of people are not much more broad-minded than they were forty years ago'.[34] Her refusal to cave to objections to her appearance flew in the face of societal expectations that a woman should dress to conform and to please rather than to express her unique identity even if that meant that it would offend the everyday viewer. Jordan's defiance against conventional femininity often put her at odds with potential male partners who were threatened by her originality and the independence that it signified. She notes that 'not a lot of men have taken me on, because I am very strong and witty and a lot of men don't like to be matched … I have to be with someone who will allow me to be me'.[35] But like other women in the scene, Jordan faced sexism in spite (or perhaps because) of her rejection of gender norms. She recounts an episode at the 1976 'Valentine's Ball' hosted by the sculptor and performance artist Andrew Logan in his London studio. This event was one of the Sex Pistols' early gigs and the band's manager, Malcolm McLaren, hoped to create a buzz around the group. Jordan recalls that 'Malcolm … was really excited because [the music journalist] Nick Kent was in attendance. He rushed up to me saying: "The *NME* are here! Do something, Jords! Take your clothes off, girl!" … I said I wouldn't do it unless John [Johnny Rotten] took control of the situation; otherwise it would just reduce me to being like a stripper'.[36] During the performance, Jordan instructed Rotten to theatrically embody the anger expressed in the lyrics that he was performing and to direct that anger towards her. It was agreed that he would tear off her top and pin her to the floor and that she would respond passively. To provide context for the blank expressions captured on photographs of the event, Jordan explains that 'I'm not reacting. Which is my sort of feminism. … What I'm trying to get at is that women can come out on top in that situation.'[37] But despite the power that she claims to have asserted in the moment, both McLaren's comment and the Sex Pistols' performance literally stripped Jordan of her carefully crafted identity and reduced her to the status of an object. As Jordan's role in the punk scene changed from that of the store clerk and fan to the manager of Adam and the Ants and her husband's junk-funk band Wide Boy Awake, she discovered that she was not immune from the gender biases of the music industry, either, despite her resistance to conventional femininity. Perhaps the most egregious example occurred when she attempted to explain her vision for Wide Boy Awake's song, 'Billy Hyena' (RCA 1984) during a production meeting at RCA. Jordan recalls that

> I had really bad experiences with the record company. Very sexist, awful things were said to me. And it was always one-to-one, so no one was ever around to witness it. We wanted to hire real helicopters to get the noise for the single, rather than use the *Apocalypse Now* soundtrack noise, and … [an unnamed male employee at RCA] said; 'why don't you just fuck off out of here, go home and open your legs like all women do … that's all women are good for'.[38]

Reflecting on her divorce from Mooney in 1984, Jordan expresses some sadness about her lost opportunity to become a mother and she reveals that she had an abortion shortly after her marriage to Kevin. She confesses that 'it was my second in two years and it weighs heavily on me to this day; I can still remember how much my body wanted to go against my decision … I just never wanted to have a child that I couldn't have looked after properly. In retrospect, I did make the right decision'.[39] Instead, she explains that she turned her attention to cat breeding and veterinary medicine as the next phase in her life.

Like Albertine's life narrative, *Defying Gravity* concludes with some reflections on the enduring role of punk in reshaping popular culture, spurred on, in this account, by the death of Malcolm McLaren in 2010. Jordan suggests that 'after Malcolm's death came an exhumation of the remains of punk, with anniversaries noted and what began as a bunch of misfits meeting on the King's Road to dream and scheme of something better becoming the subject of university courses, symposiums and huge retrospective exhibitions around the world'.[40] Her life narrative fittingly concludes with some reflections on the importance of women like Jordan to punk's rebellion against social norms. The photographer and former member of the Bromley Contingent Simon Barker contends that

The real creative force behind punk was women. All the blokes would have been in rock 'n' roll bands anyway, I think. It was you [Jordan], Vivienne, Sioux, Poly Styrene, The Slits who were the real originals. They're the ones you think: Where did that come from? You couldn't identify what the points of reference were. You couldn't explain where the look came from. You've seen it since, but you'd never seen it before.[41]

Celeste Bell, *Dayglo: The Poly Styrene Story* (2019)

Poly Styrene (née Marian Elliott-Saïd, b. 1957, d. 2011) was one of the few women of colour on the British punk scene and her life narrative reveals some of the challenges that she experienced as a mixed-race woman in Britain and in British punk. Her father was a Somali dockworker in London's East End who abandoned his family when Poly was a child; her mother was a British-born white woman. Prior to meeting Poly's father, her mother had spent time in an institution to recover from the trauma she had experienced as a teenager during the Blitz. Celeste Bell, who created this life narrative about her mother, notes that 'it was a pioneering time in terms of treatments and therapies, some more unsavoury than others, like electric shock treatment. [Poly's mother] had that'.[42] Bell discloses that, decades later, her mother would undergo a similar treatment after being misdiagnosed with schizophrenia (diagnosed correctly in 1991 as bipolar disorder). Neurodivergence is a prominent theme in *Dayglo* and is described early in this life narrative as childhood attention-deficit disorder and, in adulthood, as depression and paranoia. Through interviews with family and friends and from passages from Styrene's diaries and media interviews, Bell also chronicles how Poly's childhood in Brixton was affected by the absence of her father, poverty, and racism. She discloses that Poly was teased at school because she was Black, and she notes that her mother's lyrics and poetry would later reflect her personal experiences of racism. Bell recalls that 'Mum would talk about race a lot in interviews, it affected her a lot – being asked about it all the time ended up annoying her but generally she did want to talk about it. There are lyrics of hers that are very obviously about race and identity'.[43]

Because of her struggles in school, Poly left at the age of fifteen and went to work in London, where she met her future manager and romantic partner, Falcon Stuart, at a theatre workshop. He helped to guide her towards music and he produced her first single, a reggae track entitled 'Silly Billy' (GTO 1976), with Eric Bell and GT Moore on guitars. According to Moore, 'she had a lot of guts because … she was such a little girl trying to make it in London.'[44] After seeing the Sex Pistols at Hastings Pier Pavilion on 3 July 1976, Poly shifted from the novelty song format and began to incorporate more political substance into her work. Jayna Brown (2011) explains that her 'lyrics politicized the quotidian. Her visions were prescient, speaking of a present of monstrous waste, oppression, and consumerism, but also looking to a dystopian future.'[45] The theme of mindless consumerism shaped the image that Poly created for herself from plastic jewellery, repurposed clothing and accessories, and bin liners. She opened a stall in the Beaufort Market on the King's Road, where she sold her DIY fashion. Synthetic materials like polystyrene (the word that she adopted as her stage name) were a reflection of the artificiality of modern life. Asked about her stage name, she explained that 'I wanted to have a total obsession about synthetic things and the modern world, so therefore I dressed to fit, it went with the name and the songs and everything.'[46] This obsession would also feed her creative work in music. In 1976, Poly placed an advertisement in *Melody Maker* and *NME* in search of 'young punx' with whom to form a band. Among others, the sax player Lora Logic answered the ad and was enlisted to provide the band's unique sound. X-Ray Spex would be managed by Falcon and would feature songs written by Poly. *Dayglo* reveals that the band's first song, 'Oh Bondage Up Yours!' (Virgin 1977) was inspired by a bondage outfit that Poly saw in the window of Westwood's Seditionaries store. Poly explains that 'it was more about slavery, the Suffragette movement and the silencing of women, but her clothing had such strong imagery; when you looked at them, a million ideas flooded to mind.'[47] X-Ray Spex recorded the single with Virgin records in 1977 and followed up a year later with their first album, *The Day the World Turned Dayglo* (EMI 1978) and a promotional North American tour in March 1978. As the band gain popularity, Poly struggled with depression and paranoia. The British musician and punk scholar Vivian Goldman explains that this was particularly acute during the band's overseas tour because 'there was what you might call a darkness to the New York scene … much as it was artistic and experimental and that's all fabulous, it was much more accepting of heavy drug use.'[48] Poly describes the pressures placed on her by her fans and the music industry when she recalls that 'because you're a performer, they think you're supposed to be entertaining everybody all of the time, they think you're having a nervous breakdown if you don't want to see anybody.'[49] A combination of nerves and drugs triggered a breakdown when the band returned to England: after a gig in Doncaster, Poly claimed to have seen a UFO floating outside her hotel room window and was hospitalized for treatment. She explains that 'they gave me tons of tranquillisers and tried to make me forget that I saw it. It was horrible to be put into that situation.'[50] But because Poly had become a product for consumption by her fans, she was expected to return to her band once she completed her treatment. The band was booked as headline act at the Rock Against Racism concert on 30 April 1978, followed by an appearance on *Top of the Pops* on 18 May 1978. In January 1979, Poly was the subject of the documentary film 'Who Is Poly Styrene?', which aired on the *BBC Arena* series in January 1979. Ana da Silva, from The Raincoats, credits Poly for one of her band's most iconic singles, 'Fairytale in the Supermarket' (Rough Trade, 1979), when she recalls that 'I saw the television programme … and at that time I had a song on the go that I had been writing. When I saw her, going through the supermarket and getting all this stuff, products of the consumerist society, I thought … "these are like fairytales, but in a supermarket."'[51] Bell notes that, in her view, the film also highlighted Poly's depression. A few months after the documentary, Poly decided to leave her band, explaining that 'I wanted to get away from punk and anything that went with it. I remember being quite scared when all these punks with mohawks turned up, hanging out, all drunk and wasted on the Kings Road, I remember thinking, "This is all my fault, I've done this."'[52]

In June 1980, Poly met her future husband, Adrian (Ady) Bell, and recorded her first solo album, *Translucence* (United Artists 1981), which was critically panned because it was so different from her work with her band. Poly had her only child, Celeste, in August 1981, and she divorced her husband in 1983 to join the Hare Krishnas in Herefordshire. She lived for five years as a Krishna convert, and her daughter, Celeste, was eventually placed in the care of her grandparents. Celeste later observed that 'Krishna Consciousness, as blissful as it had been, was not enough to keep the demons from coming back.'[53] Poly continued to be haunted by imposter syndrome and to find live performances challenging. In 2008, she was invited to reconvene the band for a concert at London's Roundhouse to commemorate the thirtieth anniversary of the release of *Germ-Free Adolescents*. The show was a great success, so Poly began to work on a new album, *Generation Indigo* (Future Noise Music 2011). The popular music scholar Lucy O'Brien argues that, throughout her life, Poly's solo work has not received the kind of critical attention that it deserves and she maintains that 'when it came to her final album, some magazines and newspapers looked slightly askance at her bringing out an album, whereas it if had been one of the Sex Pistols or a former member of The Clash, there would have been acres of newsprint about it'.[54] This final return to the recording studio would yield Poly's last project. She died of metastatic breast cancer on 25 April 2011.

Pauline Murray: *Life's a Gamble* (2023)

Unlike Albertine, Mooney, and Styrene, whose geographical proximity to London placed them at the epicentre of the city's punk scene, Pauline Murray (b. 1958) was born and raised in County Durham, about 270 miles (434 kilometres) north of London. Her life narrative describes a happy childhood in the town of Waterhouses. In 1966, the coal mine in which her father worked closed and the family relocated to Ferryhill (about 25 miles south of Newcastle), where her father found work in a munitions factory. As a child, she was exposed to music through the Waterhouses Colliery Brass Band and through her mother, who sang with her sister and a friend as a part of vocal trio. Murray recalls her mother's regrets at not pursuing a career in music and how they fuelled her determination to become a musician. In her teens, Murray's musical horizons were expanded when she met Peter Lloyd, an older teenager who introduced her to such bands as Status Quo, T. Rex, David Bowie, the New York Dolls, and Roxy Music, and whom she would marry in March 1978. Together, they would attend concerts in Yorkshire and London, among which included early and historic concerts by the Sex Pistols, the Buzzcocks, Eddie and the Hot Rods, and others. Murray recalls that, at the time,

> unconventional female voices were making their way into my consciousness … I'd heard 'Piss Factory' by Patti Smith and later that year, her debut album *Horses*. I didn't always understand what she was talking about, but I liked her guttural vocal delivery, freedom of expression and the fact that it was like nothing I'd heard before. I admired the way she dressed, understated and masculine with a white shirt and tie. She exuded a confident, strong and independent attitude.[55]

Murray's initial engagement with punk was shaped by her geographical location and by the community of punks who inhabited such Northern cities as Leeds and Manchester. Inspired by the Sex Pistols, she formed a band in 1976 with her former Ferryhill classmate, Robert Blamire, and a friend of Lloyd's, Gary Smallwood. They took their name, Penetration, from the title of a song by the Stooges. While women were active in the London punk scene, Murray had few female role models in the Northern scene that surrounded her. She describes that scene as a 'cultural vacuum' that provided few creative resources for a budding female punk artist and notes that

> While some might have considered a young woman fronting a punk band as
> unusual, even scandalous, my gender was something I didn't even think about.
> I was the singer, I wrote the words, fronted the band and wanted to do the job
> to the best of my ability … I considered myself an equal member of the band,
> presenting myself on stage as asexual so that the music would speak for itself.
> As far as I am aware, both the band and the audience could see that I was a fully
> integrated member and I didn't feel pressurised [*sic*] to flaunt my sexuality to
> further our aims.[56]

Murray's attitude towards gender is reflected in the way that she tells her life
narrative. With the exception of a few diary entries drawn from the period, *Life's
a Gamble* tends to describe the events of Murray's career somewhat objectively
and provides an insider-account of punk that is detached to a degree from any
gendered experiences of its author within the scene. This life narrative focuses
largely on the geographical challenges faced by a band that recognized London
as a mecca for punk.

As London began to figure more prominently in punk, Pauline and her band,
Penetration, tackled the unique challenges of access that they faced, which were
complicated by the expenses associated with travel. Their first London gig was
on 9 April 1977, supporting Generation X at the Roxy Club, followed the next
day by a gig at the Bonham Carter House with The Adverts. Unlike those bands,
Penetration had travelled a considerable distance to participate in these gigs.
Murray recalls that 'seven hours in the back of a Luton-style box van … sitting
on equipment that was sliding about, wasn't the safest or most comfortable
way to travel'.[57] Nevertheless, Penetration made its mark on the London scene
through its sheer determination to succeed in a city that was central to British
punk. By the end of 1977, Jon Savage's review of the band in *Sounds* magazine
acknowledged the geographical obstacles faced by Penetration in their quest
to establish themselves in London, and proclaimed that 'Penetration: THE
FUTURE IS FEMALE!'[58] Despite the success of her band, however, Murray
recounts how their growing popularity came at the expense of her health and
how the endless cycle of songwriting and performing left little time for anything
else. She speaks candidly about various health issues that emerged from the
stress and how these were exacerbated by the pressures of touring in Europe,
the United States and Canada in 1979. Murray recalls that 'the situation I found
myself in [at the end of 1979] was a far cry from the joy, innocence, punk ideals
and musical creativity that I had started out with and I now felt like a prisoner
in a nightmare from which there was no escape … I was clearly on the edge of

a nervous breakdown'[59]. The band split up on 5 November 1979, leaving their record company with a net loss of £6,204.

As Penetration disintegrated, so did Murray's marriage. She turned to her former bandmate Robert Blamire to create a new band, Pauline Murray and the Invisible Girls, and she would eventually marry him in 1992 and have two children. At the same time, she built Polestar Rehearsal Studios in Newcastle to provide rental spaces for aspiring musicians. Murray notes that

> I was busy with my life and rarely thought about Penetration. … Punk had been analyzed to death by fans, academics and journalist who'd picked at the flesh and then the bones, to the point that all that remained was a pile of dust. I wasn't interested in the punk revival. I *lived* through those times and my own punk past had followed me around like a ghost.[60]

However, in 2001, she agreed to join a reformed version of Penetration, and the band played their first gig on 1 December 2001 in Heaton. She asked herself what her former persona would have thought of this new iteration of Penetration. 'I believe she would have said "Go lady! You've got balls – you're resolving unfinished business." And I was.'[61] In 2012, Murray was invited to appear as a solo artist at an event in Gateshead that was headlined by Viv Albertine, Gina Birch (The Raincoats), and Helen McCookerybook (The Chefs). One outcome of the geographical distance faced by Penetration was that she had 'never met any of these female punk contemporaries before, although they all knew each other and had already stepped out as solo performers … I found the experience [of playing as a solo artist] extremely exhilarating and liberating'.[62] Murray subsequently launched a successful solo career without the stress that she had experienced as a nineteen-year-old who aspired to success in punk.

Rethinking history through life narratives

The title of this epilogue derives from Penetration's song 'Nostalgia' (*Moving Targets*, Virgin 1978), whose lyrics play with a 'future and past that are presently disarranged' that leave the protagonist with 'nostalgia for an age yet to come'. The song's lyrics play with a chronological model of time, noting that 'yesterday never comes'. In reminiscing about the future, and not the past, the song's central message is aspirational: the lyrics express a yearning for a future that is better than the present. Given that Murray would write her life narrative forty-five years later, the song also seems poignant and prescient. In the life narratives examined in this chapter, each author describes how she (or, in the case of Poly Styrene, how her subject) emerged from certain struggles in her life to finally find recognition for her contributions to popular culture later in life.

Life narratives written by women, like those examined here, reveal certain aspects about experiences in punk that are rarely discussed in histories of punk that centre male perspectives. These narratives fill gaps in our knowledge about punk by privileging the experiences of women in the subculture. The life narratives examined here demonstrate how four women contested gender norms by creating their own standards of female beauty, by demanding attention at the front of the stage and on the city sidewalks, by creating a body of work that often resisted songwriting conventions and by engaging with female-focused themes within that work. They provide context for some of the songs that were composed and performed by bands like The Slits, X-Ray Spex and Penetration. Further, they reveal the drive to create work to reflect the experiences of women and to provide a space for female voices. These stories confirm some of my own suspicions about the influences on female punk songwriters – for example, the impact of performers like Patti Smith, the cross-fertilization among British female punks and the engagement of female punk songwriters with folk songs and nursery rhymes. Without exception, these artists reveal their determination to create a space for women's voices in punk by their refusal of established principles of songwriting and performance conventions (in the case of Albertine) and by their focus on themes and topics from a female point of view (like consumerism and the idealization of women in the media explored by Poly Styrene and Albertine). While musicians like Albertine and Murray might have relied on male colleagues to initiate them into the music scene and to learn basic music skills, these life narratives also expose the extent to which women in the scene were committed to creating music that would reflect their unique gendered perspectives. Having said that, Murray's life narrative downplays gender as a motivating factor in her band and represents Murray's belief that punk's DIY ethos allowed women to determine the extent to which they would engage with gender in their music, if at all.

Despite the positives that they describe, these life narratives also illustrate various challenges (or as Robson describes them, wounds) that these women faced because of their association with punk. They recount various threats that women endured to their personal safety in clubs or on the street, where their outward expressions of punk were often met with contempt, derision or worse. Albertine, for example, recalls how the streets of London were unsafe at night for women who were often left to find transportation home after the clubs closed. In one harrowing story, she reveals that her bandmate, Ari Up, was sexually assaulted when she accepted a ride from a group of strangers at the end of an evening out with friends. Similarly, Jordan's life narrative describes her experiences of harassment and threats of violence during her daily commute into London because of the way that she chose to dress. Sometimes, violence was part of the subculture, as it was for Poly Styrene, whose experience in New York City triggered a psychotic episode. According to various interviews with some of her friends and associates, Poly found the city to be frightening and dangerous in comparison to London. Some of these life narratives describe the intense pressure imposed upon women to live up to assertions that 'females represented the future of punk', as Savage proclaimed in 1977. Murray and Poly experienced severe physical and mental health crises in response to increasing demands by fans and to the pressure to produce new songs while touring. In Jordan's life narrative, gender-based violence asserted itself both within punk and, later, in the music industry. Her experience of sexism in punk is reflected in the ways in which she was used by Malcolm McLaren as a prop for the Sex Pistols, and this trivialization extended into the music industry, where she was reduced to the status of a sex object during a meeting at RCA records. Class origins are central to all four life narratives, which trace a narrative arc from the working-class origins of their subject to punk, where these women had relationships, formed bands and interacted with their working-class male counterparts. The drive to succeed is rooted largely in class, but also in race, in the case of Poly Styrene. Her experiences of classism and sexism intersect with racism to shape an artist who learnt to fight for her beliefs at a very early age, according to her daughter.

Because of seemingly inescapable gender norms, life after punk seems to be prefigured in each of these life narratives. Each of these women eventually married and, in three cases, had children. Norma Coates (1998) argues that, because male bodies show no obvious signs of parenthood, fatherhood can be hidden and ignored in the rock arena. She notes that 'rock sexuality is synonymous with unbridled, unfettered sexuality: sexuality without consequences, and particularly, sexuality without children'.[63] In the case of female sexuality in rock, the potential for pregnancy challenges this fundamental assumption of rock sexuality. Coates suggests that mothers have tended to be ostracized in the rock arena as somehow 'softer' or 'weaker' than their pre-maternal selves, and therefore no longer credible as rock musicians. She illustrates her point with negative media responses to Patti Smith when she announced the birth of her first child in 1982. In the case of Albertine, Poly Styrene and Murray, marriage and childbirth similarly interrupted each of their careers in music: after a successful post-punk career in film and television, Albertine returned to music in 2009, Poly spent some time in the Krishna movement before returning to music in 2008, and Pauline Murray returned to music in 2013 after establishing Polestar Studios with her second husband. The trajectory from childless punk to post-punk motherhood is a common thread in these life narratives and distinguishes the experiences of women in the scene from those of men, whose careers often continued despite fatherhood (and in whose biographies fatherhood is rarely even mentioned). But each life narrative also concludes with a trajectory from motherhood back to music, with a final reflection on the enormous impact that each author had on the punk scene that she helped to create. In the retrospective that concludes each of these life narratives, old wounds are healed and gaps in the historical record have begun to be filled.

In their study of recent life narratives in punk, David Wilkinson, Matthew Worley and John Street (2017) argue that

> the existence of alternative [in this case, life] narratives, and the potential for further exploration, suggests the historian has work to do. They allow opportunity to make better sense of punk's origins, complexities, contradictions, and contested forms. They enable a challenge to the popular historical accounts that may well represent the obsessions and imaginings of their authors, but lose sight of the evidence and the wider context. More crucially, they hint toward a need to identify the empirical basis upon which any theoretical framework may help link processes and forms of cultural practice and production to social and political change.[64]

A study of the life narratives written by women in the early British punk scene fills glaring gaps in the history of punk by providing the perspectives of those who have been traditionally excluded from punk histories by virtue of gender and race. Life narratives bridge that gap with first-hand accounts of the unique experiences of women in the scene. This knowledge helps us to reevaluate the significant contributions made by women to the British punk scene, in terms of the narratives that women recounted in their lyrics and autobiographies, the rich contributions made by women to punk art and fashion, and the unique musical and performance aesthetics that were created and embodied by women in Britain during punk's first wave.

Notes

1   George Grinnell, 'No Future in Retrospect', *Journal of Popular Music Studies* 36/3 (2024), 50.

2   Sidone Smith and Julia Watson, *Reading Autobiography: A Guide for Interpreting Life Narratives* (Minneapolis, MN: University of Minnesota Press, 2010), 4.

3   G. Thomas Couser, 'Genre Matters: Form, Force, and Filiation', *Life Writing* 2/2 (2005), 140–1.

4   Aleida Assmann, 'Re-framing Memory: Between Individual and Collective Forms of Constructing the Past', in *Performing the Past: Memory, History, and Identity in Modern Europe*, eds. Karin Tilmans, Frank van Vree, and Hay Winter (Amsterdam: Amsterdam University Press, 2010), 35–50 .

5   Grinnell, 53.

6   Assmann, 37.

7   Abigail Gardner, *Ageing and Contemporary Female Musicians* (London: Routledge, 2019), 16.

8   J. Jack Halberstam, 'Go Gaga: Anarchy, Chaos, and the Wild', *Social Text* 31/3/(116) (2013), 129.

9   Viv Albertine, *Clothes, Clothes, Clothes. Music, Music, Music. Boys, Boys, Boys.* (London: Faber & Faber, 2014), ix.

10   Cathy Caruth, *Unclaimed Experience: Trauma, Narrative, and History* (Baltimore, MD: John Hopkins University Press, 1996), 4.

11   Caruth, 4.

12   Kathryn Robson, *Writing Wounds: The Inscription of Trauma in Post-1968 French Women's Life-Writing* (Amsterdam: Brill, 2004), 12.

13   Robson, 14.

14   Albertine, 263.

15   Albertine, 323.

16   Albertine, 27.

17   Albertine, 286.

18   Albertine, 294.

19   Albertine, 44.

20   Albertine, 49. Albertine's reflections on the lack of role models for aspiring female guitarists have been explored in Green (1997) and Clawson (1999a, 1999b).

21   Albertine 104.

22   Albertine, 232–3.

23   Albertine, 208.

24   Albertine, 156.

25   Albertine, 177.

26 Albertine, 125.

27 Albertine, 357.

28 Albertine, 126.

29 Jordan Mooney, *Defying Gravity: Jordan's Story* (London: Omnibus, 2019), 103. For further research on Jarman's short films, I refer the reader to Martin Frey, *Derek Jarman, Moving Pictures of a Painter: Home Movies, Super 8 Films, and Other Small Gestures*, trans. Michael Wetzel (La Vergne, TN: Ingram Press, 2016).

30 For an analysis of Jordan's performance in *Jubilee*, also see Karen Fournier, 'The Politics of Representation in Early British Punk Videos: *Détournement* and the Moving Image', in *The Bloomsbury Handbook of Popular Music Video Analysis*, eds. Lori Burns and Stan Hawkins (New York: Bloomsbury Academic Press, 2019), 129–42.

31 Mooney, 144.

32 Mooney, 75–6.

33 Mooney, 89.

34 Jordan Mooney interviewed in *Jordan: Fear and Loathing* fanzine (2014), online. http://www.fearandloathingfanzine.com/jordan.html.

35 Mooney, 91.

36 Mooney, 143.

37 Mooney, 143.

38 Mooney, 379–80.

39 Mooney, 373–4.

40 Mooney, 418–19.

41 Simon Barker quoted in Mooney, 424.

42 Celeste Bell and Zoë Howe, *Dayglo! The Poly Styrene Story* (London: Omnibus, 2019), 16.

43 Bell, 42.

44 Bell, 38.

45 Jayna Brown, '"Brown Girl in the Ring": Poly Styrene, Annabelle Lwin, and the Politics of Anger', *Journal of Popular Music Studies* 23/4 (2011), 461.

46 Bell, 46.

47 Bell, 61.

48 Vivian Goldman quoted in Bell, 107–8.

49 Bell, 111.

50 Bell, 113.

51 Ana da Silva quoted in Bell, 100.

52 Bell, 142.

53 Bell, 168.

54 Lucy O'Brien quoted in Bell, 194.

55 Pauline Murray, *Life's a Gamble: Penetration, The Invisible Girls and Other Stories.* London: Omnibus Press, 2023), 32.

56 Murray, 45.

57 Murray, 47.

58 Jon Savage, 'Penetration: The Future Is Female', *Sounds*, 17 December 1977.

59 Murray, 117–18.

60 Murray, 165.

61 Murray, 166.

62 Murray, 171.

63 Norma Coates, 'Moms Don't Rock: The Popular Demonization of Courtney Love', in *'Bad' Mothers: The Politics of Blame in Twentieth-Century America*, eds. Molly Ladd-Taylor and Lauri Umansky (New York: New York University Press, 1998), 322.

64 David Wilkinson, Matthew Worley, and John Street, '"I Wanna See Some History": Recent Writings on British Punk', *Contemporary European History* 26/2 (May 2017), 403.

Works Cited

Albertine, Viv (2014), *Clothes, Clothes, Clothes. Music, Music, Music. Boys, Boys, Boys.*, London: Faber & Faber.

Albiez, Sean (2003), 'Know History! John Lydon, Cultural Capital, and the Punk/Prog Dialectic', *Popular Music* 22(3): 357–74.

Alexander, Peter and Rick Halpern (2000), *Racializing Class, Classifying Race: Labour and Difference in Britain, the USA and Africa*, London: Macmillan Press.

Assmann, Aleida (2010), 'Re-framing Memory: Between Individual and Collective Forms of Constructing the Past', in Karin Tilmans, Frank van Vree, and Hay Winter (eds.), *Performing the Past: Memory, History, and Identity in Modern Europe*, Amsterdam: Amsterdam University Press, 35–50.

Atkinson, J. Maxwell (1984), *Our Masters' Voice: The Language and Body Language of Politics*, London: Methuen.

Auslander, Philip (2004), 'I Wanna Be Your Man: Suzi Quatro's Musical Androgyny', *Popular Music* 2(1): 1–16.

Bakhtin, Mikhail (1984), *Rabelais and His World*, Bloomington, IN: Indiana University Press.

Ballion, Susan/Siouxsie Sioux (2009), 'The Movie That Changed My Life', BBC podcast, 31 July, https://www.bbc.co.uk/programmes/b00lv1g4.

Bangs, Lester (1988), *Psychotic Reactions and Carburetor Dung*, New York: Anchor.

Barkin, Elaine and Lydia Hamessley, eds. (1997), *Audible Traces: Identity, Gender, and Music*, Zurick: Carciofoli Verlashaus.

Barron, Lee and Ian Inglis (2002), '(Re)Constructing the Carnival: Continuity and Change in Contemporary British Popular Music', *International Review of Aesthetics and Sociology of Music* 33(1): 95–112.

Barthes, Roland (1977), *Image Music Text*, trans. Stephen Heath, New York: Hill and Wang.

Bayton, Mavis (1997), 'Women and the Electric Guitar', in Sheila Whitely (ed.), *Sexing the Groove: Popular Music and Gender*, London: Routledge, 37–49.

Bayton, Mavis (1998), *Frock Rock: Women Performing Popular Music*, Oxford: Oxford University Press.

Bell, Celeste and Zoe Howe (2019), *Dayglo! The Poly Styrene Story*, London: Omnibus Press.

Bennett, Andy (2006), 'Punk's Not Dead: The Continuing Significance of Punk Rock for an Older Generation of Fans', *Sociology* 40(2): 219–35.

Binns, Rebecca (2022), *Gee Vaucher: Beyond Punk, Feminism and the Avant-Garde*, Manchester: Manchester University Press.

Biskind, Peter and Barbara Ehrenreich (1987), 'Machismo and Hollywood's Working Class', in Donald Lazare (ed.), *American Media and Mass Culture: Left Perspectives*, Berkeley, CA: University of California Press, 201–15.

Bourdieu, Pierre (1984), *Distinction: A Social Critique of the Judgement of Taste*, Cambridge, MA: Harvard University Press.

Brown, Jayna (2011), '"Brown Girl in the Ring": Poly Styrene, Annabelle Lwin, and the Politics of Anger', *Journal of Popular Music Studies* 23(4): 455–78.

Buhl, Mary Jo (1998), *Feminism and Its Discontents: A Century of Struggle with Psychoanalysis*, Cambridge, MA: Harvard University Press.

Burolo, Franko (2022), 'Brains on the Asphalt: Three Punk Expressions of Crisis', *Punk & Post-Punk* 11(1): 35–49.

Caruth, Cathy (1996), *Unclaimed Experience: Trauma, Narrative, and History*, Baltimore, MD: John Hopkins University Press.

Cateforis, Theo (2011), *Are We Not New Wave? Modern Pop at the Turn of the 1980s*, Ann Arbor, MI: University of Michigan Press.

Caws, Mary Ann (1997), *The Surrealist Look*, Cambridge, MA: MIT Press.

Chapple, Steve and Reebee Garofalo (1977), *Rock and Roll Is Here to Pay: The History and Politics of the Music Industry*, Chicago, IL: Nelson-Hall.

Clawson, Mary Ann (1999a), 'Masculinity and Skill Acquisition in the Adolescent Rock Band', *Popular Music* 18(1): 99–114.

Clawson, Mary Ann (1999b), 'When Women Play the Bass: Instrument Specialization and Gender Interpretation in Alterative Rock Music', *Gender and Society* 13(2): 193–210.

Coates, Norma (1997), 'Mom's Don't Rock: The Popular Demonization of Courtney Love', in Molly Ladd-Taylor and Lauri Umansky (eds.), *'Bad' Mothers: The Politics of Blame in Twentieth-Century America*, New York: New York University Press, 319–33.

Cogan, Brian (2012), 'Typical Girls?: Fuck Off, You Wanker! Re-evaluating the Slits and Gender Relations in Early British Punk and Post-Punk', *Women's Studies* 41(2): 121–35.

Cohen, Sara (1997), 'Men Making a Scene: Rock Music and the Production of Gender', in Sheila Whitely (ed.), *Sexing the Groove: Popular Music and Gender*, London: Routledge, 17–36.

Cohen, Sara (1999), 'Scenes', in Bruce Horner and Thomas Swiss (eds.), *Key Terms in Popular Music and Culture*, Oxford: Blackwell, 85–100.

Couser, G. Thomas (2005), 'Genre Matters: Form, Force, and Filiation', *Life Writing* 2(2): 139–56.

Dale, Pete (2012), *Anyone Can Do It: Empowerment, Tradition and the Punk Underground*, Farnham: Ashgate.

Dale, Pete (2020), 'Punk as Folk: Continuities and Tensions in the UK and Beyond', in George McKay and Gina Arnold (eds.), *The Oxford Handbook of Punk Rock*, New York: Oxford University Press, online.

Davies, Helen (2001), 'All Rock and Roll Is Homosocial: The Representations of Women in the British Rock Music Press', *Popular Music* 20(3): 301–19.

de Beauvoir, Simone (1954), *The Second Sex*, trans. Howard Madison Parshley, New York: Bantam. (First published as *La deuxième sexe*, Paris: Gallimard, 1949).

Debord, Guy (1967), *Society of the Spectacle*, Paris: Buchet-Chastel.

Debord, Guy and Gil Wolman (1956), 'Mode d'emploi du détournement', *Les Lèvres Nues* 8: 2–9. Reprinted in *Inter: Art actuel* 177 (Spring 2014), May: 23–6.

Deleuze, Gilles (1991 [1967]), 'Coldness and Cruelty', in Jean McNeil (trans.), *Masochism*, New York: Zone Books, 9–142.

Dibben, Nicola (1999), 'Representations of Femininity in Popular Music', *Popular Music* 18(3): 331–5.

Dines, Mike and Matthew Worley, eds. (2016), *The Aesthetics of Our Anger: Anarcho-Punk, Politics and Music*, Colchester: Minor Compositions.

Drayton, Tony (2018), *Ripped and Torn: 1976–1979*, London: Ecstatic Peace Library.

Dunn, Leslie and Nancy Jones (1997), *Embodied Voices: Representing Female Vocality in Western Culture*, Cambridge: Cambridge University Press.

Eileraas, Karina (1997), 'Witches, Bitches & Fluids: Girl Bands Performing Ugliness as Resistance', *The Drama Review* 41(3): 122–39.

Elger, Dietmer and Uta Grosenick (2004), *Dadaism*, Cologne: Taschen.

Ensminger, David A. (2011), *Visual Vitriol: The Street Art and Subcultures of the Punk and Hardcore Generations*, Jackson, MS: University of Mississippi Press.

Evans, Caroline and Minna Thornton (1991), 'Fashion, Representation, Femininity', *Feminist Review* (38): 48–66.

Fisher, George and Judith Lochhead (2002), 'Analyzing from the Body', *Theory and Practice: The Journal of the Music Theory Society of New York State* (27): 37–67.

Fonarow, Wendy (2006), *Empire of Dirt: Aesthetics and Rituals of British Indie Music*, Middletown, CT: Wesleyan Press.

Fournier, Karen (2016), 'Nazi Signifiers and the Narrative of Class Warfare in British Punk', in Mirko Hall, Seth Howes, and Cyrus Shahan (eds.), *Beyond No Future: Cultures of German Punk*, New York: Bloomsbury, 91–108.

Fournier, Karen (2019), 'The Politics of Representation in Early British Punk Videos: *Détournement* and the Moving Image', in Lori Burns and Stan Hawkins (eds.), *The Bloomsbury Handbook of Popular Music Video Analysis*, New York: Bloomsbury Academic Press, 129–42.

Freud, Sigmund and Joseph Breuer (2004 [1893]), *Studies in Hysteria*, trans. Nicola Luckhurst, New York: Penguin Books.

Frey, Martin (2016), *Derek Jarman, Moving Pictures of a Painter: Home Movies, Super 8 Films, and Other Small Gestures*, trans. Michael Wetzel, La Vergne, TN: Ingram Press.

Friedan, Betty (1964), *The Feminine Mystique*, New York: Dell.

Gaar, Gillian (2002), *She's a Rebel: The History of Women in Rock & Roll*, New York: Seal.

Gamson, William A., David Croteau, William Hoyes, and Theodore Sasson (1992), 'Media Images and the Social Construction of Reality', *Annual Review of Sociology* (18): 373–93.

Garbaye, Romain and Gérôme Guibert, eds. (2024), *Musical Scenes and Social Class: Debating Punk and Metal*, London: Palgrave Macmillan.

Gardner, Abigail (2019), *Ageing and Contemporary Female Musicians*, London: Routledge.

Garrigós, Cristina (2024), 'We Were There: Individual, Social, and Cultural Memory in Punk Memoirs by Women', *The European Journal of Life Writing* (13): 259–77.

Gavron, Hannah (1966), *The Captive Wife: Conflicts of Housebound Mothers*, London: Routledge and Kegan Paul.

Gay, Peter (1984), *The Education of the Senses (Volume 1) The Bourgeois Experience: Victoria to Freud*, New York: Oxford University Press.

Gimarc, George (2005), *Punk Diary: The Ultimate Trainspotter's Guide to Underground Rock 1970–1982*, New York: Hal Leonard.

Glasper, Ian (2004), *Burning Britain: The History of UK Punk 1980–1984*, London: Cherry Red Books.

Glasser, Ralph (1967), *The New High Priesthood: Social, Ethical, and Politic Implications of a Marketing-Oriented Society*, London: Macmillan.

Goldman, Vivien (2019), *Revenge of the She-Punks: A Feminist Music History from Poly Styrene to Pussy Riot*, Austin, TX: University of Texas Press.

Gorman, Paul (2001), *The Look: Adventures in Pop and Rock Fashion*, London: Sanctuary.

Gorman, Paul (2008), *Reasons to Be Cheerful: The Life and Work of Barney Bubbles*, London: Adelita.

Gough-Yates, Anna (2003), *Understanding Women's Magazines: Publishing, Markets, Readerships*, London: Routledge.

Green, Lucy (1997), *Music, Gender, Education*, Cambridge: Cambridge University Press.

Greer, Germaine (1971), *The Female Eunuch*, New York: Paladin.

Grinnell, George (2024), 'No Future in Retrospect: On Punk Memoirs', *Journal of Popular Music Studies* 36(3): 49–68.

Grossberg, Lawrence (1990), 'Is There Rock after Punk?' in Simon Frith and Andrew Goodwin (eds.), *On Record: Rock, Pop, and the Written Word*, New York: Pantheon, 92–104.

Haddon, Mimi (2019), 'Not Playing Properly: Amateurism as Generic Choice in Three Postpunk Case Studies', *Women and Music: A Journal of Gender and Culture* (23): 159–83.

Haddon, Mimi (2020), *What Is Post-Punk? Genre and Identity in Avant Garde Popular Music, 1977–1982*, Ann Arbor, MI: University of Michigan Press.

Halberstam, J. Jack (2013), 'Go Gaga: Anarchy, Chaos, and the Wild', *Social Text* 116 31(3): 123–34.

Hall, Stuart and Tony Jefferson, eds. (1975), *Resistance through Rituals: Youth Subcultures in Post-War Britain*, London: Hutchinson.

Haraway, Donna J. (1991), *Simians, Cyborgs, and Women: The Reinvention of Nature*, New York: Routledge.

Hebdige, Dick (1979), *Subculture: The Meaning of Style*, London: Routledge.

Hesmondhalgh, Desmond (1997), 'Post-Punk's Attempts to Democratize the Music Industry: The Success and Failure of Rough Trade', *Popular Music* 16(3): 255–74.

Horney, Karen (1967), *Feminine Psychology*, New York: Norton.

Irigaray, Luce (1985), *The Sex Which Is Not One*, trans. Catherine Porter and Caroline Burke, Ithaca, NY: Cornell University Press.

Jones, Steve (1992), *Rock Formation: Music, Technology, and Mass Communication*, Newbury Park, CA: Sage.

Juno, Andrea (1996), *Angry Women in Rock*, New York: Juno Books.

King, Deborah K. (1988), 'Multiple Jeopardy, Multiple Consciousness: The Context of a Black Feminist Ideology', *Signs: Journal of Women in Culture and Society* (14): 42–72.

Klorman-Eraqi, Na'ama (2019), *The Visual Is Political: Feminist Photography and Countercultural Activity in 1970s Britain*, New Brunswick, NJ: Rutgers University Press.

Klorman-Eraqi, Na'ama (2021), 'Radical Feminism and Punk: Visual Cultures of Affect and Disruption', *Photographies* 14(2): 357–78.

Kousha, Mahnaz (1999), *Neither Separate nor Equal: Women, Race, and Class in the South*, Philadelphia, PA: Temple University Press.

Kouvaras, Linda (2004), 'Two Domestic Prison Scenarios', in Michael Ewans, Rosalin Halton, and John Phillips (eds.), *Music Research: New Directions for a New Century*, London: Cambridge Scholars, 215–29.

Laing, Dave (1985), *One Chord Wonders: Power and Meaning in Punk Rock*, Milton Keynes: Open University Press.

Lamy, Philip and Jack Levin (1985), 'Punk and Middle-Class Values: A Content Analysis', *Youth & Society* (17): 157–70.

Langhamer, Claire (2005), 'The Meanings of Home in Post-War Britain', *Journal of Contemporary History* 40: 341–62.

Le Guin, Elizabeth (2005), *Boccherini's Body: An Essay in Carnal Musicology*, Berkeley, CA: University of California Press.

Leblanc, Lauraine (2001), *Pretty in Punk: Girls' Gender Resistance in a Boys' Subculture*, New Brunswick, NJ: Rutgers University Press.

Leonard, Marion (2007), *Gender in the Music Industry: Rock, Discourse, and Girl Power*, Aldershot: Ashgate.

Lewis, Jane (1992), *Women in Britain since 1945: Women, Family, Work and the State in the Post-War Years*, Oxford: Blackwell.

Lock, Graham (1984), 'The Raincoats: Moving', *New Musical Express*, 4 February.

MacPhee, Josh and Erik Reuland, eds. (2007), *Realizing the Impossible: Art against Authority*, Edinburgh: AK Press.

Makholm, Kristin (1997), 'Strange Beauty: Hannah Höch and the Photomontage', *The Museum of Modern Art* (24): 19–23.

Malawey, Victoria (2020), *A Blaze of Light in Every Word: Analyzing the Popular Singing Voice*, London: Oxford University Press.

Marcus, Griel (1990), *Lipstick Traces: A Secret History of the Twentieth Century*, Cambridge, MA: Harvard University Press.

McDonnell, Evelyn and Ann Powers (1995), *Rock She Wrote: Women Write about Rock, Pop, and Rap*, New York: Cooper Square Press.

McDowell, Linda (1991), 'Life without Father and Ford: The New Gender Order of Post-Fordism', *Transactions of the Institute of British Geographers* 16(4): 400–19.

McDowell, Linda (2001), 'Father and Ford Revisited: Gender, Class and Employment Change in the New Millennium', *Transactions of the Institute of British Geographers* 26(4): 448–64.

McLeod, Kembrew (2002), 'Between a Rock and a Hard Place: Gender and Rock Criticism', in Steve Jones (ed.), *Pop Music and the Press*, Philadelphia, PA: Temple University Press, 93–113.

McMullen, Tracy (2006), 'Corpo-Realities: Keepin' It Real in "Music and Embodiment" Scholarship', *Current Musicology* (82): 61–80.

McNeil, Legs (1996), *Please Kill Me: The Uncensored Oral History of Punk*, New York: Grove Press.

McRobbie, Angela, ed. (1991), *Feminism and Youth Culture*, London: Routledge.

McRobbie, Angela (1999), *In the Culture Society: Art, Fashion and Popular Music*, Oxford: Routledge.

McRobbie, Angela and Jenny Garber (2006), 'Girls and Subcultures', in Stuart Hall and Tony Jefferson (eds.), *Resistance through Rituals: Youth Subcultures in Post-War Britain*, 2nd edition, London: Routledge, 209–22.

Mead, Andrew (1999), 'Bodily Hearing: Physiological Metaphors and Musical Understanding', *Journal of Music Theory* 43(1): 1–19.

Mealing, Stuart (2003), 'Value-Added Text: Where Graphic Design Meets Paralinguistics', *Research in Communication Design* 37(1): 43–58.

Metzl, Jonathan (2003), *Prozac on the Couch: Prescribing Gender in the Age of Wonder Drugs*, Durham, NC: Duke University Press.

Micale, Mark S. (2008), *Hysterical Men: The Hidden History of Male Nervous Illness*, Cambridge, MA: Harvard University Press.

Middleton, Richard (1999), *Voicing the Popular: On the Subjects of Popular Music*, New York: Routledge.

Midgley, Mary (2003), *The Myths We Live By*, London: Routledge.

Mitchell, Juliet, ed. (1986), *The Selected Melanie Klein*, New York: Penguin.

Mooney, Jordan and Cathi Unsworth (2019), *Defying Gravity: Jordan's Story*, London: Omnibus.

Mueller, Charles (2017), 'Seduction and Subversion: Sexual Strategies of Siouxsie and the Banshees', *College Music Symposium* 57, online journal.

Murray, Pauline (2023), *Life's a Gamble: Penetration, The Invisible Girls and Other Stories*, London: Omnibus.

Nachmann, Ron (2009), 'The Slits Continue to Give Wild Women a Place in Punk', *San Francisco Weekly*, 9 December.

Neal, Jocelyn (2007), 'Narrative Paradigms, Musical Signifiers, and Form in Country Music', *Music Theory Spectrum* 29(1): 41–72.

Needham, Alex (2025), '"I Was Always Obsessed with Death": How Linder Turned Pornography and Trauma into Art', *The Guardian*, 10 February, online. https://www.theguardian.com/artanddesign/2025/feb/10/i-was-always-obsessed-with-death-how-linder-turned-pornography-and-trauma-into-art.

Nehring, Neil (1991), 'Revolt into Style: Graham Greene Meets the Sex Pistols', *PMLA* 106(2): 222–37.

Noble, Trevor (1985), 'Inflation and Earnings Relativities in Britain after 1970', *British Journal of Sociology* 36(2): 238–58.

O'Brien, Lucy (2002), *She-Bop: The Definitive History of Women in Rock, Pop and Soul*, London: Continuum.

O'Brien, Lucy (2005), 'Identity? How 1970s Punk Women Live It Now', in George McKay and Gina Arnold (eds.), *The Oxford Handbook of Punk Rock*, New York: Oxford University Press, 281–94.

O'Brien, Lucy (2012), 'Can I Have a Taste of Your Ice Cream?', *Punk & Post-Punk* 1(1): 27–40.

Ogg, Alex (2006), *No More Heroes: A Complete History of UK Punk from 1976 to 1980*, London: Cherry Red Books.

Ogg, Alex (2013), 'Poly Styrene Interview', *Punk & Post Punk* 2(2): 197–204.

O'Hara, Craig (2001), *The Philosophy of Punk: More than Noise*, Stirling: AK Press.

Olwage, Grant (2004), 'The Class and Colour of Tone: Essay on the Social History of Vocal Timbre', *Ethnomusicology Forum* 13(2): 203–26.

O'Meara, Catherine (2003), 'The Raincoats: Breaking Down Punk's Masculinities', *Popular Music* 22(3): 299–13.

Osgerby, Bill (1999), '"Chewing Out a Rhythm on My Bubble-Gum": The Teenage Aesthetic and Genealogies of American Punk', in Roger Sabin (ed.), *Punk Rock: So What? The Cultural Legacy of Punk*, London: Routledge, 154–69.

Partridge, Christopher (2010), *Dub in Babylon: Understanding the Evolution and Significance of Dub Reggae in Jamaica and Britain from King Tubby to Post-Punk*, London: Equinox.

Perry, Mark (2000), *Sniffin' Glue: The Essential Punk Accessory*, London: Sanctuary.

Pinkus, Karen (1996), 'Self-Representation in Futurism and Punk', *South Central Review* 13(2/3): 180–93.

Polita, Gea (2007), 'Ana da Silva' (Interview)', *Flash Art* (40): 127.

Press, Joy (1997), 'Shouting Out Loud: Women in U.K. Punk', in Barbara O'Dair (ed.), *Trouble Girls: The Rolling Stone Book of Women in Rock*, New York: Random House.

Raha, Maria (2005), *Cinderella's Big Score: Women of the Punk and Indie Underground*, Emeryville, CA: Seal Press, 293–302.

Railton, Diane (2001), 'The Gendered Carnival of Pop', *Popular Music* 20(3): 321–31.

Reddington, Helen (2003), 'Lady Punks in Bands: A Subculturette?' in David Muggleton and Rupert Weinzierl (eds.), *The Post-Subcultures Reader*, Oxford: Berg, 239–51.

Reddington, Helen (2007), *The Lost Women of Rock Music: Female Musicians of the Punk Era*, Aldershot: Ashgate.

Reddington, Helen (2018), 'Détournement and Female Punk Bands of the 1970s', in Gavin Lee (ed.), *Rethinking Difference in Gender Sexuality, and Popular Music: Theory and Politics of Ambiguity*, London: Routledge, 34–51.

Reddington, Helen (2020), 'Space to Play: The Sound of British Female Punk Music and Its Engagement with Reggae in the 1970s', *Popular Music History* 13(1): 235–53.

Reddington, Helen (2025), 'Danger, Anger, and Noise: The Women Punks of the Late 1970s and Their Music', in George McKay and Gina Arnold (eds.), *The Oxford Handbook of Punk Rock*, New York: Oxford University Press, 115–32.

Reid, Jamie (2021), *Rogue Materials*, London: L-13 Light Industrial Workshop.

Reid, Jamie and Jon Savage (1987), *Up They Rise: The Incomplete Works of Jamie Reid*, London: Faber & Faber.

Reik, Theodor (1948), *Listening with the Third Ear*, New York: Grove Press.

Reynolds, Simon (1992), 'Belting Out That Most Unfeminine Emotion', *New York Times* Section 2: Arts and Leisure: 27, 2 September.

Reynolds, Simon (2005), *Rip It Up and Start Again: Postpunk 1978–1984*, London: Faber & Faber.

Reynolds, Simon and Joy Press (1994), *The Sex Revolts: Gender, Rebellion, and Rock 'n' Roll*, London: Serpent's Tail.

Robb, John (2012), *Punk Rock: An Oral History*, San Francisco, CA: PM Press.

Robson, Kathryn (2004), *Writing Wounds: The Inscription of Trauma in Post-1968 French Women's Life-Writing*, Amsterdam: Brill.

Romero, Mary (1994), *Maid in the U.S.A.*, New York: Routledge.

Romero, Mary and Abigail Stewart, eds. (1999), *Women's Untold Stories: Breaking Silence, Talking Back, Voicing Complexity*, New York: Routledge.

Rowbotham, Sheila (1969), *Women's Liberation and the New Politics*, Nottingham: Bertrand Russell Peace Foundation.

Rubenstein, Ruth (1994), 'Review: Valerie Steele, *Women of Fashion: Twentieth Century Designers*', *Women's Art Journal* 15(1): 42–4.

Samuels, Robert (1998), *Hitchcock's Bi-Textuality: Lacan, Feminisms, and Queer Theory*, Albany, NY: State University of New York Press.

Sanders, Marlene and Marcia Rock (1994), *Waiting for Prime Time: The Women of Television News*, Urbana, IL: University of Illinois Press.

Savage, Jon (1977), 'Penetration: The Future is Female', *Sounds*, 17 December.

Savage, Jon (2002), *England's Dreaming: Anarchy, Sex Pistols, Punk Rock, and Beyond*, New York: St. Martin's Press.

Scull, Andre (2009), *Hysteria: The Biography*, London: Oxford University Press.

Sierra, Maria (2005), 'Oblique Views: Artistic Doubling, Ironic Mirroring and Photomontage in the Works of Norah Lange and Norah Borges', *Revista Canadiense de Estudios Hispánicos* 29(3): 563–84.

Silverman, Kaja (1986), 'Fragments of a Fashionable Discourse', in Tania Modledski (ed.), *Studies in Entertainment: Critical Approaches to Mass Culture*, Bloomington, IN: Indiana University Press, 139–54.

Silverman, Kaja (1993), 'Masochism and Male Subjectivity', in Constance Penley and Sharon Willis (eds.), *Male Trouble*, Minneapolis, MN: University of Minnesota Press, 33–64.

Simonelli, David (2002), 'Anarchy, Pop and Violence: Punk Rock Subculture and the Rhetoric of Class, 1976–1978', *Contemporary British History* 16(2): 121–44.

Simonelli, David (2013), *Working Class Heroes: Rock Music and British Society in the 1960s and 1970s*, Plymouth: Lexington Books.

Smith, Sidone and Julia Watson (2003), *Interfaces: Women, Autobiography, Image, Performance*, Ann Arbor, MI: University of Michigan Press.

Smith, Sidone and Julia Watson (2010), *Reading Autobiography: A Guide for Interpreting Life Narratives*, Minneapolis, MN: University of Minnesota Press.

Sontag, Susan (1977), *On Photography*, New York: Farrar, Straus, and Giroux.

Spelman, Elizabeth V. (1988), *The Inessential Woman*, Boston, MA: Beacon Press.

Sterling, Linder (2006), *Linder: Works 1976–2006*, Lionel Bovier (ed.), Zurich: JRP-Ringier.

Sterling, Linder and Jon Savage (1978), *The Secret Public*, self-published.

Taylor, John (2017), '"Society Stinks": Suburban Alienation and Violence in the Early Films of Penelope Spheeris', in David Forrest, Graeme Harper, and Jonathan Rayner (eds.), *Filmurbia: Screening the Suburbs*, London: Palgrave Macmillan, 13–28.

Thornton, Sarah (1996), *Club Cultures: Music, Media, and Subcultural Capital*, Middletown, CT: Wesleyan University Press.

Toynbee, Jason (2019), 'The Clash, Revolution and Reverse', in Colin Coulter (ed.), *Working for the Clampdown, the Clash, the Dawn of Neoliberalism and the Political Promise of Punk*, Manchester: Manchester University Press, 35–51.

Triggs, Teal (2006), 'Scissors and Glue: Punk Fanzines and the Creation of a DIY Aesthetic', *Journal of Design History* 19(1): 69–83.

Triggs, Teal (2010), *Fanzines: The DIY Revolution*, San Francisco, CA: Chronicle Books.

Ward, Jessica Blaise (2019), 'Who Remembers Post-Punk Women?', *Punk & Post-Punk* 8(3): 379–97.

Ware, Evan (2014), 'Food for Thought: Sid Vicious's Cannibalization of Frank Sinatra's "My Way"', in Eric James Abbey and Colin Helb (eds.), *Hardcore, Punk, and Other Junk: Aggressive Sounds in Contemporary Music*, Lanham, MD: Lexington Books, 1–20.

Wiener, Nathaniel (2018), '"Put on Your Boots and Harrington!": The Ordinariness of 1970s Punk Dress', *Punk & Post-Punk* 7(2): 181–202.

Wilkinson, David, Matthew Worley, and John Street (2017), 'Review: "I Wanna See Some History": Recent Writings on British Punk', *Contemporary European History* 26(2): 397–411.

Williams, Robert and Carlo McCormick (1995), 'Cartoon Surrealism', *Grand Street* (52): 47–57.

Wiseman-Trowse, Nathan (2008), *Performing Class in British Popular Music*, London: Palgrave Macmillan.

Wolf, Naomi (1991), *The Beauty Myth: How Images of Beauty Are Used against Women*, New York: Morrow.

Worley, Matthew (2017), *No Future: Punk. Politics and British Youth Culture, 1976–1984*, Cambridge: Cambridge University Press.

Worley, Matthew (2024), *Zerox Machine: Punk, Post-Punk and Fanzines in Britain, 1976–88*, Chicago, IL: University of Chicago Press.

Zak, Albin (2001), *The Poetics of Rock: Cutting Tracks, Making Records*, Berkeley, CA: University of California Press.

Discography of punk albums

(Original release dates)

The Adverts, *Crossing the Red Sea with The Adverts*, Bright Records, 1978.

Au Pairs, *Playing with a Different Sex*, Human Records, 1981.

Au Pairs, *Sense and Sensuality*, Kamera Records, 1982.

Au Pairs, *Equal but Different, BBC Sessions 79–81*, RPM Records, 1994.

Crass, *The Feeding of the 5000*, Crass Records, 1978.

Crass, *Penis Envy*, Crass Records, 1981.

Delta 5, *See the Whirl*, PRE, 1981.

Delta 5, *Singles and Sessions 1979–1981*, Kill Rock Stars, 2006.

Liliput/Kleenex, *Liliput*, Rough Trade, 1982.

Penetration, *Moving Targets*, Virgin Records, 1978.

Poison Girls, *Hex*, Small Wonders, 1979.

The Raincoats, *The Raincoats*, Rough Trade, 1979.

The Raincoats, *Odyshape*, Rough Trade, 1981.

The Raincoats, *The Kitchen Tapes*, ROIR Records, 1983.

The Rezillos, *Can't Stand the Rezillos*, Sire Records, 1978.

Sick Things, *The Legendary Sick Things*, Chaos Records, 1983.

Siouxsie and the Banshees, *The Scream*, Polydor, 1978.

Siouxsie and the Banshees, *Join Hands*, Polydor, 1979.

Siouxsie and the Banshees, *Kaleidoscope*, 1980.

The Slits, *Cut*, Island, 1979.

The Slits, *The Peel Sessions 1977–1981*, Rough Trade, 1989.

Various, *No Thanks! The '70s Punk Rebellion*. 4 CD set. Rhino, 2008.

Various, *Left of the Dial: Dispatches from the 80s Underground*. 4 CD set. Rhino, 2004.

X-Ray Spex, 'Oh Bondage Up Yours!' / 'I Am a Cliché', Virgin Records, 1977.

X-Ray Spex, *Germ-Free Adolescents*, EMI, 1978.

Referenced images

Barney Bubbles (artist), cover artwork for The Adverts' 'One Chord Wonders', https://www.discogs.com/release/668913-The-Adverts-One-Chord-Wonders-Quick-Step.

Gee Vaucher (artist), cover sleeve artwork for Crass, *The Feeding of the 5000*, https://en.wikipedia.org/wiki/The_Feeding_of_the_5000_(album).

Pennie Smith (artist), cover photograph for The Slits' *Cut*, https://en.wikipedia.org/wiki/Cut_(The_Slits_album).

Linder Sterling (artist), cover artwork for The Buzzcocks, 'Orgasm Addict', https://en.wikipedia.org/wiki/Orgasm_Addict.

Unknown artist, cover sleeve artwork for Siouxsie and the Banshees' 'Hong Kong Gardens', https://en.wikipedia.org/wiki/Hong_Kong_Garden_(song).

Unknown artist, cover sleeve artwork for X-Ray Spex, *Germ Free Adolescents*, Wikipedia: https://en.wikipedia.org/wiki/Germfree_Adolescents.

Index